The Americanisation of Ireland

Irish emigration to America is one of the clichés of modern Irish history; much less familiar is the reverse process. Who were the people who chose to return to Ireland? What motivated them? How did this affect Irish society? While many European countries were somewhat Americanised in this period, the Irish case was unique as so many Irish families had members in America. The most powerful agency for Americanisation, therefore, was not popular culture but circumstantial knowledge and personal contact. David Fitzpatrick demonstrates the often unexpected ways in which the reverse effects of emigration remoulded Irish society, balancing original demographic research with fascinating individual profiles to assemble a vivid picture of a changing Ireland. He explores the transformative impact of reverse migration from America to post-Famine Ireland, and offers penetrating insights into its growing population of American-born residents.

PROFESSOR DAVID FITZPATRICK (1948–2019) was a member of the Royal Irish Academy and a Fellow Emeritus of Trinity College Dublin where he lectured from 1979 to 2015. He pioneered many fields within modern Irish history, including the analysis of personal testimony to illustrate migration and the Irish diaspora, the Irish experience of revolution and civil war as revealed in local sources, the transformative impact of the First World War, and the underlying affinities between Ireland's Protestant and Catholic communities. His understanding of such complexities was enhanced by living in Belfast from 1999 to 2019. His most recent books include *Descendancy: Irish Protestant Histories since 1795* (2014) and *Ernest Blythe in Ulster: The Making of a Double Agent?* (2018).

The Americanisation of Ireland

Migration and Settlement, 1841–1925

David Fitzpatrick

Trinity College, Dublin

CAMBRIDGE
UNIVERSITY PRESS

University Printing House, Cambridge CB2 8BS, United Kingdom

One Liberty Plaza, 20th Floor, New York, NY 10006, USA

477 Williamstown Road, Port Melbourne, VIC 3207, Australia

314–321, 3rd Floor, Plot 3, Splendor Forum, Jasola District Centre,
New Delhi – 110025, India

79 Anson Road, #06–04/06, Singapore 079906

Cambridge University Press is part of the University of Cambridge.

It furthers the University's mission by disseminating knowledge in the pursuit of
education, learning and research at the highest international levels of excellence.

www.cambridge.org
Information on this title: www.cambridge.org/9781108486491
DOI: 10.1017/9781316999516

First published 2020

Printed in the United Kingdom by TJ International Ltd, Padstow Cornwall

A catalogue record for this publication is available from the British Library.

Library of Congress Cataloging-in-Publication Data
Names: Fitzpatrick, David (David Patrick Brian), author.
Title: The Americanisation of Ireland : migration and settlement, 1841–1925 /
David Fitzpatrick.
Description: Cambridge, United Kingdom ; New York, NY, USA : Cambridge
University Press, 2019. | Includes bibliographical references and index.
Identifiers: LCCN 2019014213 | ISBN 9781108486491 (hardback) |
ISBN 9781108707756 (pbk.)
Subjects: LCSH: Return migration–Ireland. | Leitrim (Ireland :
County)–Population. | Ireland–Emigration and immigration–History–19th
century. | Ireland–Emigration and immigration–History–20th century. |
United States–Emigration and immigration–History–19th century. | United
States–Emigration and immigration–History–20th century. | Americans–
Ireland–History–19th century. | Americans–Ireland–History–20th century. |
Ireland–Social conditions–19th century. | Ireland–Social conditions–20th
century.
Classification: LCC JV7716 .F57 2019 | DDC 304.8/41507309034–dc23
LC record available at https://lccn.loc.gov/2019014213

ISBN 978-1-108-48649-1 Hardback

Contents

A plate section can be found between pp 208 and 209.

Charts, Maps and Tables

CHARTS

MAPS

TABLES

Prologue: Ireland's American Question

How insular was pre-revolutionary Ireland? To most outside observers, both before and after the Great Famine, it seemed self-evident that a country notorious for its persistent poverty, slow urbanisation, patchy industrial development, and relentless emigration must also be insular and traditionalist in its culture. While Britain became increasingly cosmopolitan as its empire, economy, and trading networks expanded, 'the south of Ireland' represented the very negation of British modernity. That stereotype was reinforced after partition, when the Irish Free State in particular was widely portrayed as narrowly nationalist, resistant to innovation, and anti-modern. Until recently, few historians challenged this Manichaean interpretation, preferring to argue about who or what was to blame for Ireland's apparent failure to match its neighbour's transformation.

Perhaps in response to the spectacular and undeniable 'globalisation' of the Irish over the last decade or so, and growing public impatience with a world-view blinkered by the Anglo-Irish nexus, historians have begun to look for signs of globalisation in Ireland's past. Processes such as endemic migration and Anglicisation, once dismissed as purely negative forces, are being reassessed. Emigration was not simply a loss to the national stock, but an agency for learning more about the wider world either in person or at second-hand. Anglicisation was no longer regarded primarily as a menace to traditional Irish culture and language, but as an essential tool for equipping Irish people in the global competition for jobs and status. Historians began to celebrate 'multiple identities', acknowledging the possibility of being both Irish and cosmopolitan, of using globalisation to enhance life in Ireland and Irishness to pursue global ambitions. The novel phenomenon of large-scale immigration from an ever-widening range of countries and cultures became a source of particular self-congratulation, as the 'Ireland' brand was modified to embrace the newcomers. 'Ireland' and 'the Irish' had come of age, so liberal wisdom affirmed.

Globalisation, suggesting inexorable convergence towards a global (or American) norm, is a blunt instrument for sifting out the consequences of mass human migration. 'Transnationalism', another neologism coined by Norman Angell in the aftermath of the First World War, provides a more flexible framework for trying to reconcile Ireland's lingering trad-itionalism with the unmatched intensity of Irish long-distance emigration over the century following the Famine. It encourages us to picture Ireland as a migratory hub, experiencing, absorbing, and resisting the impact of the great human outflow. Emigration stimulated reverse flows not merely of people, but of money, sentiment, information, tastes, values, and skills, bombarding the residual Irish population with images of alternative ways of life in all the countries of Irish settlement.

Since the majority of post-Famine emigrants chose the United States, the most powerful reverse flows were of American origin. There is a strong case for attributing the partial 'Americanisation' of Ireland not just to cultural invasion by movies or jazz, but to the cumulative impact of the human 'exodus'. Long before 1900, almost every inhabitant of Ireland had complex personal connections with that 'New World'. When Douglas Hyde composed his celebrated manifesto on 'the necessity for the de-Anglicisation of Ireland' in 1892, he would have done better to call for its de-Americanisation.

This book is intended as a first step towards a comprehensive explor-ation of the sometimes unexpected ways in which the reverse effects of emigration remoulded Irish society. As a necessary prelude to recovering the full story of Americanisation, it assembles statistical and official data illuminating human movement from America to Ireland from the 1840s to the 1920s. 'Return' movement, long assumed to have been negligible, is given its proper place in an introductory survey of paths of migration far more convoluted than a one-way exodus from Ireland. Part of that movement may be traced by analysis of published birthplace returns in the Irish census (1841–1911), demonstrating the growing dominance of Americans in Ireland's foreign-born population, and the spectacular contrast between the profile of Ireland's 'Americans' and other alien sub-groups.

This provides demographic context for detailed dissection of several databases assembled from records relating to individual migrants. Close scrutiny of selected family census schedules (1901–11) allows us to reconstruct the household environment of the American-born, and thus to identify Irish-born parents who would not otherwise have been unmasked as 'returned Yanks'. The 'modern' face of America in Ireland is embodied in a collective profile of about one thousand American-born visitors, mainly enumerated in Dublin, Belfast, and Cork, who were selected by occupation to represent the professional, clerical, artistic, and moneyed elite. This is complemented by a special study of Co. Leitrim (homeland of my Fitzpatrick ancestors), which by 1911 was the county with the heaviest concentration of American natives as well as the highest intensity of outward migration. These incarnations of America in Ireland, mainly living on small farms in humble circumstances, surely undermined the assumption that emigration typically offered a path to riches or at least security.

In addition to examining over four hundred household census returns, I have brought the elusive category of short-term visitors from the United States into focus by analysing about five hundred applications for passports by naturalised American citizens (or their relatives) born in Leitrim (mainly issued between 1919 and 1925).[1] Together, these illuminate the social profile and socio-geographical background of the reverse flow from North America to the most 'backward' region of rural Ireland, which was also the most cosmopolitan. The passport applications are unique in providing evidence of motive and intended destination, elucidating the bonds and rivalries that suffused Irish rural families even when their members were scattered across the globe. Though some streams of human movement from America to Ireland have eluded documentation, this book offers the first systematic impression of the gathering backwash generated by the Irish 'exodus'.

My use of the term 'American' is deliberately ambiguous and open-ended. When comparable data are accessible, I have included Canada as well as the United States, since patterns of migration to and from North America transcended state boundaries. The myriad Americans whose personal experiences impinged on Irish society and culture were not confined to any single category defined by birthplace, residence, or citizenship. The best documented group were those born in North America who were enumerated in the census, yet (being mainly young children) they probably had less direct influence on how American life was envisaged in Ireland than their Irish-born parents. The category of adults born in America ranged from tourists and temporary visitors to settlers, often of Irish background, whose experience of American life might have lasted for decades or for a few years of infancy. As in any study based on official returns, superficially cohesive categories conceal an incongruous miscellany.

The category of those who emigrated to America and subsequently went to Ireland is equally convoluted. Apart from census returns documenting the Irish families of American-born visitors and settlers, the only systematic dossier of 'returned Americans' is the vast collection of post-1914 United States passport applications analysed in the last three chapters. Since passports were issued only to naturalised American citizens and their families who declared their intention of returning from overseas after a year or so, most returning emigrants were excluded. These undocumented groups include emigrants who returned within 4 years of arrival before qualifying for naturalisation, who chose to remain British subjects thereafter, or who decided to return home permanently. My aim is not to assemble a comprehensive or coherent profile of 'Americans' who spent time in Ireland, but to sift and sort the imperfect available data in order to display the complexity of an elusive element of post-Famine Irish society.

My deployment of tendentious terms such as 'cosmopolitan' and 'Americanisation' (or 'Americanization' if fully realised) is intended as a provocation. In a demographic study such as this, it is obviously impossible to tease out precisely what influences exotic human agents exercised on those with whom they interacted in Ireland. The fact that someone was born outside Ireland does not of itself imply the importation of 'cosmopolitan' values, apart from the inevitable imprint of having lived in more than one country. A child of Irish parents born in India but reared at home was presumably only faintly Indian, whereas a Jewish pedlar from Lithuania would never lose his exoticism however long he might live in Dublin or Cork. So Chapter 2 on 'Cosmopolitan Ireland' is really a survey of those who, having been born outside Ireland, *might* have exposed Irish people to other ways of life, and *might* have assumed dual 'ethnic identities'.

'Americanisation' undoubtedly embraced a multitude of influences on Irish culture, society, economic organisation, and politics. These influences were not exerted by some homogeneous 'Americanism', but by a variety of practices associated with particular sub-groups of Americans. Because America was a chaotically multicultural country, its influence on Ireland must also have been chaotically multicultural. Any sustained analysis would have to set that basic context against the widespread belief in Ireland that (white) 'American' culture was homogeneous, apart from the gulf between 'Irish America' and a dominant, sometimes hostile, host culture. None of these nuances can be explored in this book. Instead, Americans in Ireland are treated as potential agents of every conceivable form of Americanisation. By examining their profile and distribution, it is possible to identify the regions and classes most susceptible to such influences, but not to specify *how* they were Americanised. The cultural impact of a rich American traveller in the Shelbourne Hotel surely differed from that of a poor foster-child in a remote farmhouse, but my speculations about 'winners' and 'losers' cannot be tested on the basis of demographic evidence.

The design of this book is deliberately unconventional, embodying the multiple perspectives that I have applied to an open-ended topic. Statistical analysis of each database alternates with brief accounts of hundreds of individual cases, the effect being to undermine otherwise plausible generalisations. The focus of study is progressively narrowed from a broad conspectus of neglected migration trajectories in Chapter 1 to a minute perusal of passport photographs in Chapter 10. The survey of Ireland's foreign-born in Chapter 2 provides essential context for the chapters specifically on Americans, by showing just how aberrant the American profile was. It also sets the Irish case in a broader British context, as this book is intended to contribute to the general history of migration. My analysis of Ireland's American-born elite (Chapters 3, 4, and 5) is swollen by the need to do justice to the many strands comprising that elite (yet another open-ended category). This invites comparison with American elites in Britain and beyond, though these appear to be ill-served by demographic studies. The most striking Irish anomaly is the concentration of Americans in rural regions, the discovery that inspired me to write this book. The astonishingly homogeneous profile of the American-born in one rural county (Leitrim) is explored in Chapters 6 and 7, followed by an examination of temporary visitors born in the same county who applied for American passports (Chapters 8, 9, and 10).

Some will be perplexed by my concentration on a single county when examining the American presence in rural Ireland, and by my deliberate selection of a county that was extreme, rather than 'representative', in its recorded rates of emigration and American settlement and in its social demography. Leitrim's extreme position in the rural spectrum provides insight into an American sub-population that was atypically unitary. Since 'Ireland' is itself a political and cultural construct, it should not be necessary to justify a microstudy focused on a particular sub-region. Even so, every available statistical series is deployed to show where Leitrim ranked among Irish counties, and comparisons are drawn with Diane Rose Dunnigan's pioneering study of passport applicants from the entire province of Connaught. By limiting my focus to a single county, I have been able to link nominal data from several intricate data-sets, so greatly enriching what could be gleaned from each collective profile in isolation.

With unlimited time and resources, it might have been possible for an immense team to have assembled comparable data for the entire country. The resultant dossier would either have been unreadable or devoid of personal examples and *nuances*, and I cannot predict what intellectual benefit, if any, would have resulted from asking the same questions about thirty-two counties instead of one. Meanwhile, my demographic exploration of Leitrim has cleared the way for any future holistic micro-study of the impact of Americanisation in a socially homogeneous environment.

In my attempt to recover the submerged history of American move-ment into Ireland, I have been encouraged by the ever-growing interest of scholars in the complexities of human migration, especially short-term and short-distance movement, long-distance reverse movement, and continuing movement following the initial act of emigration. European scholars such as Dirk Hoerder and the brothers Lucassen have helped to reconfigure migration as a global and multi-faceted phenomenon, sub-verting the former American emphasis on long-distance one-way emigra-tion, inspired by poverty or persecution in Europe compounded by the irresistible lure of the 'New World'. Distinguished British scholars, including Tom Devine and the late Eric Richards (my lamented fellow-conspirator in trying to recast Australia's migration history), have like-wise liberated Scottish, English, and imperial migration from obsolete models.

Cormac Ó Gráda, Kerby Miller, and Don Akenson led the way in complicating the story of Irish migration, tethering it securely to verifi-able facts, and devising testable explanatory models. Crusaders pursu-ing 'global' or 'transnational' approaches to migration, such as Don MacRaild, Kevin Kenny, and Enda Delaney, are rapidly transforming the focus and terminology of the subject. The study of immigration to Britain and European countries, long a major topic for sociologists, has been projected back into historical contexts, initially to provide back-ground for analysis of contemporary problems. In the Irish case, this has led to innovative studies of inward movement by Ó Gráda, Marjo-lein 't Hart, Dunnigan, and most recently Irial Glynn. The outstanding work of many of these pioneers is acknowledged in later chapters. Without their influence and example, this book would not have been written.

Nor would it have come to fruition in difficult circumstances without the encouragement and promptitude of Liz Friend-Smith and her perceptive readers at Cambridge University Press, and the support of my friends and family. Cormac Ó Gráda and David Dickson spurred me on and arranged technical assistance (especially the maps so rapidly and elegantly designed by Matthew Stout). Georgina and Sheila Fitzpatrick offered vital moral support and meticulous comments on all chapters. I have been encouraged and uplifted by my elder 'children', Brian Fitzpatrick and Meg D'Ortenzio, whose visits from Australia (along with those of Georgina and Sheila) fired up the last stages of writing. Above all, I have been sustained and inspired by the steadfast presence of Jane Leonard and our daughters Julia and Hannah, my beloved companions.

Belfast, January 2019.

Map 1.1 Ireland, showing administrative boundaries

1 Beyond Emigration

I   Migration and Emigration

The transformation of Irish society and culture after the Great Famine was shaped in large part by personal interaction between those at home and outsiders. Some of those outsiders were immigrants or temporary visitors to Ireland, mostly born in Britain but also increasingly from India, the dominions, Russia, to some extent Europe, and especially the United States. This neglected cosmopolitan presence is anatomised in the next chapter. Most overseas-born incomers were less exotic than might be assumed, having been drawn to Ireland by strong prior connections with the country. Many were the wives or children of Irish migrants, and the wives were often themselves of Irish or British descent, even if born in India or Italy. By far the largest and most influential foreign element were the Americans, whose increasingly conspicuous presence in Ireland is the subject of this book.

Yet no analysis of incomers to Ireland can ignore the multitude of 'insider–outsiders' who never revisited their home place, but typically remained in contact through correspondence or indirect accounts brought home by friends or relatives. These were the 7 million people who left Ireland between the 1840s and the 1920s, leading to almost continuous depopulation throughout the century after the Famine. Their decisions about settlement, family formation, and social interaction shaped the origins and outlook of most of the foreign-born 'outsiders' who went on to visit or settle in Ireland. The extraordinary profile of the Irish 'diaspora' is well documented and more or less familiar to students of international migration. I shall therefore confine myself to summarising some of its most noteworthy features.

First, no other European country had such high and sustained rates of net outward migration throughout the later nineteenth century, and none experienced depopulation. Second, the most intense emigration occurred after rather than during the Famine, quickly becoming an expected and 'normal' event in the life cycle of the majority of each cohort. Third, despite the expense and riskiness of long-distance migration, its ubiquitous appeal to the post-Famine Irish quickly broke down social and economic inhibitions and obstacles. By the later nineteenth century, the most intense movement was from the poorest, least urbanised, and most 'backward' regions of the Atlantic seaboard, the Leinster midlands, and mid-Ulster. Fourth, habitual emigration was mainly funded not by the state or landlords, but by previous emigrants who supplied remittances or pre-paid passages for friends and relatives ('chain migration'). Fifth, whereas all other European migrations were male-dominated (with occasional Scandinavian exceptions), both sexes left Ireland in roughly equal numbers with two periods (around 1855 and 1900) in which women outnumbered men. Sixth, Irish emigrants (unlike Germans or Italians) settled almost exclusively in the Anglophone world, mostly in the United States but also in Britain, the dominions, and Argentina with its well-established 'Inglès' elite. Seventh, despite their overwhelmingly rural origins, most Irish emigrants settled in foreign cities, being clustered within the United States (even more than the Germans or Italians) in New York, Boston, and the urban north-east.[1]

This vast, relentless, and largely voluntary displacement of the Irish population generated a less obvious but equally relentless backwash in the human form of emigrants and their families who returned 'home'. Before riding the American rip in that human backwash, it must be understood that even Irish migration was never an irreversible translation from 'home' to some far-distant place of settlement. Since that simplistic model remains powerful in popular imagination, despite decades of scholarly refutation, this chapter is intended to demonstrate the importance of short-distance, circular, and reverse migration over the period of the Anglo-Irish Union (1801–1922). After brief discussions of the extent of internal displacement between Irish counties and seasonal movement to Britain, a sustained attempt is made to measure reverse migration from overseas and from the United States in particular.[2] How widespread was the exposure of the home population to each of these migratory flows, and by extension to the attendant cultural detritus?

II   Internal Migration

A distinguishing feature of Irish migration was the relative rarity of movement between Irish counties, the best documented form of internal migration. Relocation within Ireland was discouraged by the slow pace of urbanisation, the weakness of industrialisation outside north-eastern Ulster, and low wage levels by comparison with Britain or America. Census statistics of birthplace and residence give no indication of local movement within counties, which must have been considerable as the result of marriage, changed employment, or displacement from one holding to another. Some hint of short-distance movement during the Famine is provided by returns of poor relief, which distinguish the proportion of recipients who had not lived in the immediate locality for at least thirty of the preceding 36 months. The mean proportion of migratory paupers was usually about one-seventh, being slightly higher in the summer months of most acute shortage. It was relatively low in major centres such as Dublin, Belfast, and Galway, but extremely high in certain western poor law unions in Munster and Ulster.[3]

The convulsions of the Famine decade brought only a modest increase in the number displaced from their county of birth to some other Irish county. That number never exceeded 560,000, even in 1851, though as a proportion of Ireland's population it rose from 5% in 1851 to 9% by 1871. About two-thirds of those inter-county migrants had merely crossed county borders. Dublin was the only major city to draw migrants from a broad catchment zone, to the extent that nearly one-third of its population in 1851 had been born in other counties. Displacement both inwards and outwards was most intensive in the east, being relatively rare along the Atlantic seaboard and in much of Ulster. The regional patterns of displacement changed very little between 1841 and 1871, reflecting the static distribution of employment opportunities and the slow pace of urban and industrial expansion.[4]

The character of demand for labour in nineteenth-century Ireland was also evident in the distributions of inter-county migrants by sex and occupation. Except in parts of the west, females slightly outnumbered males among those resident away from their counties of birth. Women often migrated as a consequence of marriage; but those with specific occupations were disproportionately likely to be teachers or domestic servants, predictably often spinners or dressmakers, and seldom weavers or farmers. Male migrants were heavily over-represented in the professional and clerical categories of the census between 1841 and 1861. Skilled tradesmen, grocers and dealers, domestics, and car men were other favoured groups, whereas labourers as well as farmers were disinclined to migrate between counties.[5] Thus, Irish inter-county migration was particularly scanty in poorer regions and among the unskilled rural population.

No information on migrant occupations was published after 1861, but the female majority still applied in 1911. The concentration of population displacement in eastern counties also persisted, maintaining strong positive correlation between the county distributions for 1871 and 1911, though the Belfast region developed rapidly as a magnet for internal migrants in competition with Dublin.[6] By 1911, 13% of the Irish-born population were living outside their native counties, the absolute number (558,000) having scarcely risen since 1851. Despite the clamour to promote internal migration as an alternative to emigration, from both Catholic and Protestant clergy and politicians such as Parnell, it proved impracticable to deploy 'internal colonisation' as an instrument for spiritual or material modernisation. Even so, short-distance migration introduced hundreds of thousands of country people to urban life, and many others to the images of urban life that the migrants conveyed to relatives who remained at home.

III   Seasonal Migration

Seasonal migration from Ireland to Britain, though superficially irrelevant to the American presence in Ireland, contributed indirectly to long-distance migration. The relationship between seasonal, 'permanent', and indeterminate migration is of course tangled, since many Irish people who left for Britain intending to undertake a season's farm work went on to find casual labour in towns or seek poor relief, often settling in the regions of Britain with which they became familiar or moving further afield, particularly to the United States. In terms of Irish mentality, seasonal migration had countervailing influences on the disposition to resettle abroad. By accustoming home communities to British *mores* and wages it strengthened the 'pull' across the water, yet by propping up the home economy through seasonal earnings it mitigated the 'push' out of Ireland.

Data on seasonal migration before 1880 is haphazard and uncertain. The Irish reaper was already a familiar figure in the summer landscape of eighteenth-century England, and by about 1834 it seems from the Poor Inquiry's parish survey that some 40,000 reapers were migrating annually to Britain. A defective count during the 1841 season recorded nearly 60,000 departures of deck passengers to Britain, but these seem to have included visitors and jobbers as well as seasonal workers. Six-sevenths of these travellers were male and three-fifths were aged between sixteen and thirty-five.[7] Historians have disagreed about changes over time in the pattern of seasonal migration, but Ó Gráda indicates that the volume continued to increase during and after the Famine to a peak of about 100,000 in the mid-1860s.[8]

Seasonal workers came broadly from the same regions as Britain's Irish-born population as returned at the census, which from 1851 onwards occurred in spring before the seasonal influx had begun. In 1841, one-third of the migrants came from Ulster, of whom three-quarters were bound for Glasgow. Over two-fifths were from Connaught, and all but one-seventh of these proceeded to Liverpool. The surveys of 1834 and 1841 indicate that seasonal migration was already concentrated in the impoverished north-western counties well before this applied to 'permanent' emigration from Ireland, and it was always to remain a far more localised phenomenon. In 1841, Donegal, Leitrim, Mayo, Roscommon, and Sligo were all sending out at least sixteen migrants per thousand of population, whereas half of the counties of Ireland sent less than five. Inter-county variation was more than three times as marked as that for post-Famine permanent migration.[9]

Despite fluctuations in demand and diversion into non-agricultural work, seasonal migration remained a significant component of the British farm labour force up to the First World War. As usual, detailed enumeration began only when the flow was slackening and therefore countable. Official statistics for 1880–1915 show a reduction in the number of migratory workers known to the Royal Irish Constabulary from 20,000 to 8,000, interrupted by a brief surge at the turn of the century.[10] Conflicting returns from railway and shipping companies, though confirming this trend over time, suggest that the actual annual movement from Ireland to Britain was about twice as great. Part of the difference is attributable to the widespread practice of making two annual visits with an interval at home. The magnitude of regular annual migration was evidently even higher in the 1870s, the subsequent decrease usually being ascribed to the gradual substitution of machinery for labour in British farming. An inquiry in 1883 suggests that this applied most of all to the western counties of northern England and southern Scotland. The general decrease in Irish seasonal migration to eastern and midland counties, stretching from Yorkshire to Edinburgh, was seldom attributed to mechanisation, and may represent failure of labour supply rather than demand as longer-distance migrants drifted into urban industry.

Donegal, together with Armagh and the five counties of Connaught, provided virtually all regular migratory labour from pre-war Ireland. In 1880, these seven counties contained four-fifths of all migratory labourers counted by the constabulary, a proportion that reached 97% before the end of the century. Mayo's contribution ranged between half and three-fifths during the three decades after 1886, while the proportion of migrants from Donegal doubled to one-fifth. The recovery in migration from Donegal was reflected in the proportion of migrants making for Scotland, which attracted few workers from other counties apart from north Leitrim. Seasonal migration, to a far greater extent than in pre-Famine times, was a highly localised movement between certain districts in north-western Ireland and a shrinking belt of agricultural Britain (a few also found seasonal employment elsewhere in Ireland). It was composed largely of men rather than women, and of farmers' sons rather than landholders, who, when they did migrate, were usually very small farmers.

Thus, in a few districts, seasonal migration provided an alternative to permanent emigration for the surplus population of young unmarried adult males. For many of these, it was in fact the prelude to a less easily reversible departure. It provided both a taste of life elsewhere and the means for indulging that taste. Indeed, seasonal and permanent migration were often complementary rather than alternative experiences, seasonal movement being a normal adolescent episode whereas emigration occurred slightly later in the male life cycle, often when the transfer of farm occupancy was being accomplished. The counties of heavy seasonal migration all had high emigration rates, and this relationship also applied to smaller districts within counties such as Donegal, Mayo, and Leitrim. Here seasonal migration propped up a singular demographic system whereby frequent marriage and rapid natural increase were counteracted by heavy net emigration. Yet the practice of annual migration to Britain survived the gradual reduction in permanent emigration after the 1880s, so that in Mayo (1901) the number of regular harvesters almost equalled the entire recorded male emigration over the subsequent decade. Though diminishing, seasonal migration remained as a relic of the transience and impermanence that had once typified the Irish experience in Britain.

The net financial return from seasonal work alone may well have amounted to one-third of the remittances received from overseas emigrants, which served similar functions in the home economy by facilitating payment of shop debts, rent, and tickets to America. Apart from its economic functions, seasonal migration to Britain (like movement between Irish counties) tended to break down parochialism and introduce exotic practices to the most remote and 'backward' districts of Ireland. By accustoming certain regions of Ireland to other ways of life, it helped to undermine Irish insularity.

IV   Reverse Migration

Vast in magnitude and tortuous in path, it has generally been assumed that nineteenth-century Irish emigration was seldom reversed. The striking similarity between estimates of gross and net movement out of post-Famine Ireland suggests that few of those leaving Ireland returned to live in their native country. The shortage of land and employment that encouraged emigration also discouraged permanent return, especially since those left behind were presumably reluctant to readmit well-heeled expatriates to the restrictive markets of rural Ireland. Whereas the predominantly male 'new' immigrants from southern or eastern Europe often preferred to spend a few years in the United States, saving for their eventual marriage and resettlement at home, the Irish of both sexes usually intended from the outset to marry and settle abroad. Though some left with the dream of retirement and 'death in Erin', their determination tended to soften into ineffectual nostalgia after experience of relative liberty and prosperity elsewhere. Or so historians of migration have speculated in the absence of credible statistics of reverse passenger movement before 1895.

Those who did return faced an uneasy blend of resentment arising from their assets or accents, and contempt for their evident inability to 'make it' overseas: 'Oh, that is a man who has come home; he has failed through his own fault.'[11] The 'Yank' or 'Returned Yank' nevertheless became a familiar figure in rural folklore, a symbol of loneliness: the woman bringing home a fat fortune with which to find a husband and 'redeem' his farm; the man flourishing ready cash to secure land or pub; the lost offspring summoned home to take over from faltering parents. As early as 1835, a Sligo witness referred to 'many instances of persons having saved money in America, and having returned in their old days to their place of birth, where they have given excessive prices for small portions of land'.[12] The accuracy of such stereotypes is even more difficult to assess than the frequency of reverse migration.

Analysis of passenger lists from America assembled in connection with the Fenian scare (1858–67) suggests that the typical reverse migrant was very unlike the stereotype distilled from folklore surveys by Schrier. Since two-thirds of those sampled were male, while half of the female minority were already married, it is clear that husband-hunters did not predominate. The median age of returning men was 29.8 years compared with 26.5 years for women, indicating a sojourn in the United States of only 7 and 4 years, respectively. In occupational distribution they differed little from America's resident Irish population, though labourers and servants were far less conspicuous among returning than departing emigrants. 'Yanks' seem to have been unusually inclined to settle in the north-west or in north Leinster, where the land market was probably more open than in the south and west of the country.[13] Returned migrants undoubtedly helped to diffuse information about foreign lands and so to facilitate further emigration.

By the 1870s, reverse movement to Ireland had become significant and widely noticed. The halving of the east-bound fare in 1874 was reported to have provoked a 'rush of steerage passengers' from the United States to Liverpool and Glasgow.[14] In 1876, when emigration fell to its lowest level since the 1830s, the number of passengers leaving Irish ports for extra-European destinations only just exceeded the number returning. Passenger traffic from the United States to Irish ports actually surpassed the westward movement.[15] Admittedly, the remarkable reversal of the familiar pattern in 1876 was a short-lived aberration, reflecting the coincidence of recession in North America and strong demand for labour in the British Isles and Europe. For all passengers of British or Irish origin ('nationality'), excluding tens of thousands of foreigners passing annually through the British Isles, the 'repatriant ratio' of inward to outward passengers in a particular year fell sharply from parity (100%) in 1876 and 62% in 1878 to only 22% in the following year, when crop failure in Ireland contributed to the scramble for jobs in the reviving American economy. In making sense of these abrupt variations, we should realise that the volume of eastward movement was a product of previous westward movement, so that past surges in out-migration tended to produce surges in reverse migration a few years later, even in the absence of enhanced economic incentives to return from America.

Subsequent changes confirm Thomas's hypothesis that transatlantic passenger flows were deeply influenced by the fact that the European and American business cycles moved in roughly opposite phase throughout the half century before the First World War. The repatriant ratio from the United States to the British Isles recovered from 16% in 1882 to a minor peak of 42% in 1885, dipping to 29% in 1887, reaching 49% in 1890 and 80% in 1894 before falling to 56% in 1895. Further minor peaks were recorded in 1898, 1904, 1908, and 1911, with troughs in 1903, 1906, and 1910. Discounting short-term fluctuations, the ratio of inward to outward movement, for Canada as well as the United States, was most pronounced in the later 1870s and later 1890s, subsiding somewhat in the Edwardian decade but recovering just before the First World War.[16]

Reverse migration to Europe was encouraged not merely by variations in economic push and pull, but by cut-throat competition between the major transatlantic shipping companies to make more efficient use of passenger vessels on the reverse journey to Europe. By offering bargain berths for eastward travellers, even at a nominal loss, it proved possible to subsidise the westward journey by increasing overall occupancy in the manner of discount airlines today. Rather than slashing fares, the subsidy was typically invested in superior regularity, safety, accommodation, and provisions, making the week-long voyage a comfortable cruise instead of the grim and prolonged incarceration endured by earlier steerage passengers. Business historians have documented the success of pre-war

British, German, and American shippers in attracting tourists, business travellers, and settlers wishing to visit relatives at home.

They also catered for emigrants struggling to mitigate the impact of seasonal or cyclical unemployment, who increasingly circulated between Europe and North America in order to optimise their income or (perhaps more crucially) their access to social support.[17] By 1913, the success of the shippers' strategy for filling up their vessels was reflected in the monthly calendar of migration of British subjects between the United States and the British Isles. Almost 30% of passengers leaving the United States in that year travelled in the final quarter of the year, whereas only 17% travelled in the opposite direction during that quarter. Since 30% of *temporary* migrants to the United States travelled in the first quarter of the year, it would appear that these passengers were disproportionately inclined to visit the British Isles over the winter despite the inhospitable weather and long nights.[18] The dynamics of Irish reverse migration are best understood in the broader context of transatlantic economic and business history.

The earliest systematic returns of Irish reverse migration were compiled in 1895, when inward passenger traffic from extra-European ports was first tabulated by nationality on the basis of shipping manifests submitted to the Board of Trade. Separate figures were given for British subjects of English, Irish, and Scottish nationality, and for 'foreigners' or 'aliens'. From 1908, Welsh nationality was belatedly recognised and a new category was introduced for passengers of British colonial birth, an important strand of migration hitherto distributed among the home nationalities on the basis of assumed 'origin'. Admittedly incomplete, these returns of 'immigration' included not only those who planned to change their country of residence, but also temporary visitors, business travellers, and passengers en route for countries outside the United Kingdom.

Between 1895 and 1911, about 47 Irish passengers returned for every 100 passengers who left, compared with 52 English and 42 Scots (see Tables 1.1 and 1.2). The Irish repatriant ratio ranged between 40 in 1906 and 60 in 1908, exceeding 50 in five individual years. Whereas the British repatriant ratio fell sharply after 1899, there was no clear decline in the Irish case. Irish reverse movement was most pronounced from India and Ceylon (120) and British South Africa (77), lowest from British North America (30), and intermediate from Australasia (48). Irish reverse migration from the United States fell slightly short of the British level, the Irish repatriant ratio (1895–1911) being 46 compared with 48 for the Scots and no fewer than 58 for the English. These findings suggest that Irish reverse movement was more common than is usually assumed, with little difference between the repatriant ratios for Ireland and Britain. Chart 1.1 plots year-by-year fluctuations in the volume of inward movement from the United States, while Chart 1.2 traces the repatriant ratios for Irish and British passengers.

The predominance of America[19] as the epicentre of Irish migration is highlighted in Table 1.1. This shows that 31% of passengers from the

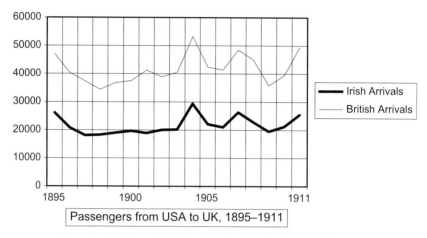

Chart 1.1 Irish and British repatriant ratios between USA and UK, 1895–1911

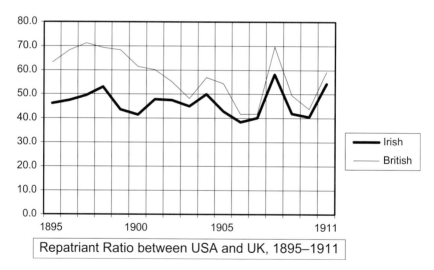

Chart 1.2 Irish and British passengers from USA to UK, 1895–1911

United States to the British Isles between 1895 and 1911 were Irish, whereas Irish passengers accounted for only 5% of those travelling from other countries. The same pattern was evident in outward movement, 35% of passengers to the United States being Irish compared with 4% to other destinations. Irish pre-eminence in pre-war American migration is undeniable, for Ireland housed only about one-tenth of the United Kingdom's population. Whereas only about two-fifths of British migrants moved to or from the United States, that country accounted for 86% of Irish incomers and 87% of Irish outgoers.

Furthermore, the profile of Irish–American migration differed sharply from the British movement. Children were notably under-represented (as in all axes of migration except Indian), while the majority of Irish–American migrants in both directions were women (56% of incomers and 55% of outgoers). By contrast, women consistently accounted for only about two-fifths of British passengers to and from the United States, confirming the unique and long-standing prominence of women and the relative scarcity of children in Irish migration. A female majority of Irish passengers from the United States was recorded in every year between 1895 and 1911 and in all but four individual years for outgoing passengers. This singularity applied only to the American case, men forming a marked majority of both Irish and British movement across all other major axes of migration.

It would appear from this analysis of Irish passenger statistics that reverse migration from the United States had become commonplace by the turn of the century, with about two passengers leaving for each one who returned. Yet these calculations leave important issues unresolved. Because of the increasing prevalence of short-term visitors and travellers in transit, the official passenger returns had long since ceased to represent the underlying patterns of long-term emigration and immigration. During 1912, the Board of Trade introduced new regulations for all ships entering or leaving the United Kingdom from outside Europe, requiring masters to record the 'permanent residence' of travellers both before the voyage and afterwards. This was indicated by the countries in which they had previously resided, and in which they intended to reside, for at least one year.

Briefly, between April 1912 and December 1913, Irish migration was documented by two parallel sets of published statistics. The 'passenger' returns were sub-divided not by nationality, as before, but by the country of permanent residence within (or beyond) the United Kingdom, tabulating outward passengers formerly resident in Ireland or elsewhere, and incoming passengers intending to settle in Ireland or elsewhere. A second set of returns showing long-term movement excluded those who did not intend to change their 'permanent' residence. Thus, 'emigration' was restricted to residents of the United Kingdom who proposed to settle outside Europe, while 'immigration' comprised residents of the empire or foreign countries who proposed to settle in the United Kingdom. In all cases, separate tabulations were provided for British subjects and for aliens, in an attempt to establish how many aliens were merely in transit through British ports or other short-term visitors. Production of these elaborate returns fell victim to 'wartime economy' from 1914, but they offer a unique snapshot of the complexities of what is loosely termed 'migration', and the peculiar profile of movement into and out of Ireland just before the First World War.

The returns of long-term migration summarised in Table 1.3 confirm the long-standing predominance of women and the scarcity of children in Irish–American migration in both directions, reinforcing the contrasts between Irish and British movement displayed in Table 1.1. Additional tabulations by age show that adult emigrants from Ireland tended to be much younger than those from Britain, only 15% being over 30 compared with 40% of adult Britons. British subjects immigrating into Ireland were also less likely to exceed 30 than those settling in Britain, though the contrast was less marked. Immigrants in general (often being former emigrants) tended to be older than emigrants: 43% of immigrants into Ireland had reached 30 compared with 53% of immigrants into Britain.

A crude attempt was also made to classify the occupations of long-term migrants in four categories, as summarised in Table 1.4. This shows that male emigrants from Ireland to the United States were still mainly classified as farmers (34%) or labourers (48%), no less than 87% of female emigrants being in service (typically, no doubt, within the family home). By contrast, almost four-fifths of male emigrants from Britain to the United States were in skilled or white-collar occupations, as were two-fifths of occupied female emigrants. In the case of emigration to other countries, Irish over-representation of farmers and labourers was far weaker, with no significant Irish–British contrast among female emigrants. The occupational profile of immigrants from the United States is particularly interesting. Though farmers and labourers remained far more prominent among men settling in Ireland by comparison with Britain, almost half of those entering Ireland were skilled or white-collar workers compared with less than one-quarter of emigrants from Ireland.

There was less evidence of upward mobility among female immigrants from the United States, most of whom remained in service. But the female proportion classified under 'teachers, clerks, and professions' was notably greater among immigrants, accounting for one-twelfth of occupied women entering Ireland and one-quarter of those bound for Britain. This professional element was far greater among immigrants from the dominions to Ireland, approaching one-quarter of those from Canada and Australasia and half of those from British South Africa. Overall, reverse migration into Ireland drew from a broader occupational spectrum than emigration, without eliminating the British advantage. Thus, some incomers, but by no means all, gave the appearance of having raised their social status during their residence overseas (though it is possible that the repatriant ratio was higher for emigrants of initially superior status).

The final column of Table 1.3 shows the repatriant ratio of long-term immigrants to long-term emigrants in 1912–13. The Irish repatriant ratio from the United States (11%) fell well short of the British ratio (22%), whereas there was no marked British–Irish difference in the case of non-American migration (21% in each case). These figures reflect the truism that reverse movement is far less prominent in long-term than short-term (typically two-way) migration. Whereas the repatriant ratio was only 11% for long-term migration between Ireland and the United States in 1912–13, the ratio for Irish–American passenger movement between 1895 and 1911 was 48%. The corresponding ratios for British–American movement were 22% (1912–13) and 56% (1895–1911). These contrasts appear to demonstrate that statistics based on total passenger flow exaggerate the frequency of long-term reverse migration, through the inclusion of tens of thousands of temporary visitors travelling annually in both directions.

Admittedly, this inference relies on the assumption that the migration flows of British subjects recorded for 1912–13 were broadly in keeping with previous patterns. That assumption may be tested by disaggregating the newly compiled returns in order to distinguish between 'permanent' and 'temporary' migration (defined by the difference between total passenger movement and 'permanent' migration). Virtually all outward passengers previously resident in the United Kingdom were long-term emigrants, whereas nearly one-third of inward passengers intending to reside in the United Kingdom were temporary migrants who had not previously resided overseas. The very high repatriant ratios for temporary migrants (277% for Ireland and 153% for Britain) ensured that the ratio for all passengers with residence in the United Kingdom was 29% compared with only 20% for permanent migrants alone. Even after adjustment, this ratio might suggest an abrupt short-term decline in reverse migration, since the ratio for all passenger movement of British subjects between 1908 and 1911 had been 47%.

Closer inspection (see Table 1.5) reveals that this abrupt decline was a statistical by-product of replacing 'nationality' by domicile when categorising United Kingdom passenger movement of British subjects. If we incorporate British subjects domiciled outside the British Isles both before and after migration, who were much more likely to enter than to leave the United Kingdom, the overall repatriant ratio for 1912–13 rises to 47%.[20] This index of reverse movement is identical to the ratio for aggregate passenger movement of British subjects over the four preceding years.[21] We may infer that the patterns reported for 1912–13 were not an aberration of that particular accounting period, and that in this era the true repatriant ratio for long-term migration between Ireland and the United States was indeed only about one-tenth. The true rate of reverse movement among 'permanent' migrants, though higher than generally assumed, was well below the level suggested by the deceptive returns of passenger flow.

As Table 1.6 indicates, there was relatively little temporary passenger flow between Ireland and extra-European ports in 1912–13. 79% of British subjects landing in Irish ports were 'permanent' immigrants compared with 68% of those landing in British ports. In the case of outward migration, there were 99 emigrants previously resident in Ireland for every 100 passengers leaving Irish ports, compared with 94% in the British case.[22] This pattern was replicated for migration to and from all major extra-European countries. The net outflow from Ireland of permanent migrants exceeded 70,000, whereas there was a small net inflow of less than 2,000 temporary migrants into Irish ports. Because so many Canadian residents travelled via New York or Boston rather than Canadian ports, it is not possible to make precise comparisons between British North America and the United States when computing temporary migration levels. However, the combined North American figures presented in Table 1.6 indicate that temporary inward movement to Ireland from North America was considerably more common than temporary movement from Australasia, South Africa, or India. Given the greater expense in time and money in travelling from those distant countries, this contrast is not surprising.

The distinctive patterns of Irish migration are perhaps most clearly evident in Table 1.7, which confirms the unique predominance of America. Three-quarters of all those bound for Ireland, whether as permanent or temporary migrants, came from North America, compared with less than half of permanent immigrants into Britain and three-fifths of temporary migrants disembarking at British ports. Table 1.7 also shows how few temporary migrants passed through Irish ports (less than 5% of United Kingdom incomers and only 2.6% of United Kingdom outgoers). All of these findings, it should be recalled, exclude aliens as well as British subjects without any residence in the United Kingdom. Since most British and Irish emigrants to the United States eventually became naturalised Americans and therefore 'aliens', it is worth asking how many aliens entered Ireland in the only period for which such returns were published (1912–13). The number was inconsiderable: 336 alien immigrants intended to take up residence in Ireland, including 308 from the United States. The number of alien emigrants from Ireland was only slightly greater: 468 passengers, including 392 bound for the United States.[23] Since some of these alien migrants were presumably not of Irish origin, it is clear that naturalised Americans were not yet a major element of permanent reverse movement into Ireland. The extent of short-term visits by naturalised Irish settlers with American residence cannot, alas, be ascertained from the published returns.[24]

Attempts to compute the balance of inward and outward flow, and to discriminate between permanent and temporary migration, had already been made by statisticians in the United States. Using a variety of criteria, Gould has computed repatriant ratios for the Irish and other alien groups in the United States just before the First World War. According to one specification, for every alien intending to emigrate to Ireland there were sixteen Irish residents immigrating to the United States, the lowest repatriant ratio for any major country of origin.[25] Irish expatriates were far more inclined to return home as visitors than to resettle in Ireland. It should be noted, however, that all American-generated repatriant ratios understate the true reverse flow because they exclude passengers who had repudiated their Irish or British nationality by taking out American citizenship. As shown in Chapter 8, a significant flow of naturalised American visitors to rural Ireland had developed by the early twentieth century. The fact that most Irish reverse movement was temporary does not diminish its cultural impact and contribution to 'Americanisation'.

Though most emigrants did not return permanently to their homeland, the 'returned Yank' had become a familiar figure in rural Ireland by the 1890s. In terms of occupation and material success, as already suggested, the home-comers were not easily reducible to any simple stereotype. Local response to their arrival was correspondingly ambivalent, ranging from admiration through envy to contempt. Return, like departure, generated fierce and conflicting emotions. A Donegal man who embarked from New York at the beginning of the twentieth century remembered that 'the shouting, the roaring, and the lamentation of the people on the quays would deafen you'; whereas when he left Derry about 4 years earlier there had been no quayside farewell.[26] Arrival home was often a muted occasion marked by awkwardness, alienation, and mutual wariness. Hosts and guests alike would be eager to impress each other: the Yankee would 'provide a bit of a feast' for the villagers, who in turn might have brought an outside car to the station to make his homecoming as 'dacent' as possible.[27]

Despite dancing, drinking, and gossiping, alienation often predominated. On his first trip to Inishmaan, J. M. Synge witnessed 'the return of a native who had spent five years in New York'. He paced about 'in his neat suit, looking strangely foreign to his birthplace ... When the curraghs were in their places the men crowded around him to bid him welcome. He shook hands with them readily enough, but with no smile of recognition. He is said to be dying.'[28] Other reports stress the conspicuousness in 'dress, manner, and appearance' of repatriates, such as the girl who 'in her well-fitting cloth dress and jacket, looked strangely out of place in the small cottage where I found her' (near Westport, Co. Mayo, in 1893).[29] Some Yanks were tactful enough to discard their finery after a couple of days, like the girls whom the novelist 'George Birmingham' observed chatting in Irish and raking the hay in crimson flannel petticoats.[30]

Yet re-assimilation into Irish life was difficult even for those who had found out that America 'did not suit them, and that they did not get their health there, and the working hours were too long and too different'.[31] Those who had failed abroad tended to be despised at home, while those who had succeeded were greeted with resentment. As Birmingham wrote:[32]

We do not, as a rule, much like them either as settlers or visitors. If they come home for good and all, they put up the price of land, bidding up small holdings which happen to be for sale to quite ridiculous prices. Then they build houses which are out of keeping with our humble dwellings. Their ways of life are a continual reproach to our easy-going habits ... If they come as visitors their conversation annoys us.

Irish networks of kinship and friendship, so efficient in overcoming physical separation, came under severe strain when that separation was unexpectedly terminated.

As before, the successful returned emigrant was often stereotyped as either a woman in search of a husband or a man in search of property. In north Longford it was the custom for returning women to devote their ample fortunes to rescuing debt-burdened farmers, so earning the epithet 'redeemer'.[33] In 1907, the Dudley Commission was told that numerous girls returned from America to Knock, Co. Mayo, with fortunes of £100 or £200, so being 'sure to get husbands'. In Carna, Co. Galway, girls brought back dowries of between £50 and £300, while the range reported in Roscommon was £50–£200.[34] Occasionally, men came home in search of Irish wives, as in the case of a reformed alcoholic who returned in the 1860s from the Victorian gold diggings 'to the Old Land with the reward of his labour, and seriously talked about "picking up some young woman" to shed the radiance of her smiles within his cottage home of ease'.[35]

The prominence of Yanks in purchasing tenant right, often at inflated prices, is confirmed by testimony from counties as disparate as Wexford and Donegal (1880), Cork and Galway (1897), and Leitrim (1907). In Dungloe, Co. Donegal, a small farmer cum shopkeeper claimed that 'the American money raised the price of land. Many who paid large prices for farms on their return with their savings from America have, since the bad times, had to go back to the States.'[36] A similar case was reported from Carna (Connemara), where a Boston man bought for £28 four adjacent holdings whose tenants had been evicted:[37]

The man returned from America, when his relative bought the places, and he expended about £40 or £45 on it, and made a very superior country house. When he had all that done the land was incapable of improvement, and he failed on the spot and sold it, with his house, for £30, and went off to America.

In Mallow, Co. Cork, two Americans returned in the mid-1880s with capital raised from diamond-mining and sheep-farming, and 'at once picked up' any farms that had since come on to the market.[38] Local hostility was aroused not only by the alleged inflation of land prices, but also by the readiness of returned emigrants to 'grab' evicted farms and by their agricultural incompetence. An organiser of the United Irish League in Mohill, Co. Leitrim, asserted that the only farmers able to buy land were returned or returning Americans: 'I never saw one of them fit for a spit in agriculture. They have exhausted their energies in America earning this money.'[39]

Those who returned as settlers or tourists, though often greeted with reserve and suspicion, helped to bridge the cultural gap between Ireland and the urban world. Their speech, clothing, and manners inevitably infected the home population, producing a droll blend of Ireland, Britain, and America. The evident possibility of return encouraged emigrants to leave Ireland with less fuss than before. Even in 1871, Wexford people were matter-of-fact about going to America: 'in fact, they speak of it now as they spoke formerly about going from one county into another'.[40] The American wake and wail were still reported, but as Robert Lynd remarked of emigrant girls boarding trains in Connemara, 'sometimes, the lamenting girl seems to lose her grief as suddenly as she found it, and as she arrives at various railway stations she leans out of the window to see if there is any friendly face about which be wakened into interest by her momentary tragedy'.[41]

In 1882, James Hack Tuke described the departure of his second shipload of assisted emigrants from Clifden, Co. Galway: 'I did not hear a single "wail" as we left the ship; but before we steamed out a multitude of hand-shakings and blessings were showered upon me, and three cheers rang across the bay.'[42] As Monsignor O'Riordan observed in 1905:[43]

the 'American wake' has ceased to be what it once was. The wailing which was once witnessed at the parting of old friends and the separating of families is heard no more. Most of our present emigrants are leaving friends at home only to join others beyond the sea. Children learn from their childhood that their destiny is America; and as they grow up, the thought is set before them as a thing to hope for.

Pity, once lavished upon Ireland's 'exiles', now consoled those who had failed to escape.

V   Cosmopolitan Emissaries

'Provincial' Ireland was clearly less insular and inward-looking than its denigrators suggested. Internal migration helped to sharpen and personify regional and inter-county rivalries, and to replenish the battery of stereotypes, usually withering, associated with Kerry or Cork or Belfast. It also gave human shape to metropolitan cultures, embodied in the steady flow of officials and professionals from Dublin to the provinces. Seasonal movement had a highly localised impact, introducing certain counties of Connaught to rural society in northern England and southern Scotland, which would have seemed almost as alien as life in the industrial towns that drew long-term emigrants across the water.

The most important cultural import was embodied in returning emigrants and their children, whose behaviour and appearance conveyed contradictory messages about the attractions of life beyond Ireland. Though almost always dwarfed by outward migration, reverse movement from North America and Australasia was sufficient to ensure that most pre-war Irish people became eye-witnesses to the human consequences of emigration. In order to grasp the scale and character of this cosmopolitan intrusion into Ireland, especially into its most 'backward' regions, we must examine the profile of non-natives recorded in the decennial census from 1841 onwards. Where did these immigrants and visitors originate, where did they reside in Ireland, and what is known about their collective profile? What does this suggest about the relative impact of Anglicisation and Americanisation on rural Ireland? How cosmopolitan was the population of post-Famine Ireland?

Table 1.1 *Sex and age of passengers entering and leaving the UK, 1895–1911*

Nationality	Ann. Av.	% of UK	% of AC	% Female	% <12	% Im:Em
Irish	18,666	30.9	85.9	56.1	9.3	
British	41,724	69.1	41.6	38.6	11.2	
Irish	40,693	35.2	87.5	54.7	6.8	45.9
British	74,772	64.8	37.2	40.8	13.4	55.8
From Other Countries						
Irish	3,052	5.0	14.1	34.8	10.6	
British	58,522	95.0	58.4	36.9	14.3	
To Other Countries						
Irish	5,788	4.4	12.5	37.2	11.7	52.7
British	126,314	95.6	62.8	37.9	15.3	46.3

Note: Inward passengers are British subjects contracted to land in the UK from extra-European ports. Outward passengers are British subjects embarking from the UK and contracted to land in extra-European ports. Proportions refer to percentage of (1) all UK passengers belonging to each nationality, excluding 'British Colonial' (separately returned from 1908); (2) all passengers who embarked to (or from) all countries (AC); (3) all passengers who were female; (4) all passengers who were under 12 years; (5) inward passengers to outward passengers from the UK. Totals exclude the final such return covering January–March 1912. *Source: Copy of Tables relating to Emigration and Immigration from and to the UK in the Year [1895–1911]*: HCP.

Table 1.2 *Sex and age of passengers entering and leaving the UK, 1895–1902 and 1903–11*

Nationality	Ann. Av.	% of UK	% of AC	% Female	% <12	% Im:Em
1895–1902						
From USA						
Irish	18,094	31.6	89.9	55.4	9.7	
British	39,192	68.4	49.1	39.8	12.9	
To USA						
Irish	38,701	38.7	91.9	56.7	6.5	46.8
British	61,201	61.3	49.5	41.0	12.2	64.0
From Other Countries						
Irish	2,031	4.8	10.1	36.8	13.1	
British	40,599	95.2	50.1	38.2	15.9	
To Other Countries						
Irish	3,413	5.2	8.1	36.3	9.1	59.5
British	62,533	94.8	50.5	36.5	12.9	64.9
1903–1911						
From USA						
Irish	19,174	30.4	82.9	56.7	8.9	
British	43,974	69.6	37.1	37.6	9.9	
To USA						
Irish	42,465	32.8	84.3	53.0	7.0	45.2
British	86,835	67.2	32.2	40.8	14.2	50.6
From Other Countries						
Irish	3,959	5.0	17.1	33.9	9.5	
British	74,453	95.0	62.9	36.3	13.5	
To Other Countries						
Irish	7,899	4.1	15.7	37.6	12.6	50.1
British	183,008	95.9	67.8	38.4	16.0	40.7

Note: See Table 1.1.

Table 1.3 *Sex and age of UK immigrants and emigrants, 1912–13*

Residence	No.	% of UK	% of AC	% Female	% <12	% >30	% Im:Em
From USA							
Ireland	6,709	21.4	59.8	55.8	10.4	43.1	
Britain	24,636	78.6	18.4	41.5	13.3	52.8	
To USA							
Ireland	60,406	34.6	73.6	54.4	6.2	14.7	11.1
Britain	113,968	65.4	18.0	46.1	16.4	40.0	21.6
From Other Countries							
Ireland	4,508	4.0	40.2	37.7	14.5	52.0	
Britain	109,537	96.0	81.6	40.5	17.5	52.4	
To Other Countries							
Ireland	21,648	4.0	26.4	41.7	14.8	26.7	20.8
Britain	520,331	96.0	82.0	44.7	20.2	36.6	21.1

Note: 'Immigrants' are British subjects leaving extra-European ports, previously resident in the stated country for at least 12 months, and contracted to land in the UK with the intention of residing in the stated country for at least 12 months. 'Emigrants' are British subjects leaving the UK, previously resident in the stated country for at least 12 months, and contracted to land in extra-European ports with the intention of residing in the stated country for at least 12 months. Proportions refer to percentage of (1) all UK migrants who intended residence in each country; (2) all migrants who were previously resident in all countries (AC); (3) all migrants who were female; (4) all migrants who were under 12 years; (5) all adult migrants (over 12 years), excluding those of unstated age, whose age exceeded 30 years. The only available tabulations for each country within the UK cover April 1912–December 1913. *Source: Copy of Tables relating to Emigration and Immigration from and to the UK in the Year [1912, 1913]*: HCP.

Table 1.4 *Occupations of UK immigrants and emigrants, 1912–13*

Occupation	M: Agric.	Lab.	Com.	Sk.	F: Service	Trades	Prof.
From USA							
To Ireland	9.4	41.5	22.0	27.1	84.2	7.5	8.3
To Britain	5.6	14.0	31.3	49.0	60.2	15.3	24.5
To USA							
From Ireland	33.6	48.2	8.2	9.9	87.1	9.7	3.2
From Britain	6.2	15.3	24.4	54.1	60.0	25.3	14.7
From Other Countries							
To Ireland	19.3	26.0	26.3	28.4	58.4	13.3	28.3
To Britain	12.7	15.6	29.0	42.7	58.4	10.0	31.6
To Other Countries							
From Ireland	30.7	34.7	19.7	15.0	76.3	12.3	11.4
From Britain	23.9	21.5	20.1	34.5	77.1	12.5	10.3

Note: Proportions refer to the percentage of men and women of all ages returned under the stated occupational groups, excluding those of 'miscellaneous' or unstated occupations. Men were classified as (1) 'agricultural', (2) 'commercial and professional', (3) 'skilled trades', (4) 'labourers'; and women as (5) 'domestic and other service', (6) 'dressmakers and other trades', (7) 'teachers, clerks, and professions'.

Table 1.5 *Nationality vs. residence of British subjects entering and leaving the UK, 1908–13*

Country	USA			Other Countries			All Countries		
	In	Out	RR	In	Out	RR	In	Out	RR
% by Nationality, 1908–11									
English & Welsh	54.4	48.4	60.9	66.9	74.0	41.0	62.3	65.6	48.3
Scottish	13.6	19.0	38.8	13.4	18.7	32.7	13.5	18.8	34.8
Irish	28.1	31.6	48.1	4.4	3.9	51.0	13.1	13.0	48.7
British Colonial	3.9	1.0	216.4	15.3	3.4	202.6	11.1	2.6	204.3
Total British subjects	100	100	54.2	100	100	45.4	100	100	48.3
% by Permanent Residence, April 1912–December 1913									
England & Wales	31.4	50.4	38.5	47.4	69.6	28.4	41.8	64.5	30.5
Scotland	6.0	14.0	26.2	8.6	15.5	23.2	7.7	15.1	23.9
Ireland	6.2	27.5	13.9	2.2	3.5	26.3	3.6	9.8	17.1
British Colonies	10.6	2.4	276.0	37.7	10.3	152.4	28.3	8.2	161.8
Foreign countries	45.8	5.7	499.8	4.2	1.1	156.2	18.6	2.3	377.9
Total British subjects	100	100	61.8	100	100	41.7	100	100	47.0

Note: For categories, see notes to Tables 1.1 and 1.3. 'Permanent residence' is defined as the last country in which outgoing passengers had resided for at least 1 year or the country in which incoming passengers intended to reside for at least 1 year. The category 'British Colonial' (separately returned from 1908) refers to those born in British colonies or possessions, previously distributed among the home nationalities. The 'repatriant ratio' (RR) gives the number of inward passengers as a percentage of outward passengers. Statistics refer to British subjects, excluding 'foreigners' (1908–11) and 'aliens' (1912–13), and omit the last set of returns under the old categorisation (January–March 1912).

Table 1.6 *Distribution of UK permanent and temporary migrants, 1912–13*

	Net Flow		Repatriant Ratio		% Permanent	
Residence	Perm.	Temp.	Perm.	Temp.	In	Out
All Countries						
Ireland	70,837	−1,940	13.7	277	78.7	98.7
Britain	500,126	−22,059	21.2	153	67.9	93.9
USA						
Ireland	53,697	[−712]	11.1	[161]	78.1	[98.1]
Britain	89,332	[3,366]	21.6	[89]	47.6	[78.9]
British North America						
Ireland	13,139	[−930]	12.7	[−76]	82.7	[103.6]
Britain	283,466	[−21,203]	12.6	[−103]	79.1	[103.3]
Total North America						
Ireland	*66,836*	*−1,642*	*11.4*	*358*	*79.1*	*99.2*
Britain	*372,798*	*−17,837*	*14.9*	*189*	*63.4*	*95.6*
Australia & New Zealand						
Ireland	3,639	−93	22.5	338	88.9	99.2
Britain	115,061	−253	16.1	108	87.1	97.9
British South Africa						
Ireland	75	−52	90.4	286	89.8	96.5
Britain	2,821	−1,492	86.4	148	79.5	86.9
India & Ceylon						
Ireland	22	−20	94.0	161	86.7	91.8
Britain	2,099	−609	83.0	137	81.4	87.9

Note: See Table 1.4.

Table 1.7 *Location of UK permanent and temporary migrants, 1912–13*

Residence	% by Residence in UK				% by Country			
	Inward		Outward		Inward		Outward	
	Perm.	Temp.	Perm.	Temp.	Perm.	Temp.	Perm.	Temp.
All Countries								
Ireland	7.7	4.6	11.5	2.6	100	100	100	100
Britain	92.3	95.4	88.5	97.4	100	100	100	100
USA								
Ireland	21.4	6.5	34.6	3.7	59.8	61.9	73.6	[106.6]
Britain	78.6	93.5	65.4	96.3	18.4	42.7	18.0	[73.7]
British North America								
Ireland	4.5	3.6	4.4	4.8	17.1	13.2	18.3	[−48.4]
Britain	95.5	96.4	95.6	95.2	30.4	17.0	51.1	[−25.3]
Total North America								
Ireland	11.6	5.7	14.7	3.1	76.9	75.1	92.0	58.2
Britain	88.4	94.3	85.3	96.9	48.7	59.7	69.1	48.4
Australia & New Zealand								
Ireland	4.6	3.9	3.3	1.3	9.4	4.4	5.7	3.6
Britain	95.4	96.1	96.7	98.7	16.4	5.1	21.6	7.3
British South Africa								
Ireland	3.8	1.7	3.6	0.9	6.3	2.6	1.0	2.6
Britain	96.2	98.3	96.4	99.1	13.3	7.3	3.3	7.6
India & Ceylon								
Ireland	3.4	2.3	3.0	2.0	3.1	1.7	0.4	3.0
Britain	96.6	97.7	97.0	98.0	7.3	3.5	1.9	3.9

Note: 'Permanent migrants' are those intending to reside for at least 12 months in another country. Figures for 'temporary migrants' were obtained by subtracting the number of 'permanent migrants' from that of all passengers previously resident for at least 12 months in Ireland or Britain and contracted to land in the stated country, or intending to so reside after arrival in the UK from the stated country. For each sub-category, the '% by residence in UK' shows the proportion whose UK domicile was in Ireland and Britain, respectively. The '% by country' shows the proportion of those with British and Irish residence, respectively, migrating to or from the stated country outside the UK. See also Table 1.4.

2   Cosmopolitan Ireland, 1841–1911

I   Sources

How should the lack of any comprehensive study of immigration into nineteenth-century Ireland be rectified? Demographic historians, who have done so much to clarify the profile and dynamics of the Irish 'diaspora', have mostly glossed over the human counter-flow into Ireland, with the exception of penetrating studies of Jewish, Italian, and Scottish immigration.[1] Though dwarfed by outward movement, the scale of immigration and return movement was clearly sufficient to expose a large proportion of the Irish people to the direct personal influence of those who had lived elsewhere. It is easy to explain academic concentration on outward movement: its much greater magnitude; the passionate debates that it engendered; the beguilingly elaborate enumeration of emigrants; and the inexhaustible personal documentation to be found in emigrant letters and testimonies. My intention in this chapter is to show that inward movement to pre-war Ireland from many countries of origin also deserves sustained examination. By assembling a statistical profile of non-natives enumerated in the Irish census, I hope to illuminate the emergence of cosmopolitan Ireland within the shell of the Union.[2]

This chapter supplies a broader context for the ensuing study of Americans in Ireland from two perspectives. First, it compares the statistical profile of non-natives in Ireland with those enumerated in Britain, in order to assess the relative concentration of human agents of 'cosmopolitanism' in both parts of the United Kingdom. Second, it shows that the American presence in Ireland diverged radically from the profile of any other group of settlers and visitors from outside the country. This fact, hitherto undiscussed, is my key justification for writing a book on Americans in Ireland rather than outsiders in general, and for preparing the way for a broader analysis of 'Americanisation' rather than 'globalisation' or 'cosmopolitanisation'. But the place of Americans in

Irish society cannot be understood without preliminary exploration of those wider settings.

In the absence of inward passenger returns specifying nativity before 1895, historians must rely primarily on the statistics of birthplace assembled for the decennial census between 1841 and 1911.[3] Heads of 'family' (household) were asked to state the birthplace of each household member (by county within Ireland and otherwise by country). As with all census returns, the outcome was somewhat unreliable: apart from lapses of memory, knowledge, and veracity, the enumerators had to contend with many anomalous and idiosyncratic entries (a particular problem was the ambiguous term 'America'). Anomalous birthplace entries were so widespread that those responsible for digitising the family forms for 1901 and 1911 have been unable to classify hundreds of thousands of entries, with baneful consequences for statistical analysis based on computer searches.[4] The census commissioners and their staff were punctilious in translating informal entries into standard categories, but ambiguities remained, and many relevant cross-tabulations were inevitably omitted from the brilliantly devised series of published reports (few family forms survive except for 1901 and 1911). From 1841 to 1861, no clear distinction was drawn between those of colonial and foreign birth; and even after the reorganisation of the Irish census to make it more compatible with British practice, the Irish did not follow the British example by distinguishing British from foreign subjects. With all their limitations, what do census returns reveal about the cosmopolitan presence in Ireland?

II   Ireland and Britain

How far did Ireland lag behind Britain in its intake of outsiders?[5] By the early twentieth century, the scale of overseas immigration into Britain (particularly of Lithuanian Jews from the Russian empire) was arousing intense controversy, whereas movement into Ireland was scarcely noticed. Table 2.1 dissects the Irish component of immigration to the British Isles. At first glance, this does not suggest rampant cosmopolitanisation in Ireland. Ireland's overseas population, as a proportion of the overseas population of the United Kingdom, declined steadily from 9.3% in 1841 to 4.6% in 1911. Why so? As the bottom line of the table suggests, this decline must be set against the continuous depopulation of Ireland during a period of steady growth in Britain, the Irish component of the United Kingdom's population having fallen from 30.6% in 1841 to 9.7% in 1911. In that year, Ireland accounted for only 4.9% of colonials and 2.1% of non-American foreigners in the United Kingdom.

Ireland's share of the colonial population reached its peak (9.4%) in 1871, two decades later than its highest share of the foreign population (11.9%). These proportions were dwarfed by Ireland's share of the resident American population, which rose almost uninterruptedly to 41.3% in 1911. Something odd was going on.

The overseas-born proportion of each country's population was indeed much smaller for Ireland than for England or Scotland. Yet, in Ireland as in Britain, that proportion rose steadily throughout the period 1841–1911, and the gap narrowed over time (Table 2.2). In 1841, 4,500 of Ireland's 8 million inhabitants had been born overseas – equivalent to 5 per 10,000, one-fifth of the English proportion. By 1911, despite continuous depopulation, the Irish component had risen to almost half of the British figure. Ireland's 28,000 immigrants accounted for 64 per 10,000 of the Irish population, compared with 148 for England and Wales and 112 for Scotland. Ireland (like Scotland) housed almost half as many colonials as foreigners, a much higher ratio than that for England. Admittedly, by the standards of our own day, only a tiny part of the Irish population had been born overseas. Yet the cultural impact of 28,000 cosmopolitans in a country of 4 million people was potentially immense, when we consider the intricate personal networks of neighbourhood, workplace, and school fostered by Irish sociability.

The rapid growth of immigration to every province of Ireland is manifest in Table 2.3, which traces its development in each province between 1841 and 1911. The largest absolute increment outside Connaught occurred in the 1860s, but the proportionate increase was greatest over the Famine decade. The overseas component was invariably greatest in Leinster and lowest in Connaught, with similar proportions in Munster and Ulster. In 1851, the overseas proportion was already 22 per 10,000 in Leinster but only 5 in Connaught, the province most notorious for poverty, insularity, backwardness, and heavy emigration. By 1911, following a remarkable upsurge in immigration to Connaught over the preceding decade, the proportion had risen to 47 in Connaught and 84 in Leinster. Connaught's overseas proportion thus exceeded that for the entire country only two decades earlier (45).

The strikingly stable geography of cosmopolitan Ireland is revealed by ranking the thirty-two counties of Ireland according to the overseas proportion of their population in census years ranging between 1841 and 1911. At every census, Dublin headed the overseas league, with very high overseas proportions in the urbanised counties embracing Belfast, Londonderry, and Cork. Already in 1841, Dublin had 27 overseas-born per 10,000, rising to 59 in 1851, 73 in 1861, 103 in

1871, and 127 in 1911. Despite variations in county rankings from census to census, the county distribution in 1861 accounted for almost two-thirds of the variation in 1911, and over three-quarters of that in 1841.[6] These findings suggest the persistent strength of pull-factors, such as urbanisation and the location of ports, in determining where outsiders chose to locate themselves within Ireland.

Table 2.3 also records the much more visible presence of natives of Great Britain, who likewise multiplied steadily throughout the period (from 38 per 10,000 in 1841 to 293 in 1911). By 1911, almost 129,000 embodiments of native Britishness were living in Ireland, admittedly a much smaller presence than the reverse displacement of Irish natives in Britain. Yet, when measured against the host population, the British presence in Ireland was more than twice as great as the Irish presence in Britain.[7] A substantial but usually unrecorded minority of Ireland's Britons were military and naval personnel (excluded from the birthplace returns in 1841 and 1851).[8] Most were short-term but highly visible visitors, whose custom was invaluable to many pubs and merchants in the vicinity of army barracks and naval stations. Once again, the British presence was predictably highest in Leinster, lowest in Connaught, and intermediate in Munster and Ulster. Connaught was the only province not experiencing a continuous increase in the British proportion, pre-sumably because of fluctuations in its military population.

Alongside the relentless post-Famine 'recolonisation' of Ireland by Britons, the overseas component was growing even more rapidly. In 1861, there were only 15 overseas-born in Ireland for every 100 born in Britain; five decades later, the ratio of overseas-born to Britons had risen to 22. The most spectacular and continuous rebalancing was in Con-naught, where the ratio soared from 20 in 1861 to no less than 57 in 1911. By this measure, the poorest province was leading the race against insularity. If the size of the British presence provides a crude indicator of 'Anglicisation', then the countervailing influence of cosmopolitanism, betokened by the overseas presence, was offering serious competition as Ireland prepared for Home Rule.

By far the greatest influx came from America.[9] Table 2.4 compares the inexorable growth of Ireland's American population with that of other foreigners, excluding sailors and seamen because of wild fluctu-ations in the number of foreign ships which happened to be berthed in Irish ports on successive census nights. We are fortunate that the Irish census commissioners, unlike their British counterparts, invariably published returns of the major occupations followed by each national-ity. These reveal that the perplexing peak of 1851 was generated by 2,789 foreign sailors, compared with just 27 in 1841 and 808 in 1861.

Excluding sailors, the foreign-born population rose quite steadily from 3,580 in 1841 to 5,089 in 1851 and 7,459 in 1861.[10] The number of Americans increased in every intercensal period between 1841 and 1911, rising from below 2,000 to nearly 13,000, with particularly rapid advances in the 1850s and 1870s. Meanwhile, Ireland's non-American foreign population expanded only from 1,600 to 5,700. The American proportion of the foreign population rose fairly steadily from 43% in 1851 to 69% in 1911. Though the presence of up to 13,000 Americans in Ireland was dwarfed by the 2 million natives of Ireland in North America, it is clear that the vast exodus to America was generating substantial reverse movement.[11]

What were the origins of Ireland's immigrants? Table 2.5 unveils a startlingly diverse foreign population even before the Great Famine. Ireland's interaction with the empire was reflected in the presence of 500 (East) Indians and over 350 West Indians, doubtless for the most part the wives or children of Irish soldiers, administrators, and planters (no record was kept of colour or race). About one-quarter of each colonial category were living in Dublin, but the rest were sprinkled throughout the country: even Leitrim had attracted 5 Indians and 3 West Indians by 1841. Europe was represented by 445 French, 241 Spaniards, 180 Germans and Poles, and 96 Italians. The largest contingent (almost 2,000, or 44% of the total) hailed from 'America', reflecting extensive pre-Famine emigration to British North America as well as the United States.

The Famine decade, notorious for unprecedentedly heavy mortality and emigration, also witnessed a sharp increase in the overseas population. It seems perplexing that so many foreigners were attracted to a country whose society and economy had scarcely begun to recover from the disaster by 1851. Overall, the number of incomers more than doubled, with marked growth among the Indians (211 in 1851 for every 100 in 1841), Italians (282), and Germans and Poles (467), and the amalgam of 'other' nationalities not separately tabulated (506). The Famine expansion was less marked for the French (179), West Indians (177), Americans (118), and Spaniards (115). It seems equally odd that, during the decade of economic recovery after 1851, every overseas contingent shrank except for Italians (106 in 1861 for every 100 in 1851), Indians (151), and Americans (153).

The general expansion of immigration masked notable variation between nationalities. Movement from France, India, and the British empire stabilised after increasing sharply in the 1860s. The German and Italian presence increased fairly slowly after 1861,[12] while the Spanish population tended to fall. Among the foreigners first separately enumerated in 1871, the most spectacular subsequent expansion was that of 'Russians' (almost all Jews and mainly, it appears, subjects of the Russian empire who had left Lithuania). By 1901, Russians outnumbered all other foreign groups except Americans with nearly 2,000 representatives. There were also small but fairly stable contingents from central Europe and the Low Countries, and fluctuating groups of Scandinavians. Ireland's exotic newcomers in 1911 included 128 Chinese and 73 Egyptians. Admittedly, a digital search unearthed only one native of China with a Chinese name (Kwao Yuen Tsan), a 30-year-old commercial traveller of no religious profession staying in a Belfast hotel.[13]

Settlers and visitors from the British empire and dominions, separately classified from 1871 onwards, outnumbered non-American foreigners at every census thereafter. The colonial population was dominated by natives of the Indian empire, numbering about 3,500 at each census between 1881 and 1911. By comparison, there were over 12,000 natives of Ireland in India by 1911.[14] Otherwise, Ireland's colonials were not distinguished by national origin in any published report after 1861. A digital search of the family returns for 1911 reveals about 800 Canadians and 1,000 Australians (concentrated in or near major cities).[15] These immigrants from the dominions were vastly outnumbered by the Irish in Canada (93,000) and in Australia (140,000).[16] The county distributions of colonials, Britons and non-American foreigners, likewise clustered in Dublin and urbanised regions, were closely inter-correlated.[17] All three were negatively correlated with the distribution of Americans in 1911, reflecting the increasing concentration of Americans in relatively poor and rural counties.[18]

III   Ireland's Immigrants

Sharper insight into the profile of Ireland's immigrants is provided by census returns for each nationality tabulated by sex, age, and locality (Table 2.6). Invariably, just over half of the Irish population was female. Except in 1851, the number of male and female immigrants was also quite evenly balanced overall. The female proportion of Americans, the largest nationality, varied only between 50% and 52% over the period 1851–1911. Males were always outnumbered among Indians and colonials, probably reflecting marriages between Irishmen and women of colonial birth. Except in 1841, however, men predominated among non-American foreigners and also British settlers (a disparity accentuated after the inclusion of servicemen in 1861). By 1911, the female component for foreign nationalities ranged between 13% for Danes and

64% for Swiss; six other small nationalities also had female majorities. The distribution of nationalities according to sex was fairly stable, almost half of the variance in 1911 being 'explained' by that in 1871.[19] Whereas an even sex-balance may point towards family migration, male predominance suggests an influx of unmarried men (such as soldiers or merchant seamen) on short-term assignments in Ireland.[20]

These surmises are consistent with statistics showing the proportion of children and minors for each nationality. In 1841, nearly half of the entire Irish population was under 20 years of age, a proportion that declined unevenly to 39% in 1911. Between 1841 and 1861, the only years for which ages were tabulated for colonials and Britons in Ireland, the colonial age distribution resembled that for the Irish population, whereas adults comprised more than two-thirds of Britons by 1861. Immediately before and after the Famine, the same applied to Ireland's American population. By contrast, between 1861 and 1911, minors accounted for about two-thirds of Americans (61%–72%). Over the same period, the proportion for non-American foreigners fell from 32% to 14%, indicating that very few European immigrants had come to Ireland with children, most being unmarried adults. In 1911, the proportion of minors ranged between zero for Greeks and 75% for Egyptians, exceeding one-fifth in only five cases (Table 2.7). The distribution of nationalities according to age was even more stable than that for sex.[21] By contrast with most European nationalities, the presence of so many young Americans reflected a form of family migration which requires further investigation. With its even sex-balance and high child proportion, the American population was clearly shaped by reverse migration, whether by family groups or by American-born children whose emigrant parents were temporarily unable to maintain them.

Predictably, the immigrants tended to cluster in the major towns and ports. Most nationalities were concentrated in Dublin, which accounted for almost one-quarter of foreigners but only 4.6% of the Irish population in 1841. The Europeans (notably the Germans) were even more metropolitan than the colonials, whereas less than one-tenth of the Americans were in Dublin. These contrasts between nationalities were broadly replicated between 1851 and 1911. Between 22% and 34% of the overseas population at each census were enumerated in Dublin, incorporating even higher proportions for non-American foreigners and sometimes for colonials. The British-born were likewise clustered in Dublin, the Dublin component ranging between 21% in 1871 and 29% in 1851. By 1911, Dublin housed 22% of Britons, 28% of colonials, and

40% of non-American foreigners. The most metropolitan nationality were the Russians, of whom 60% were Dubliners in 1901 and 56% in 1911. The distribution of nationalities according to the Dublin component fluctuated somewhat, but was fairly stable from 1881.[22] Once again, the Americans bucked the prevailing pattern. The Dublin component peaked at just 15% of Americans in 1861, thereafter declining steadily to less than 8% in 1911 despite Dublin's continuing expansion (the city and county comprised 10.9% of the Irish population by 1911). Reflecting the geographical origins of the emigrants themselves, the American newcomers were the only immigrant group to be widely distributed throughout the country.

Ireland's share of immigration to the British Isles likewise varied sharply between nationalities. The recorded Irish component in 1911 (Table 2.7) was relatively high for Africans (14%) and Chinese (8%), but negligible for Dutch, Swedes, and Russians (1%).[23] Taken as a group, Ireland's share of non-American foreigners was only 2%. By contrast, over two-fifths of recorded Americans in the United Kingdom were enumerated in Ireland in 1911, reflecting the far greater intensity of transatlantic emigration from Ireland by comparison with Britain.[24] The inhabitants of Ireland were three or four times as likely as their British contemporaries to have American neighbours.

IV   Occupations

What were the occupations of Ireland's immigrants and visitors, and how did these vary between nationalities? Unfortunately, the 1861 census report was the last to incorporate comprehensive occupational statistics by birthplace (Table 2.8). Official employment, overwhelmingly in the army, accounted for 46% of occupied British men, along with 44% of Indians, 28% of West Indians, and 17% of Americans (including Canadians). The importance of seafaring as a cosmopolitan conduit is apparent in the predominance of merchant seamen in most European nationalities (23% of occupied Spaniards, 36% of Germans, 40% of Italians, and 44% of 'other', unclassified foreigners). Frenchmen ranged more widely, 10% being teachers, 10% 'writing clerks', 12% officials, 4% clergy, 13% in domestic service or labour, and 7% in the clothing trades. Clothing also occupied 7% of Spaniards and Americans, and 9% of West Indians. Farming provided little employment for any nationality except the Americans, 19% of whom were returned as farmers or their servants and labourers. Domestic service was a major occupation for women of all nationalities, ranging between 27% of West Indians and 45% of

British women, while the proportion in clothing ranged between 13% of Germans and 45% of Americans. Teachers and governesses were prominent among the West Indians (15%), Italians (19%), French (28%), and Germans (45%).

Subsequent returns are less satisfactory, since they exclude Britons and colonials, fail to distinguish men from women, and refer only to occupational categories with more than forty foreigners. In 1911 (Table 2.9), these thirty-seven occupations accounted for 77% of all occupied foreigners. As in 1861, service was a major source of employment, especially for Germans and Italians, while clothing occupied no less than one-third of Russians (along with many general dealers). Teaching and religion were French and German specialities, while sailors still accounted for 17% of the French and 11% of all occupied Europeans. The most striking European–American contrast was in the farming and service sectors. Farming accounted for 31% of Americans but only 1% of Europeans; 16% of Americans were in service, but only 7% of Europeans. These findings confirm the contrast between a predominantly rural American population and a highly urbanised European presence.

Let us look more closely at the occupations associated with particular nationalities.[25] Between 1871 and 1911, merchant seamen invariably formed a majority of Danes, Norwegians, Swedes, and Dutch with reported occupations. In 1871 and 1881, the same was true for Greeks, Austrians, Russians, Spaniards, and Italians, but never for the French or Germans.[26] It is obvious that many of Ireland's Europeans were a floating population, shaped by which ships happened to be in Irish ports or waters when the census was taken. The same applied to fishermen, who invariably accounted for at least 30% of all the French with reported occupations (forming the majority in 1901). As the 1871 census commissioners observed, the fact that all foreign fishermen were French (apart from four Americans) was 'due to the presence in Kinsale Harbour of a fleet of small fishing smacks upon the Census night'.[27]

The predominance of seafarers among Scandinavians was not unique to Ireland, as revealed by Scottish census reports showing the proportion of foreigners enumerated on board ships in 1901 and 1911. In both years, the majority of all Swedish, Norwegian, and Danish males spent census night afloat, along with substantial proportions of the Dutch, Spanish, and Chinese.[28] Half a century earlier, the Scottish commissioners reported that 2,106 of the 3,969 foreigners 'were the crews of 300 foreign ships in the several ports of Scotland, while 139 were German emigrants wrecked on the coasts of Orkney'.[29] In their report for the same year, the English commissioners wryly remarked that 'the merchant seamen amount to 15,561, chiefly from Norway, Denmark, Sweden, and Germany, the descendants of the same races as invaded England'.[30]

If the Scandinavian seafarer and French fisherman were types firmly rooted in the occupational profile of those actually present and visible in pre-war Ireland (as in Britain), other nationalities also conformed closely to popular stereotypes. Census returns for 1871–1911 show that makers of watches and clocks accounted for up to one-quarter of occupied Germans in Ireland, while as many as 37% of the Italians were musicians or music teachers.[31] Even more noteworthy was the concentration of Italian ice-cream vendors, who in 1911 accounted for 64 of the 227 occupied Italians in Ireland (28%). A digital search identified 59 natives of Italy engaged in making or selling ice cream, along with 17 Italonyms born elsewhere and just 4 vendors without Italian names.[32] The most common Italian surnames were Forte, Fusco, Magliocca, Matassa, and Morelli, mainly families from the Casalattico district of Latium, near Rome, whose descendants still populate Irish telephone directories. Even in the 1980s, 85% of all Italians in the Republic of Ireland came from Latium, while 46% of those with occupations were ice-cream vendors.[33]

Teaching was another category strongly associated with certain nationalities, doubtless reflecting the demand for native speakers of European languages as school teachers and governesses. This applied particularly to the Swiss, whose teaching component ranged between 34% and 45%. There were also marked concentrations of French, German, and Belgian teachers in almost every census year. As 'Litvaks' multiplied in Ireland from the 1880s, they became indelibly associated with the 'rag trade', especially as pedlars, drapers, and tailors. Pedlars and hawkers alone comprised 42% of occupied Russians in 1891, 24% in 1901, and 14% in 1911.[34] It is easy to imagine the impact on Irish imaginations of personal exposure to Scandinavian seamen, Italian organ-grinders and ice-cream vendors, German watch-makers, Swiss language teachers, and Russian (Lithuanian) Jewish pedlars. Each group was justifiably viewed as exotic in its way of life, fostering cartoon-type images that ranged from quaint to menacing. In some measure, Irish stereotypes about the world at large were formed by personal observation of visitors and newcomers.

V   Digital Delvings

Thanks to the digital indexing of the census returns for 1911 (and 1901), it is possible (though arduous and hazardous) to explore several aspects of Ireland's incoming population ignored in the published reports (Table 2.10). Admittedly, the results of digital searching are far less reliable than the meticulously categorised and copy-edited tabulations in the original census reports.[35] As a result of faulty transcription and coding, searches by key word are neither comprehensive nor accurate in detail, but many omissions and anomalies may be eliminated through individual inspection of thousands of returns labelled 'other'. It is reassuring that the proportions of females and minors generated through digital searches seldom differ much from those derived from the published census (Table 2.4).[36] Though imprecise, the proportions given in Table 2.8 illuminate the age, religion, literacy, marital status, and relationship to family head of residents born in Britain and the empire as well as major foreign countries.

The religious profile of cosmopolitan Ireland is particularly interesting. The Roman Catholic component ranged from hardly any Russians to 87% of Italians. No less than 96% of the Russians returned their religion as 'Jewish', 'Hebrew', 'Israelite', 'Mosaic', 'Synagogue', or other synonyms.[37] Though Catholics dominated the Italian contingent, there were three Italian Waldensians in Ireland in 1911. There was also a large Catholic majority among the French (74%), most of the residue being Episcopalians (17%). The religious profile of Ireland's German population was predictably complex, including Catholics (33%), Episcopalians (27%), and explicit Lutherans (16%). The American religious profile is also worth noting, since all direct estimates of the religious complexion of the Irish in the United States are based on guesswork and stereotype.[38] American incomers were overwhelmingly Catholics (78%), with significant Episcopalian and Presbyterian minorities (9% each).[39]

The fact that over one-quarter of British incomers were Catholic points to a substantial presence of emigrant offspring, as in the American case. Though Episcopalians predominated among the English (58%) and Presbyterians among the Scots (38%), non-Conformists were also well represented (8% of the Welsh were Methodists). The religious profile of Canadians in Ireland resembled that of the Irish in Ontario, where the Catholic proportion was likewise 28%.[40] In the Australian case, the Catholic component (47%) was considerably below that for the Irish in Australia (71% in 1911). As in Irish Australia, however, Episcopalians (29%) outnumbered Presbyterians (17%).

Ireland's Indians were less exotic than one might hope: Catholics (43%) were slightly outnumbered by Episcopalians (47%), the residue being mainly Presbyterians (5%) and Methodists (2%).[41] The large Catholic component reflected the recent success of Irish Catholics

in penetrating the Indian administration, confirming the belief that
Ireland's involvement in the empire transcended communal and religious divisions at home.[42] Just six out of 3,600 had oriental names, while
three others were pagans. Four of the six orientals were servants. David
Pohlwà, a farm labourer, belonged like his employer in Wicklow to the
Church of Ireland. John Rasquinha, a Catholic 'Portuguese Indian'
who could neither read nor write, was butler to an Anglican captain
in the Wiltshires, resident in Fitzwilliam Square but born in London.
Mrs Kumariah Ayah, a Hindu, was a children's nurse for an Indian-born
family of Irish-speaking Catholics living in Donnybrook. Cooloo Krish-
swami, a Hindu male nurse, was employed by a Presbyterian major in
the Indian Medical Service, who explained that Cooloo could 'read and
write his own vernacular "Tamil" not English'. The other 'orientals'
were Leslie Ba Lau, an Episcopalian infant from Burma, living with
his Dublin-born mother and her parental family in Portobello, and
Maneck Dalal, a Zoroastrian 'doctor non-practising' in a Dublin
boarding house.

The three remaining Indian-born pagans were Mary Higgins,
an unmarried Hindu midwife at the Rotunda hospital, Elizabeth May
Warrington (an Irish-speaker), and her 17-year-old daughter Isobel.
The Warringtons belonged to a small Buddhist commune in Gilford
Road, Sandymount, shared with an English journalist and two Irish-
speaking medical students who had recently graduated in Arts from
Trinity College. Under the printed column-heading 'if deaf and dumb;
dumb only; blind; imbecile or idiot; or lunatic', Ralph Mecredy
wittily inscribed 'Vegetarian' for the entire household except Isobel.
His Buddhist fellow-student and boarder, Francis Clements Crosslé,
emigrated to New South Wales after achieving notice as a rugby international and a chronicler of arcane divisions within Irish
Freemasonry.[43]

The fact that personal connections with India were so common in pre-
war Ireland probably encouraged the cult of orientalism associated with
Yeats, 'AE', and the Irish literary revival. It is well known that the
Methodist James Henry Sproull Cousins, an idiosyncratic versifier and
feminist from Belfast who had belonged simultaneously to the Orange
Order and the Gaelic League, followed Annie Besant to India in 1915 to
expound his rather mawkish nationalist and theosophist ideals in a vastly
greater theatre. His infatuation with India was surely related to the fact
that the wife and eldest child of his uncle John Cousins, a Belfast
army pensioner belonging to the Brethren, were both born in India.[44]
Sentimental cosmopolitanism was fostered by practical links with other
peoples.

Literacy was almost universal among all nationalities except the Italians, of whom only 65% could read or write in any language. The low American proportion (80%) was probably due to the presence of many young children, seldom found in other nationalities. Acquaintance with the Irish language was predictably rare among foreigners, though 5% of Australians and 11% of Americans were reportedly able to speak Irish.

As in so many fields, Ireland's Americans and Russians were at opposite extremes. Whereas 82% of the Americans in 1911 were unmarried and only 16% were heads of family (or their wives), the corresponding Russian proportions were 19% unmarried and 64% heads. The unique profile of the Americans is confirmed by the distribution of children, relatives, those not described as relatives, and servants. One-tenth or less of Germans, French, and Italians were returned as children of family heads, the highest child proportion being 38% for Americans. Many other Americans were grandchildren (16%) or nephews and nieces (12%). No other nationality had more than a handful of grandchildren or nieces and nephews, the distant runners-up being Canadians (5% in each category) and Australians. Few Americans were unrelated to family heads (only 5% were lodgers, boarders, or visitors, while 3% were servants). By contrast, about one-quarter of Italians and Germans were unrelated inmates or servants.[45] In short, the American profile was conspicuous for its low proportions of literates, heads of family, and unrelated dependants, and its high proportions of Catholics, Irish-speakers, and children. The remarkable prominence of American grandchildren, nephews, and nieces strongly suggests that relatives in the homeland were routinely helping out when child-rearing became burdensome for emigrant parents.

VI   Americans in Ireland

On the eve of the First World War, Americans were by far the largest group of foreigners in Ireland, numbering nearly 13,000 and accounting for 45.3% of those born overseas (Table 2.11). In every province, the American-born component of the population had risen throughout the period 1841–1911, with rapid acceleration after 1891.[46] Yet the regional distribution of Americans changed radically over that period, reflecting the changing regional origins of those emigrating from Ireland to America and forming families there. Up to 1861, the American component was greatest in Leinster and Ulster, the provinces responsible for most pre-Famine emigration. Thereafter, Munster slowly gained on Leinster, while American settlement in Connaught accelerated until it outpaced all other provincial movements. By 1911, over four-fifths of Connaught's overseas-born were Americans, compared with only 28% in Leinster.

In other respects, there was surprisingly little variation between provinces in the American profile (Table 2.12). Between 1861 and 1911, about two-thirds of Ireland's American-born were aged under 20 years, fluctuating between three-fifths in 1911 and almost three-quarters in 1871. Though Connaught invariably had the most youthful American population (only 16% were adults in 1871), the other three provinces also had a youthful majority in every census year.[47] There was even less inter-provincial variation in the American female component, which hovered around 50% in every province and every census year from 1841 to 1911. The proportion never fell below 45% or exceeded 58%, and showed no clear tendency to rise or fall over time. Thus, the most distinctive features of Ireland's American population, its youthfulness and even sex-balance, applied throughout the four provinces.

The distribution of counties most likely to house Americans in 1871 was recognisably similar to that in 1841 (Maps 2.1, 2.2), but changed radically thereafter, so that the distribution in 1911 (Map 2.3) was only faintly correlated with that for 1871.[48] Thus, Dublin ranked third in 1841 and top of the league in 1871, but had fallen to twenty-eighth out of thirty-two counties by 1911. Conversely, Galway ranked twenty-ninth in 1841 and fourteenth in 1871, but second by 1911. Two counties were notable for their consistently high concentration of Americans: Longford ranked top in 1841 and third in both 1871 and 1911, while Londonderry ranked second in 1871, and seventh in 1911. Two Munster counties had a persistently sparse American presence. Clare ranked thirty-first in 1841, twenty-sixth in 1871, and twenty-fourth in 1911, compared with Tipperary's respective rankings of thirtieth, twenty-fourth, and twenty-seventh. Americans also remained a rarity in Mayo, which ranked bottom in 1841, 1851, and 1871, rising only to seventeenth by 1911.

Otherwise, however, the most dramatic change in the pattern of American settlement occurred in Connaught. The American colonisation of Connaught over the Edwardian decade echoed the massive exodus from the province in the 1880s, with a time lag of a couple of decades as emigrants married, bore children, and contemplated a return home. It is reassuring to find a marked correlation between the county distribution of census residents born in America and that of emigrants leaving Irish ports for the United States between 1876 and 1914 (Map 2.4). Backward Leitrim, the county with the highest American proportion by 1911, was also near the top of the emigration league table (see Chapter 6). It appears that the counties sending out the most

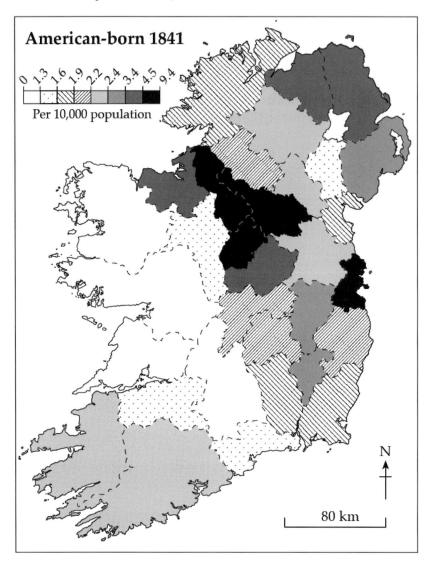

Map 2.1 American-born per 10,000 of population in each county, 1841

emigrants also tended to be those to which American-born children of those emigrants returned.[49]

Ireland's Americans were so unlike other incomers that they merit separate examination. Chapters 3, 4, and 5 scrutinise various groups of elite Americans, mainly found in cities and towns, who may be viewed as

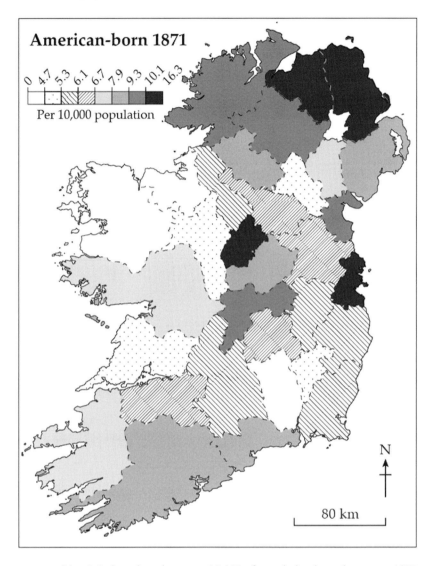

Map 2.2 American-born per 10,000 of population in each county, 1871

a showcase of American modernity exported in human form to Ireland. This is balanced by a prosopographical study of the American population of a single county, derived from family census returns for Leitrim in 1901 and 1911. Unlike most Americans enumerated in Irish cities, these were mainly the children of emigrants who had either returned home

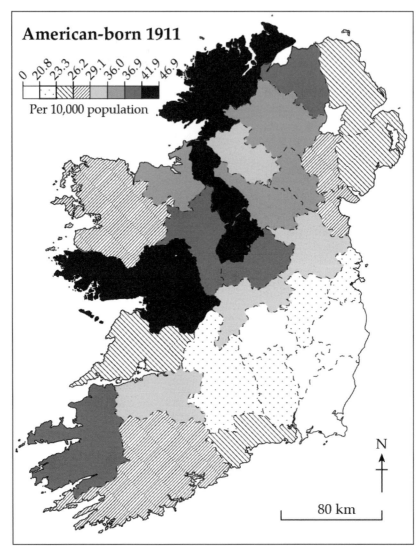

Map 2.3 American-born per 10,000 of population in each county, 1911

themselves or found it necessary to foster family members with relatives at home. By looking closely at the domestic environment of a manageable group of Americans in one of Ireland's most 'backward' counties, I hope to clarify the transnational bonds that drew emigrants and their offspring back to the homeland.

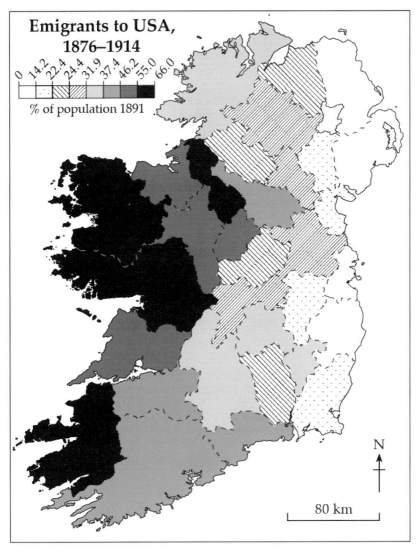

Map 2.4 Emigrants to USA, 1876–1914, % of population of each county, 1891

Table 2.1 *Percentage of UK overseas-born population in Ireland, 1841–1911*

Census	1841	1851	1861	1871	1881	1891	1901	1911
As % of UK Total								
Colonial	[38.8]	4.1	3.5	9.4	7.2	6.3	5.0	4.9
American	n.a.	n.a.	26.4	29.3	26.8	22.2	34.7	41.3
Other Foreign	n.a.	n.a.	5.7	4.3	3.8	2.8	2.5	2.1
Total Foreign	8.5	11.9	7.6	5.5	5.6	4.9	4.3	4.4
Total Overseas	9.3	8.3	5.8	6.9	6.2	5.3	4.5	4.6
Total Population	*30.6*	*23.9*	*20.0*	*17.2*	*14.8*	*12.5*	*10.8*	*9.7*

Note: UK totals exclude the Channel Islands and the Isle of Man. Irish colonial figures for 1841–61 refer only to India (East and West Indies). Those of foreign birth were classified as British or foreign subjects in British (but not Irish) census returns. Colonials resident in Britain but born in the British Empire and India were greatly under-enumerated in 1841, as the family schedule made no provision for them. British returns of specified nationalities (such as Americans) exclude those identified as British subjects, leading to over-statement of the Irish proportions of American and non-American foreigners; the 'total foreign' category (1851–1911) includes British subjects. America (all regions) includes British North America (1841–61). *Sources*: Census of Ireland (1841–1911), Great Britain (1841–61), England and Wales (1871–1911), and Scotland (1871–1911): HCP. Tables 2.1–2.5 are derived from published census reports (including Irish county and provincial reports) for the stated years.

Table 2.2 *Proportion of population of each country born overseas, 1841–1911*

Country of Residence	1841	1851	1861	1871	1881	1891	1901	1911
Colonial								
England and Wales	1	19	26	31	36	38	42	45
Scotland	1	23	25	29	34	34	36	38
Ireland	1	3	4	15	16	18	18	21
Foreign								
England and Wales	25	34	51	61	67	80	104	104
Scotland	11	15	25	27	34	40	67	75
Ireland	4	12	14	16	22	27	37	43
Total Overseas								
England and Wales	25	53	76	93	103	119	146	148
Scotland	12	37	50	56	69	74	102	112
Ireland	5	15	18	31	38	45	55	64

Note: Figures show the number per 10,000 of the censal population of England, Scotland, and Ireland born in British possessions and India (colonial), and elsewhere outside the UK (foreign).

Table 2.3 *Location of population born overseas and in Great Britain, 1841–1911*

Census	1841	1851	1861	1871	1881	1891	1901	1911
Overseas								
Leinster	9	22	30	50	59	66	77	84
Munster	4	17	16	38	39	45	53	61
Ulster	5	13	14	22	31	40	52	59
Connaught	3	5	10	11	19	23	29	47
Ireland	*5*	*15*	*18*	*32*	*38*	*45*	*55*	*64*
Number	*4,471*	*9,961*	*10,379*	*17,010*	*19,535*	*21,330*	*24,602*	*28,171*
Great Britain								
Leinster	69	117	214	286	289	333	342	406
Munster	24	57	104	151	159	177	199	218
Ulster	36	70	85	127	154	223	268	341
Connaught	15	26	51	65	82	75	59	82
Ireland	*38*	*71*	*116*	*163*	*177*	*216*	*241*	*293*
Number	*30,137*	*46,766*	*67,622*	*88,199*	*91,710*	*101,846*	*107,078*	*128,723*
% Ratio of Overseas to British-born Population								
Leinster	14	18	14	18	20	20	22	21
Munster	16	31	15	26	24	26	27	28
Ulster	14	18	17	17	20	18	19	17
Connaught	21	21	20	17	23	31	49	57
Ireland	*15*	*21*	*15*	*19*	*21*	*21*	*23*	*22*

Note: For each province, the figures show the number per 10,000 of the censal population born overseas (whether colonial or foreign) and in Great Britain. Returns for 1841 and 1851 exclude military and naval personnel. *Source:* Census of Ireland (1911), *General Report*, table 25.

Table 2.4 Foreign-born population of Ireland, excluding seamen, 1841–1911

Census	1841	1851	1861	1871	1881	1891	1901	1911
Number								
American	1,971	2,197	3,513	4,267	6,954	7,671	10,072	12,742
Other Foreign	1,609	2,892	3,946	3,054	3,424	4,489	5,821	5,676
% Intercensal Change								
American		+11	+60	+21	+63	+10	+31	+27
Other Foreign		+80	+36	−23	+12	+31	+30	−2
Proportion per 10,000 of Population								
American	2.4	3.4	6.1	7.9	13.4	16.3	22.6	29.0
Other Foreign	2.0	4.4	6.8	5.6	6.6	9.5	13.1	12.9
% of all Foreign-born								
American	55.1	43.2	47.1	58.3	67.0	63.1	63.4	69.2

Note: The top section gives the population born in America and in other foreign countries, deducting merchant seamen returned as 'sailors' or 'boatmen' (1841–61) or 'seamen' (1871–1911). Other sections show the percentage change in each category across each intercensal period; Americans and other foreigners as a proportion of the Irish population; and the percentage of all foreign non-seamen born in America.

Table 2.5 *Birthplaces of population born overseas, 1841–1911*

Census	1841	1851	1861	1871	1881	1891	1901	1911	% Ratio 1911:1881
Birthplace									
British Poss.	358	635	533	[8,367]	4,466	4,948	4,470	5,585	125
India	506	1,070	1,620	n.a.	3,859	3,482	3,591	3,681	95
America	1,982	2,336	3,577	4,354	7,034	7,705	10,120	12,763	181
France	445	795	773	1,216	1,129	1,232	1,349	1,104	98
Germany	180	840	697	787	927	940	1,037	963	104
Italy	96	271	287	642	357	263	301	417	117
Spain	241	278	214	115	133	89	104	82	62
Portugal				52	33	20	20	27	82
Greece				68	114	115	60	41	36
Russia				122	198	1,111	1,966	1,985	1,003
'Poland'				23	69	35	61	92	133
Austria				179	104	50	80	174	167
Switzerland				207	222	278	293	245	110
Belgium				107	120	163	145	177	148
Holland				66	56	44	79	106	189
Norway				324	234	374	335	133	57
Denmark				50	53	64	64	95	179
Sweden				56	95	123	120	74	78
China				42	65	112	113	128	197
Egypt				10	1	26	49	73	[7,300]
Other	663	3,358	2,719	223	266	156	245	226	85
Total Overseas	*4,471*	*9,583*	*10,420*	*17,010*	*19,535*	*21,330*	*24,602*	*28,171*	*144*

Note: America (all regions) excluded Canada and Newfoundland (1871–1911); 'British possessions' were restricted to the West India islands (1841–61); India was not separately enumerated from British possessions (1871 only); Poland was counted with Germany (1841–61); the undivided 'other' category (1841–61) incorporated Australasia, Africa, Asia, and much of Europe. The right-hand column gives the percentage ratio of the number for 1911 to that for 1881. *Sources*: Census of Ireland (1841–1911).

45

Table 2.6 *Characteristics of population born outside Ireland, 1841–1911*

Census	1841	1851	1861	1871	1881	1891	1901	1911
% Female								
Colonial	59.4	57.7	55.6	57.5	52.3	54.0	55.4	53.4
American	46.9	51.9	49.8	51.7	50.3	51.7	49.7	49.7
Other Foreign	51.1	27.4	41.9	35.8	38.5	37.5	39.0	43.4
Total Overseas	50.8	38.8	47.5	50.6	48.7	49.2	48.8	49.5
British	47.5	45.8	37.3	39.7	39.7	40.2	43.5	42.9
Total Population	*50.8*	*51.3*	*51.1*	*51.2*	*51.0*	*50.7*	*50.7*	*50.1*
% under 20 Years								
Colonial	53.4	45.4	50.1	n.a.	n.a.	n.a.	n.a.	n.a.
American	26.6	37.1	67.8	72.3	69.7	63.6	66.2	60.7
Other Foreign	30.0	17.4	32.5	21.0	18.3	21.5	19.1	14.2
Total Overseas	33.5	27.3	48.3	n.a.	n.a.	n.a.	n.a.	n.a.
British	36.5	33.5	31.5	n.a.	n.a.	n.a.	n.a.	n.a.
Total Population	*49.0*	*48.3*	*44.4*	*45.2*	*45.9*	*44.4*	*41.0*	*39.3*
% in Dublin								
Colonial	25.8	30.6	33.0	52.0	27.4	47.0	28.4	28.4
American	9.8	14.9	15.5	15.2	15.0	11.7	10.1	7.8
Other Foreign	35.6	27.3	37.1	31.9	34.2	34.5	37.4	39.8
Total Overseas	22.3	30.4	34.3	25.3	24.4	31.2	23.2	21.5
British	29.0	28.8	29.5	21.0	25.9	23.3	24.2	21.8
Total Population	*4.6*	*6.2*	*7.1*	*7.5*	*8.1*	*8.9*	*10.1*	*10.9*

Note: America (all regions) includes British North America (1841–61); 'overseas' excludes Great Britain; Dublin includes county and city (county borough); the number aged under 20 (1841–51) for each category is estimated from the number of unoccupied immigrants aged under 15, adjusted by the ratio of these two numbers for each nationality in 1861 (the only year for which both groups were tabulated). *Sources:* see Table 2.5.

Table 2.7 Characteristics of overseas population of Ireland by nationality, 1911

Characteristic	% Female	% under 20	% in Dublin	% UK Total	Population
Birthplace					
America	49.7	60.7	7.8	41.3	12,763
Colonial	59.4	53.4	25.8	4.9	9,266
Russia	45.9	10.6	56.4	[1.9]	1,985
France	41.2	14.0	26.2	3.6	1,104
Germany	45.6	7.2	40.5	1.7	963
Italy	31.2	12.5	35.0	1.6	417
Switzerland	64.1	9.0	34.7	2.3	245
Belgium	54.8	11.3	29.4	3.6	177
Austria	32.8	5.7	54.0	[1.1]	174
Norway	21.1	21.8	19.5	1.9	133
China	55.5	44.5	30.5	7.9	128
Holland	18.9	10.4	15.1	1.3	106
Denmark	12.6	16.8	9.5	1.8	95
'Poland'	38.0	19.6	34.8	n.a.	92
Spain	50.0	23.2	39.0	2.0	82
Sweden	32.4	16.2	29.7	1.1	74
Egypt	49.3	75.3	24.7	[13.9]	73
Greece	61.0	0.0	29.3	3.0	41
Portugal	59.3	7.4	37.0	3.3	27
Total Foreign	47.6	45.5	18.2	5.8	18,905

Note: Figures in brackets, showing the Irish share of each nationality, refer to Russia and Poland, Austria and Hungary, and Africa including Egypt. Nationalities with negligible presence are not separately listed.

Table 2.8 Occupations of population born outside Ireland, 1861

Birthplace	Britain	India	WI	America	France	Spain	Italy	Germany	Other	Overseas
Male										
Farming	4	5	7	19	3	6	1	0	3	6
Service	5	8	6	13	14	13	2	4	7	7
Clothing	6	5	9	7	10	7	3	6	4	6
Dealers	3	3	0	3	4	4	2	3	1	2
Officials	46	44	28	17	12	6	7	5	24	20
Sailors	13	2	10	11	3	23	40	36	44	27
Clerks	2	5	3	4	10	3	1	6	2	4
Teachers	1	2	2	2	10	0	5	5	2	3
Religious	1	1	2	1	4	1	1	0	3	2
Total Occupied	34,584	313	129	579	270	70	192	431	1,059	3,043
Female										
Farming	1	1	0	1	0	0	0	0	3	1
Service	45	34	27	32	41	38	43	31	37	35
Clothing	29	38	34	45	16	42	14	13	24	29
Dealers	3	2	0	5	1	2	0	2	2	2
Teachers	9	7	15	6	28	0	19	45	19	18
Religious	1	1	0	1	8	2	0	5	4	3
Annuitants	3	6	8	4	3	9	14	1	4	5
Total Occupied	5,681	140	71	245	159	45	21	144	278	1,103

Note: For each country of birth outside Ireland, the table shows the percentage of occupied males (or females) in selected categories: farming (farmers, farm labourers and servants, ploughmen, and gardeners); service (domestic servants and labourers); clothing (all 'ministering to clothing'); dealers (general shopkeepers and assistants, merchants, and dealers in unspecified goods); officials (all 'ministering to justice and government', mostly soldiers); sailors (not Royal Navy); writing clerks; school teachers; religious (clergy, monks, and nuns); and annuitants. There were no female officials or sailors, and only one female clerk (British); male annuitants were rare (59 British, 50 from overseas). The right-hand column refers to those born overseas, except in Britain. 'WI' refers to the West India islands; America includes all regions; Germany and Poland were counted together. Detailed tabulations by sex were published only in 1841–61 for Ireland as a whole (subsequent returns, though available by county, collated the sexes, omitted the total number with occupations, and excluded those born in Britain and the empire). *Source:* Census of Ireland (1861), *General Report*, 532–7.

Table 2.9 *Occupations of population born in foreign countries, 1911*

Birthplace	America	Europe	France	Germany	Italy	Russia	Total
Occupation							
Farming	31	1	1	1	2	0	16
Service	16	7	6	10	11	1	12
Clothing	9	12	2	2	1	33	10
Dealers	1	4	0	1	5	11	3
Officials	1	1	1	0	1	0	1
Sailors	1	11	17	5	0	2	6
Clerks	0	1	1	1	1	1	2
Teachers	2	7	9	14	3	2	5
Religious	1	5	9	9	2	2	3
Total Occupied	*4,181*	*3,992*	*975*	*697*	*294*	*1,131*	*8,251*

Note: For each country of birth outside Ireland, the table shows the percentage of all occupied persons in selected categories. These figures are based on incomplete tabulations restricted to 37 occupational categories with more than 40 foreigners of both sexes in 1911. Farming excludes ploughmen and gardeners; clothing is restricted to dressmakers, milliners, linen and flax factors, drapers, and tailors; dealers exclude merchants; officials are restricted to soldiers and NCOs and public servants; sailors are defined as seamen (merchant service). The total number occupied is recorded only for the entire foreign population, indicating that 77% of that total belonged to the 37 selected occupations; other totals in the bottom row are estimated by applying that proportion to the recorded number in the 37 occupations. *Source:* Census of Ireland (1911), *General Report*, table 86.

Table 2.10 *Characteristics of population born outside Ireland, 1911*

%	FE	U20	RC	RW	IR	SI	HW	SD	GC	NN	LBV	SE
British Empire												
Britain	42.6	29.9	26.2	88.9	2.0	59.5	34.2	23.2	2.6	2.6	7.7	3.3
India	54.1	32.1	43.2	87.8	1.8	57.8	36.3	30.3	2.0	2.8	6.8	2.6
Canada	55.5	30.5	28.2	86.3	1.6	59.1	35.9	29.5	4.7	4.8	8.2	1.8
Australia	56.3	27.6	47.0	95.4	4.5	66.6	30.3	32.1	3.0	5.5	8.6	2.6
Foreign												
America	49.4	61.7	77.9	80.0	11.1	82.2	16.1	38.3	15.9	11.9	5.0	3.0
Russia	46.0	11.0	0.7	96.2	0.3	29.4	64.0	16.5	0.1	1.0	10.9	0.2
France	47.2	13.2	74.1	91.2	0.5	53.9	27.8	5.4	0.3	1.0	9.2	5.1
Germany	46.4	7.1	32.5	96.1	0.5	47.9	46.9	4.3	0.4	0.7	16.8	7.3
Italy	30.0	12.3	86.6	64.7	0.5	38.2	53.2	10.2	0	0.5	14.7	8.6

Note: All proportions refer to the number of each major birthplace indicated by a digital search of the 1911 census (admittedly incomplete as a result of coding problems). Figures for America combine those attributed to the United States and 'America'. The columns show the proportions of the total population of each birthplace identified as female (FE), under 20 years (U20), Roman Catholic (RC), able to read and write (RW), able to speak Irish (IR), single (SI), heads of family or wives (HW), sons or daughters of heads (SD), grandchildren (GC), nephews or nieces (NN), lodgers, boarders, or visitors (LBV), servants of head (SE). In the case of smaller nationalities (excluding Britain and America), all cases of 'other' religion, literacy, marital status, and relationship to head have been inspected and reassigned, where possible, to the appropriate categories.
Source: Census of Ireland (1911), digital index to family schedules.

Table 2.11 *Characteristics of population born in America, by province, 1841–1911*

Census	1841	1851	1861	1871	1881	1891	1901	1911
Number								
Leitrim	94	16	60	37	66	101	148	298
Leinster	628	738	1,057	1,290	2,153	1,973	2,445	2,737
Munster	393	502	737	964	1,527	1,573	2,131	2,919
Ulster	706	918	1,285	1,673	2,515	3,131	4,119	4,719
Connaught	255	178	489	427	839	1,028	1,425	2,388
Ireland	*1,982*	*2,336*	*3,577*	*4,354*	*7,034*	*7,705*	*10,120*	*12,763*
Proportion of Population (per 10,000)								
Leitrim	6.0	1.4	5.7	3.9	7.3	12.8	21.3	46.9
Leinster	3.2	4.4	7.3	9.6	16.8	16.6	21.2	23.6
Munster	1.6	2.7	4.9	6.9	11.5	13.4	19.8	28.2
Ulster	3.0	4.6	6.7	9.1	14.4	19.3	26.0	29.8
Connaught	1.8	1.8	5.4	5.1	10.2	14.2	22.0	39.1
Ireland	*2.4*	*3.6*	*6.2*	*8.0*	*13.6*	*16.4*	*22.7*	*29.1*
% of Overseas Population								
Leitrim	82.5	50.0	46.2	41.6	64.1	79.5	81.3	89.2
Leinster	34.0	20.6	24.0	19.2	28.6	25.2	27.8	28.1
Munster	56.8	41.5	47.3	18.0	30.0	29.4	36.9	51.0
Ulster	42.9	15.5	31.4	42.2	46.9	48.4	50.6	46.4
Connaught	54.8	32.3	54.0	44.8	54.2	60.9	75.6	82.8
Ireland	*44.3*	*24.4*	*34.3*	*25.6*	*36.0*	*36.1*	*41.1*	*45.3*

Note: For Co. Leitrim and for each province, the table shows the number born in America, the proportion of Americans per 10,000 inhabitants, and Americans as a percentage of all those born outside the UK. Statistics refer to all persons returned as born in all regions of America, excluding military and naval personnel (1841–51) and natives of British colonies and Canada (1871–1911).

Table 2.12 *Characteristics of population born in America, by province,*
1841–1911

Census	1841	1851	1861	1871	1881	1891	1901	1911
% Female								
Leitrim	47.9	56.3	55.0	54.1	48.5	43.6	47.3	47.0
Leinster	46.3	57.5	49.0	52.2	49.4	54.4	51.1	51.2
Munster	45.0	47.6	47.1	50.1	50.2	44.9	48.6	48.7
Ulster	48.3	49.9	52.1	53.2	51.7	54.7	50.3	51.1
Connaught	47.1	51.1	50.7	48.2	48.9	47.9	46.8	46.3
Ireland	*46.9*	*51.9*	*49.8*	*51.7*	*50.3*	*51.7*	*49.7*	*49.7*
% under 20 Years								
Leitrim	n.a.	n.a.	70.0	75.7	66.7	81.2	81.8	77.2
Leinster	n.a.	n.a.	60.4	68.1	64.1	55.7	52.7	46.3
Munster	n.a.	n.a.	63.9	71.8	74.1	66.9	70.5	66.3
Ulster	n.a.	n.a.	71.8	72.9	68.0	61.3	66.3	56.9
Connaught	n.a.	n.a.	80.4	84.1	81.5	80.7	82.7	77.7
Ireland	*n.a.*	*n.a.*	*67.8*	*72.3*	*69.7*	*63.6*	*66.2*	*60.7*

Note: See Table 2.11.

3   America on Show, 1901–11: Profile

I   Sources

This chapter presents in statistical form the more exotic and conspicuous aspects of American settlement by exploring the mainly urban American-born elite.[1] The inclusion of Canadians recognises the fluidity of migration throughout North America, while also inviting contrasts arising from the radically different social, economic, and political environment of a British dominion by comparison with the United States. Those differences tended to draw distinct categories of migrants to settle in Canada, even though so many mid-nineteenth-century Irish emigrants lived temporarily in Canada before proceeding to settle in the United States. Cross-border movement was never effectively controlled, and many emigrants and their descendants worked at some time in both countries. The analysis in section II, 'Profile', below, tests the extent to which Canada departed from the United States model as a supplier of incomers to Ireland, in the context of its persistent distinctiveness as a magnet for Irish people on the move. Unfortunately, the Canadian comparison cannot be pursued in later chapters examining short-term visitors of Irish birth, because Canada offers no documentary counterpart to the dossier of American passport applications.

In the absence of an adequate occupational index, I have conjured up hundreds of key words in order to identify American residents in clerical, official, and professional occupations, along with manufacturers, transport personnel, hospitality workers, persons of independent means, and 'performers' (artists). Since occupational self-designations were sometimes ludicrously capricious, my American lexicon has been amplified by incorporation of *all* terms applied to those in similar categories who were indexed as natives of Canada (a more manageable dossier).[2] In most cases, the chosen categories involved provision of essential services to the public, ranging from the 'learned professions' to the drinks trade. My conception of 'the elite' is perhaps best delineated by what it is intended to exclude, though ambiguous terminology creates a fuzzy borderline. Exclusions cover almost all Americans in rural Ireland and humbler urbanites: farmers, labourers, domestic servants, porters, tradesmen without 'modern' skills, industrial operatives, merchants, and shopkeepers. Though a few American-born 'merchants' might have qualified through wealth, the category was excluded because others were clearly mere shopkeepers.

This incremental approach has generated a database of about one thousand north Americans in 1901–11,[3] together constituting a roll-call mingling consuls, capitalists, commercial travellers, pen-pushers, publicans, hotel-keepers, missionaries and nuns, doctors and quacks, ladies and gentlemen, and music-hall artists. Statistical analysis of the elite is followed in Chapter 4 by numerous brief accounts of named visitors and immigrants, derived from census returns, in order to display the complexity of their Irish and international connections and the diverse circumstances in which they lived. It would be impracticable to probe more deeply into the background and careers of hundreds of individuals, no matter how diverting or revealing their stories might prove to be. What was the character of Ireland's submerged American elite?

II   Profile

An elite, by its nature, is unrepresentative of the broader population. We should not be surprised that less than one-fifth of adult males born in the United States (including those from 'America' undefined) belonged to the elite analysed in this chapter. By contrast, the Canadian elite constituted a majority of resident male Canadians, pointing to a dramatically different collective profile.[4] In certain respects, these contrasts mirrored well-documented differences between the profiles of post-Famine Irish emigration to the two countries. Those bound for Canada were predominantly Protestant and of Ulster origin, whereas (despite the notorious patchiness of comparable data for the United States) it is generally agreed that most emigrants to the United States, at least from the 1840s onwards, were Catholic and of southern origin. As already shown in Table 2.10, the same contrast applied to natives of the United States and Canada enumerated in Ireland in 1911. These congruities confirm the extent to which Irish emigration indirectly shaped the foreign presence in early twentieth-century Ireland.

Table 3.1 indicates that the underlying dissimilarity between the two nativities extended to members of the elite, and pinpoints many other contrasts. It may be read in two ways, either to compare Canadians with Americans, or to compare each elite with the broader population of the same birthplace. For both nativities, the occupational elite was less likely to be female, Catholic, unmarried, aged under 20 years, and to be a child or other relation of the household head. They were more likely to be household heads themselves or to be unrelated to the head. For those born in the United States, the contrasts between the proportions for the elite and for the total American-born population were spectacular (30% and 49% female, 53% and 78% Catholic, 60% and 82% unmarried, 14% and 62% aged under 20, 26% and 40% children of household heads). Only 7% of the elite spoke Irish, compared with 11% of the entire population born in the United States. In the Canadian case, the Catholic proportion only just exceeded one-quarter for both groups, and members of the elite were actually more likely to speak Irish (admittedly, the proportions were minuscule). Far fewer Canadians were aged under 20 (31% compared with 62% from the United States), but even fewer elite Canadians were in that age group (5% compared with 14% of elite Americans). The remarkable youthfulness of Ireland's American population, by comparison with the mainly adult elite, largely explains the contrasts in marital and household status. The relative scarcity of women and Catholics in the elite may be attributed to the long-standing deficit of both groups in jobs offering higher income or greater security.

Table 3.2 pursues the comparison between the two nativities by restricting attention to members of the occupational elite. In 1901, the Canadians were less often female (26% by comparison with 38% of Americans), far less likely to be Catholics (20% and 53%), less often Irish-speakers (1% and 9%), and less often unmarried (42% and 65%). The majority of Protestants for both nationalities were Protestant Episcopalians, but there were also substantial minorities of Presbyterians and (especially among the Canadians) Methodists. The Canadians were more likely to be heads of household than the Americans, but less likely to be children or indirect relatives of heads. The Canadian age profile was markedly older, the median age being 37 years by comparison with 30, and upper quartile values of 49 and 40, respectively (signifying that one-quarter of the group exceeded the stated age). Two-thirds of each nationality were co-resident with family members, and about one-quarter were in households containing another North American. Almost half of the Canadian elite were in households with servants, far more than in the American case (38%).

These patterns of contrast were closely replicated in 1911. In certain respects, however, the American and Canadian elites had followed different trajectories over the intervening decade. Whereas the American female proportion fell sharply from 38% to 30%, the Canadian proportion rose slightly. The unmarried component fell somewhat for Americans but increased to nearly one-half for Canadians. The proportion unrelated to the household head, markedly greater for Americans in 1901, was just over one-quarter for both groups in 1911.

Table 3.3 analyses the physical environment. In 1901, the majority of elite Americans as well as Canadians lived in the three major cities, with one-quarter in Dublin and substantial settlement in Belfast and Cork. Outside the cities, the province with the largest representation was Ulster, followed by Leinster, Munster, and Connaught in descending order. Canadians were markedly more likely to reside in superior ('first class') houses, which hosted the majority of Canadians and one-third of Americans. The number in inferior housing ('third class') was negligible in both cases. The superiority of housing for Canadians was reflected in the median number of rooms (eight) and front windows (five), compared with six rooms and four windows for Americans. These calculations refer only to private dwellings, and exclude those enumerated in institutions, hotels, and the like. No major changes in the physical environment are revealed by the corresponding figures for 1911.

The religious complexion of the elite is further explored in Tables 3.4 and 3.5, which provide corresponding proportions for Catholics by comparison with Protestants. In 1901, Catholics were more likely to be female (41% as against 29%), to speak Irish (17% as against none), to be unmarried (67% and 53%), and to have no kinship with the household head (42% and 26%). Protestants were more likely to be household heads themselves (46% as against 30%), co-resident with family members (72% and 59%) and with other North Americans (29% and 22%), and to reside in households with servants (45% and 35%). There were no important differences in median age or the proportions still in Ireland 10 years later. In many respects these contrasts were replicated in 1911, when, however, both religious groups had similar proportions of household heads (two-fifths), residents unrelated to the head (one-quarter), and households shared with family members (over two-thirds in both cases) and fellow Americans (over one-quarter).

The urban concentration of the elite was particularly pronounced for Protestants (57% as against 51% for Catholics), with an even sharper disparity in 1911 (59% and 45%). Whereas Dublin, followed by Cork, accounted for most urban Catholics, Belfast was the major urban location for most Protestants. Indeed, the majority of the Protestant elite were enumerated in Ulster, whereas Catholics outside the three major cities were quite evenly distributed across the three southern provinces. Protestants were more likely to inhabit first-class houses in 1901 (46% as against 30% for Catholics), and especially in 1911 (48% and 22%). The median Protestant lived in a house with eight rooms and five windows in 1901, compared with five rooms and four windows for Catholics. Predictably, the contrasting profiles of the two religious groups closely replicated those between Canadians (predominantly Protestants) and Americans (mainly Catholics).

A critical issue for any study of foreign-born populations is the degree
to which those present on census night had demonstrable family
links with the host population. In many cases particularised in the
following chapters, American residents were co-resident with spouses,
children, parents, or relatives from several countries, though kin of Irish
birth were typically predominant. A powerful indicator of the strength of
Irish family connections is provided by the nativity of kinsfolk enumerated in 'American' households. In both census years, three-quarters of
co-resident spouses (almost always wives) were of Irish birth, about one-
third of these being natives of Ulster. One-seventh were born in Britain
and one-tenth in North America, along with a scattering of more exotic
spouses from Australia, Cape Colony, India, Sweden, and Norway.[5]

Natives of Ireland were even more predominant among co-resident
parents, who were much more likely than spouses to come from Ulster
rather than the southern provinces. Over three-quarters of mothers in
both census years were Irish, and, once again, American mothers were
outnumbered by natives of Britain.[6] A similar pattern applies to the
smaller group of co-resident fathers.[7] Admittedly, these findings exaggerate the ubiquity of Irish family connections in the American elite. Only a
minority of elite Americans were co-resident with a spouse or parent, and
the undocumented majority (including short-term visitors travelling
alone) probably included a substantially higher proportion whose parents
were American-born.[8] Nonetheless, this analysis strongly suggests that,
even within the elite, kinship connections with Ireland were in most
cases crucial to their presence in Ireland.

III   Occupational Contrasts

In order to pinpoint significant contrasts within the American elite,
I have subsumed the myriad designations inscribed on family schedules
into various broader groups. Since no useful comparison can be made
with published census returns, this classification does not accord with
any used by the census commissioners. Unlike the published census
returns, the chosen groups overlap, as many self-descriptions apply to
two or more groups. For example, there was major overlap between
those assigned to 'education' and 'religion' and likewise to the 'clerical'
and 'finance' sectors, while members of many categories were also classified under 'civil service'. In order to avoid suppression of significant
contrasts through excessive aggregation, I have adopted a dual system of
classification. First, the returns for each census were assigned to seventeen sectors of widely variant size. Second, these sectors were assigned
to four major categories of roughly equal size, labelled 'white-collar',

'official', 'professional', and 'miscellaneous'. Before delving beneath these labels, let us contrast the four major categories.

The female component in 1901 (Table 3.6) varied sharply between 8% (white-collar) and 49% (miscellaneous), along with 24% (official) and 47% (professional). The majority in all four categories were unmarried, the excess being greatest for professional workers (who, as shown below, included many nuns in education and health as well as the religious profession per se). The lowest median age was recorded in the clerical and official sectors. Nearly one-third of officials were Canadians, compared with less than one-third in the other three sectors. Catholics were a majority among officials and professionals, Protestant Episcopalians being particularly prominent among miscellaneous workers (40%). It is noteworthy that the white-collar sector had particularly heavy concentrations of Presbyterians and Methodists. The groups most likely to have co-resident relatives were white-collar workers and officials (over three-quarters), compared with miscellaneous workers (69%) and professionals (52%). Excluding those in institutions, the highest proportion with American-born co-residents were in the white-collar sector (29%). One of the most significant contrasts applies to the proportion still (or again) in Ireland in 1911, our best proxy for long-term residence. No less than 57% of white-collar workers were matched in 1911, compared with a minority ranging from 42% to 45% for the other three groups.

The patterns and contrasts just described were broadly replicated in 1911, when the size of the American elite had increased by almost one-fifth from 530 to 629 (Table 3.7). The large increase in the proportion of those who were also enumerated in the other census (from 45% to 57%) is attributable to the fact that many members of the elite of 1911 had been returned as children or dependants in 1901. It is noteworthy that the female component declined over the decade in all categories except white-collar workers. The Canadian proportion rose slightly in all sectors except miscellaneous workers. The apparent increase of 4 years in median age (from 32 to 36 years) is partly explained by the general inflation of age returns in 1911, particularly apparent in older people. Religious composition changed little apart from an increased Catholic component of officials. The proportion of inmates and Americans without co-resident family members declined slightly in most categories, while the proportion in families with other Americans increased across the board. Once again, the proportion traceable in the 1901 census was far higher for white-collar workers (two-thirds) than for the other three groups (between 51% and 57%).

The four broad occupational categories conceal notable contrasts between sub-sectors, as revealed by the returns of headship and family co-residence in Table 3.8. Peculiarities in the profile of each individual sub-sector will be summarised in the following chapter, which points out variables (such as the female or Catholic proportions) that had exceptionally high or low values for that sector. In both census years, managerial staff were much more likely to head their own households than were clerks. Among officials, only one-quarter of postal workers in 1901 and 35% in 1911 were household heads. Equally low proportions applied to professionals in education and religion. In the miscellaneous category, independents and workers in the hospitality sector were much more likely to head their own households than those practising creative arts. These contrasts were broadly correlated with the proportions co-resident with family members.

The third column for each census year shows the proportion in each sector that were traced in the other census, offering insight into which sectors were relatively settled in Ireland. In both census years, all four white-collar sectors as well as the civil service sector exceeded the aggregate proportions (45% in 1901 and 57% in 1911). The same applied to education, law, transport, and hospitality. By contrast, sectors with relatively few matched members included the forces (police and military), health, engineering, religion, the arts, and independents (predominantly those returned as annuitants or people with private means). These contrasts confirm that the American elite should not be treated as a monolith, but as a highly stratified composite of groups with very different reasons for living in Ireland and variable prospects of remaining there for prolonged periods.

Table 3.9 attempts to clarify some of the patterns of diversity by comparing the Catholic component of the seventeen sub-sectors with the proportions of female and unmarried and the median age of those in each sub-sector. The table is arranged according to the Catholic component in 1901 in descending order. The proportion of Catholics ranged from more than three-fifths for those in the postal, religion, and hospitality sectors, to barely one-sixth of manufacturing and managerial workers. It is notable that Catholics were over-represented in education, underrepresented in finance and engineering and among independents, and fairly represented in the forces, the clerical sector, and health. Despite various anomalies, the occupational distribution of Catholics in 1911 strongly resembled that for 1901.

The female component varied wildly between occupational sectors, with no women returned under law, transport, engineering, or manufacturing in either year. The female component was negligible in commerce, the forces, finance, and management. In 1901, women were predominant among independents (84%), in education (65%), and health (56%), and over-represented in religion (48%), the civil service (39%), and hospitality (38%). Once again, the pattern had changed little by 1911, with one striking exception. The proportion of female clerks trebled from 6% to 19% over the intercensal decade, reflecting the multiplication of women typists and secretarial workers throughout the Irish workforce in the Edwardian era.

Table 3.9 also records two inter-related variables, the proportion unmarried and median age. In both census years, unmarried components exceeding two-thirds were found in engineering, religion, education, the postal service, law, and the clerical sector. By contrast, less than one-third of those in managerial or manufacturing occupations were single. Median age in 1901 was highest in manufacturing (42 years), among independents (39), and in religion, commerce, the forces, finance, and management (37 in each case). The most youthful sectors of the elite were the postal service (median age 25), engineering (26), and hospitality and clerical work (28). A similar pattern applied in 1911, though median age in all but three sectors had increased by comparison with 1901. In general, it appears that the structure and profile of the American elite remained fairly stable, maintaining established hierarchies and contrasts between occupational groups.

Statistical profiles, though essential for recognising major contrasts between different sectors and categories, cannot do justice to the diversity and personal idiosyncrasies of Ireland's American elite. What follows is an attempt to personalise the analysis by briefly examining hundreds of individual cases.[9]

Table 3.1 *Characteristics of elite and total Americans by nativity, 1911*

%	USA: Total	Elite	Canada: Total	Elite
Female	49.4	30.0	55.5	26.8
Catholic	77.9	53.3	28.2	26.8
Irish Speech	11.1	6.9	1.6	2.2
Single	82.2	60.2	59.1	46.9
Aged under 20 Years	61.7	14.0	30.5	5.0
Relation to Head				
Head	16.5	38.9	38.4	49.7
Child	39.8	25.8	32.4	16.8
Other Relations	30.3	8.7	13.8	6.7
Unrelated	13.4	26.7	15.5	26.8

Note: This table compares proportions for all persons of American nativity in 1911 (see Table 2.10) with members of the American elite in the same year (see Table 3.2). Certain figures already given in Table 2.10 have been slightly adjusted to ensure consistency with criteria applied in Table 3.2. *Source*: Census of Ireland (1911), digital index to family schedules.

Table 3.2 *Characteristics of elite Americans by nativity, 1901–11*

%	USA: Total	Elite	Canada: Total	Elite
Census Match	43.3	51.1	60.9	46.9
Female	37.5	25.6	30.0	26.8
Religious Denomination				
Catholic	52.9	20.3	53.3	26.8
Episcopalian	24.9	48.1	20.2	43.0
Presbyterian	12.6	15.0	15.8	17.3
Methodist	3.3	11.3	4.4	6.7
Other	6.3	5.3	6.2	6.1
Language				
Literate	99.0	100	99.6	100
Irish Speech	9.3	1.5	6.9	2.2
Marital Status				
Single	64.7	42.1	60.2	46.9
Married	25.2	40.6	27.8	38.0
Married (spouse absent)	4.8	7.5	4.7	7.3
Widowed	5.3	9.8	7.3	7.8
Relation to Head				
Head	34.5	51.9	38.9	49.7
Child	21.4	14.3	25.8	16.8
Other Relations	9.3	5.3	8.7	6.7
Unrelated	34.8	28.6	26.7	26.8
Households Containing				
Family	65.0	68.4	70.0	69.3
Other American	27.5	23.0	28.2	27.7
Servant	38.2	48.7	29.3	44.6
Age in Years				
Lower Quartile	24	29	22	28
Median	30	37	35	41
Upper Quartile	40	49	46	51
Number	*397*	*133*	*450*	*179*

Note: Proportions relate to residents of Ireland with selected occupations born in the USA or 'America' and in Canada (located in a digital search of the family schedules). 'Census match' signifies the proportion of Americans (1901) confidently matched in 1911, and vice versa. 'Literate' refers to the proportion aged over 5 years who could read and write; every Irish-speaker was bilingual in English. Family schedules also record the relationship of each American to the 'head of family' responsible for completing the form. 'Head' includes spouse; 'child' includes step-child and in-law; 'unrelated' includes boarder, lodger, visitor, servant, etc. Proportions are given for households with an American or Canadian that also contained (1) another family member, (2) another American, and (3) a servant. The proportions for co-residence with another American exclude those in institutions, hotels, etc. (82 in 1901, 88 in 1911). *Source*: Census of Ireland (1901, 1911), family schedules.

Table 3.3 *Location and housing of elite Americans by nativity, 1901–11*

%	USA: Total	Elite	Canada: Total	Elite
Location				
Dublin City	23.9	24.1	23.3	30.7
Belfast City	17.4	15.8	17.3	16.2
Cork City	12.3	16.5	9.1	11.7
Total Urban	*53.7*	*56.4*	*49.8*	*58.7*
Leinster except Dublin	10.3	11.3	10.0	14.0
Ulster except Belfast	19.6	15.0	23.1	15.1
Munster except Cork	9.6	9.8	9.1	7.8
Connaught	6.8	7.5	8.0	4.5
Total Provincial	*46.3*	*43.6*	*50.2*	*41.3*
House Class				
1st	35.6	51.4	33.8	44.6
2nd	60.7	43.9	62.1	53.4
3rd	3.7	4.7	4.1	2.0
Median Number				
Rooms	6	8	7	8
Front Windows	4	5	4	5
Number	*397*	*133*	*450*	*179*

Note: Proportions relate to the domestic environment of residents of Ireland with selected occupations born in the USA or 'America' and in Canada (located in a digital search of the family schedules). 'Provincial' locations exclude the county boroughs of Dublin, Belfast, and Cork. Proportions are given for households with an American or Canadian that also contained (1) another family member, (2) another American, and (3) a servant. The proportions for house class, rooms, and front windows exclude those in institutions, hotels, etc. (82 in 1901, 88 in 1911). *Source*: Census of Ireland (1901, 1911), house and building returns.

Table 3.4 *Characteristics of elite Americans by religion, 1901–11*

%	1901: Catholic	Other	1911: Catholic	Other
Census Match	44.3	46.1	58.3	55.7
Female	41.4	29.0	33.7	25.2
Language				
Literate	98.7	99.7	99.7	99.7
Irish Speech	16.5	0	11.8	0.3
Marital Status				
Single	66.7	52.9	60.8	52.8
Married	23.6	33.4	27.8	33.1
Married (spouse absent)	4.2	6.5	2.4	7.9
Widowed	5.5	7.2	9.0	6.2
Relation to Head				
Head	30.4	45.7	40.3	43.4
Child	19.8	19.5	22.6	23.8
Other Relations	8.0	8.5	8.3	7.6
Unrelated	41.8	26.3	28.5	25.2

Table 3.4 (*cont.*)

%	1901: Catholic	Other	1911: Catholic	Other
Households Containing				
Family	58.6	71.7	68.8	70.7
Other American	22.5	29.1	26.7	29.2
Servant	35.3	44.8	28.8	37.0
Age in Years				
Lower Quartile	25	25	23	24
Median	31	33	36	36
Upper Quartile	40	43	47	47
Number	*237*	*293*	*288*	*341*

Note: See Table 3.2.

Table 3.5 *Location and housing of elite Americans by religion, 1901–11*

%	1901: Catholic	Other	1911: Catholic	Other
Location				
Dublin City	28.3	20.5	31.3	20.5
Belfast City	6.3	25.6	4.2	27.9
Cork City	16.5	10.9	9.4	10.3
Total Urban	*51.1*	*57.0*	*44.8*	*58.7*
Leinster except Dublin	13.9	7.8	15.6	7.3
Ulster except Belfast	8.9	26.3	12.8	27.6
Munster except Cork	14.3	5.8	14.6	3.8
Connaught	11.8	3.1	12.2	2.6
Total Provincial	*48.9*	*43.0*	*55.2*	*41.3*
Number	*237*	*293*	*288*	*341*
House Class				
1st	30.2	46.2	22.5	47.9
2nd	62.6	52.2	69.9	51.8
3rd	7.1	1.6	7.6	0.3
Median Number				
Rooms	5	8	6	8
Front Windows	4	5	4	5

Note: See Table 3.2.

Table 3.6 *Characteristics of elite Americans by occupational categories, 1901*

%	Total	A	B	C	D
Census Match	45.3	57.0	43.4	45.5	42.3
Characteristics					
Female	34.5	8.2	23.9	47.3	48.9
Single	59.1	56.3	50.4	70.3	51.1
Canadian	25.1	22.8	31.9	23.0	23.6
Median Age (years)	32	31	31	33	35

Table 3.6 (*cont.*)

%	Total	A	B	C	D
Religious Denomination					
Catholic	44.7	42.4	50.4	51.5	40.7
Episcopalian	30.8	29.1	31.0	20.0	39.6
Presbyterian	13.2	16.5	11.5	15.8	9.9
Methodist	5.3	10.1	1.8	4.8	4.4
Relation to Head					
Head	38.9	41.5	46.0	32.1	44.0
Unrelated	33.2	26.6	21.2	41.8	32.4
Households Containing					
Family	65.8	76.6	76.1	52.1	69.2
Other American	26.4	28.5	23.0	21.3	27.2
Number	*530*	*158*	*113*	*165*	*182*

Note: Proportions refer to selected occupations of Americans, including Canadians (1901), assigned to four categories: A (white-collar), B (official), C (professional), and D (miscellaneous). The proportions for co-residence with another American exclude those in institutions, hotels, etc. The sum of these four groups exceeds the grand total because many Americans were enumerated in more than one category. For occupational sectors within each category, see Table 3.8. *Source*: Census of Ireland (1901), family schedules.

Table 3.7 *Characteristics of elite Americans by occupational categories, 1911*

%	Total	A	B	C	D
Census Match	56.9	67.3	52.5	56.7	50.8
Characteristics					
Female	29.1	14.6	15.8	41.4	39.7
Single	56.4	60.0	53.3	64.5	45.8
Canadian	28.5	25.4	35.8	33.0	22.9
Median Age	36	32	37	35	40
Religious Denomination					
Catholic	45.8	36.6	57.5	49.3	46.4
Episcopalian	26.7	29.8	27.5	21.7	30.2
Presbyterian	16.2	22.4	10.8	16.7	10.6
Methodist	5.1	6.8	1.7	4.4	5.6
Relation to Head					
Head	42.0	39.0	46.7	34.5	52.5
Unrelated	26.7	15.1	23.3	41.4	25.1
Households Containing					
Family	69.8	83.9	71.7	55.7	68.7
Other American	28.1	33.0	20.8	22.1	26.5
Number	*629*	*205*	*120*	*203*	*179*

Note: See Table 3.6. *Source*: Census of Ireland (1911), family schedules.

Table 3.8 *Characteristics of elite Americans by occupational sectors, 1901–11*

%	1901	Head	Family	Match	1911	Head	Family	Match
A: White-collar								
Clerical	85	34.1	76.5	56.5	116	24.1	86.2	64.7
Finance	42	57.1	83.3	64.3	47	48.9	78.7	74.5
Managerial	18	77.8	83.3	61.1	24	75.0	79.2	75.0
Commerce	32	37.5	65.6	50.0	48	58.3	81.3	68.8
B: Official								
Civil Service	49	55.1	85.7	49.0	50	50.0	66.0	56.0
Postal Service	31	25.8	87.1	41.9	34	35.3	91.2	76.5
Forces	34	50.0	50.0	35.3	36	52.8	61.1	25.0
C: Professional								
Education	68	29.4	58.8	48.5	87	29.9	56.3	71.3
Health	39	43.6	43.6	41.0	52	30.8	48.1	36.5
Law	10	40.0	100	70.0	17	52.9	94.1	76.5
Engineering	15	13.3	66.7	33.3	19	36.8	73.7	42.1
Religion	42	23.8	21.4	42.9	46	32.6	21.7	47.8
D: Miscellaneous								
Manufacturing	6	50.0	100	66.7	10	70.0	70.0	60.0
Transport	22	50.0	77.3	77.3	18	66.2	88.9	55.6
Hospitality	34	55.9	82.4	47.1	52	59.6	76.9	53.8
Independent	74	45.9	64.9	33.8	49	57.1	65.3	53.1
Arts	45	28.9	60.0	33.3	51	37.3	58.8	43.1
Total	*530*	*38.9*	*65.8*	*45.1*	*629*	*42.0*	*69.8*	*56.9*

Note: For seventeen selected occupational sectors in 1901 and 1911, the table shows the number in each sector, the percentages who were household heads or spouses, co-resident with a family member, and matched in the other census. Sectors are arranged within the four categories analysed in Tables 3.6 and 3.8. The sum of members of these seventeen sectors exceeds the grand total because many Americans were enumerated in more than one category. *Source:* Census of Ireland (1901, 1911), family schedules.

Table 3.9 *Characteristics of elite Americans by occupational sectors, 1901–11*

%	1901: RC	Female	Single	Age	1911: RC	Female	Single	Age
Postal Service	64.5	22.6	71.0	25	79.4	20.6	73.5	31
Religion	61.9	47.6	76.2	37	58.7	50.0	73.9	45
Hospitality	61.8	38.2	47.1	28	69.2	38.5	50.0	38
Law	60.0	0	70.0	36	41.2	0	47.1	37
Education	57.4	64.7	75.0	30	57.5	54.0	74.7	28
Commerce	50.0	9.4	46.9	37	35.4	4.2	37.5	38
Clerical	48.2	5.9	68.2	28	39.7	19.0	75.0	25
Forces	47.1	2.9	38.2	37	38.9	0	25.0	45
Arts	46.7	28.9	53.3	30	37.3	33.3	54.9	36
Health	46.2	56.4	59.0	35	44.2	48.1	55.8	39
Civil Service	42.9	38.8	46.9	31	56.0	24.0	60.0	37
Transport	40.9	0	40.9	30	45.2	0	33.3	36
Finance	33.3	9.5	50.0	37	31.9	8.5	53.2	36
Engineering	33.3	0	80.0	26	36.8	0	63.2	30
Independent	28.4	83.8	56.8	39	30.6	69.4	36.7	47
Manufacturing	16.7	0	33.3	42	30.0	0	30.0	52
Managerial	16.7	5.6	22.2	37	20.8	8.3	33.3	44
Total	*44.7*	*34.5*	*59.1*	*32*	*45.8*	*29.1*	*56.4*	*36*

4   America on Show: People

I   A Middle Way

How can a measure of humanity be restored to the people who made up this eclectic exhibition of American modernity, and whose peculiarities were pulverised into the collective profile presented in the preceding chapter? One approach, which can only be applied to a few groups, is to go beyond census returns to recover individual backgrounds and life histories using wider documentation. This chapter adopts a middle way by offering an annotated catalogue of selected census returns. In order to parade the diversity of the American elite, these individual cameos typically specify religion, age, marital status, presence of servants, and housing (a crude proxy for wealth). Policemen reported the number of rooms and *front* windows in each dwelling, not troubling to plod round the side or back of a house to complete the enumeration. Though often inconsistent from census to census even when no apparent change of home had occurred, these returns have some comparative value. Social context may often be inferred from the place of residence, which in the case of Dublin and Belfast is typically located by the municipal ward and often by street name.[1]

Of crucial importance for this study is the extent to which North American settlers and visitors had family connections stretching across Ireland and beyond. A useful indicator is the nativity of co-resident parents, spouses, children, and relatives, so many cameos include brief summaries highlighting cosmopolitanism within the family. For those traced in both 1901 and 1911, any significant changes of circumstance are noted, revealing conspicuous descent as well as upward mobility. Ability to speak Irish is routinely noted, usually pointing to an upbringing in rural Ireland but also found in unexpected cases such as the Duke of Manchester. Canadians, whose collective profile differed sharply from the American norm, are specifically identified. By unleashing a cascade of names, facts, and oddities, I hope that the cumulative effect will be to create a panorama of Americans on show in pre-war Ireland.

How may such a catalogue add meaning, as distinct from colour, to the patterns revealed in statistical analysis? First, the emphasis on variety within sectors subverts crude inter-sector comparisons based on the female proportion or median house size. Most sectors covered a range of occupations with widely variant status and income, and sub-groups such as women or Canadians were typically clustered in certain bands of that spectrum. Female clerks, for example, were not simply in junior positions, but rapidly advancing between 1901 and 1911 in both number and skills (especially typing). Second, inspection of apparently homogeneous sub-groups (such as hotel-keepers) may reveal striking contrasts (a guestless lodging house with a bar was as much an 'hotel' as the Shelbourne). Third, the provision of names and addresses that interest them may challenge readers to pursue them in greater depth for themselves.

This chapter concerns Americans and Canadians who performed specialist services (excluding domestic service), ranging from clerks, commercial travellers, managers, and public servants to soldiers, doctors, teachers, and hotel staff. All of these services, delivered with an American accent, entailed extensive interaction with the general population, generating strong personal impressions of American manners and peculiarities. As in the preceding chapter, the seventeen occupational sectors have been arranged in four overlapping categories (white-collar, official, professional, and miscellaneous). To spare readers the need to refer back to the preceding statistical profile, peculiarities in the collective profile of each sector are summarised in the introduction to each section.[2] Two miscellaneous sectors are sufficiently distinctive, well-documented, and intrinsically interesting to merit more detailed treatment in the following chapter, which is devoted to independents, performers in the arts, and (as a bonus) Latter Day Saints.

II   White-Collar

The inexorable growth of the Irish white-collar and official categories was a symptom of modernisation, with its incessant demand for employees with sufficient education to handle complex transactions and records, and ever more sophisticated systems of production, management, and distribution. Those reared in American cities would have had a comparative advantage over the rural Irish in tackling such tasks. Many American-born white-collar workers, however, had come to Ireland as young children. In seeking clerical posts in the public or private sectors, they were probably driven by the same factors that influenced their Irish-born peers, especially the lack of demand for labour in most other sectors. One-quarter of all American-born white-collar workers in 1911 were already in Ireland in 1901 as 'scholars' (school children aged under 16), compared with only one-sixth in the official and professional categories. The white-collar category as a whole had the highest proportion of matches with the other census, and of elite members who were co-resident with kin and with fellow Americans. It ranked fourth and last for the proportion of female and for median age. The number of North Americans classified in the white-collar category was 158 in 1901 and 205 in 1911. They have been assigned to four overlapping sectors (clerical, financial, managerial, and commercial). Within each sector, the census records an impressive array of specific occupations and personal career trajectories.

Clerical

Eighty-five North Americans were assigned to the clerical sector in 1901, rising to 116 in 1911. Clerical workers were noteworthy for only one 'extreme' score, having an exceptionally low median age in both census years. American clerks and kindred employees were to be found in banks, law firms, commercial establishments, the railways, and the public service. Francis Xavier Boyle, a 29-year-old who had married into Cork city, was unusually versatile, doubling as clerk and musician in 1901. Ten years later, the arrival of six children and co-residence with his father-in-law (a 'private gentleman') had not dented his enthusiasm for music.

Several Americans in 1901 held more exalted clerical positions such as company secretary. Philip MacNulty was secretary of a railway company, sharing his twelve-roomed house in Clontarf with two American-born brothers, two brothers-in-law, an Irish-speaking wife from Mayo, two daughters born in Dublin, and two servants. Francis J. Mooney, 22-year-old secretary of a wine and tea company, lived with his Irish-born parents, six siblings, and a servant in a thirteen-roomed house in Ballyboggan, Finglas. Both MacNulty and Mooney were Catholics, whereas Episcopalian John Alexander McClune of Haywood Avenue, Belfast and Presbyterian Samuel Murray of Bere, Co. Cork, lived in more modest accommodation. All four remained in Ireland in 1911. MacNulty had become a transit inspector for the Department of Agriculture and Mooney a clerk for Dublin County Council, while Murray had moved to an eleven-roomed house in Dartry Road. McClune reappeared as secretary to a money-lending company, having upgraded to a nine-roomed house in Florenceville, close to his old home off the Ormeau Road.

In 1901, the clerical sector was still overwhelmingly male, with only five female infiltrators of American birth. Maria Louisa Frith, an Episcopalian, lived in Eccles Street, Dublin, with her widowed Corkonian mother and extended family (her American-born brother had failed to find an occupation). Two Catholic Americans (Florence McLoughlin in Dublin and Lila Quirk in Kilkenny) worked as clerks in butchers' shops. Ellen Mitchell, a Presbyterian Canadian boarding in Prospect Street in Belfast's Cromac ward, worked as a linen clerk. The only stenographer, soon like the typist to become a niche occupation for women taking advantage of the new secretarial colleges, was Sarah Mooney, whose brother Francis has already been introduced. Their father was a Dubliner who managed a livery business, their mother was from Cavan, and their American-born sister Julia Mary was a civil service telegraphist.

Though still a small minority of American clerks in 1911 (19%), the female proportion had trebled over the intercensal decade. Nine women were specifically returned as 'clerks' (including a 'lady clerk' and a 'clerkess') and nine were typists, along with a stenographer, two secretaries, and an office assistant. In six cases, several American siblings had found work in the sector. Mary S. and Margaret R. Anderson, Presbyterian Canadians, were both typists in a linen warehouse, living with their widowed mother from Londonderry in her ten-roomed house in Alliance Avenue, Belfast. Violet Ervin (typist) and Emily Ervin (drapery clerk), from Alabama, likewise lived with their widowed mother from Limerick in eight rooms in Oldpark Road, Belfast. Their American-born brother, Robert J. Ervin, was a grocer's bookkeeper. In 1901, when all three were still scholars, this Presbyterian family was living in Omagh. Nellie Teresa and Minnie Frances Lee were also scholars in 1901, daughters of a Catholic American railway clerk and Corkonian mother in Killarney. By 1911, now in four rooms in Adare, Co. Limerick, they were both typists.

Three American children of a Catholic rope-maker from Louth and his Dublin wife were working in the clerical sector in 1911: Teresa, Gertrude, and Leo Mulholland were employed as stenographer, typist, and clerk, respectively. Their seven-roomed house was in Shelbourne Road, Pembroke. Eileen O'Kearney White and her twin brother Ernest (both Catholic commercial clerks) were among four American-born children of a Dublin solicitor and his English wife, living in 1911 in their uncle's seven-roomed house in St Lawrence Road, Kilmainham. This catalogue indicates the comfortable background of most American women who found clerical employment in pre-war Ireland, whether from Catholic or Protestant families.

Finance

Most Americans in the financial sector worked in banking or insurance, along with bookkeepers, accountants, brokers, and pawnbrokers. Attempts had recently been made to professionalise some of these once disreputable services, with the creation of the Insurance Institute of Ireland (1885) and Institute of Bankers in Ireland (1898). Three societies competed for the affiliation of accountants (chartered, incorporated, and corporate). The number classified under finance was 42 in 1901 and 47 in 1911. The sector was notable for its extremely low proportion of Catholics, and extremely high incidence of matches with the other census. The 1901 census included five American insurance agents as well as a manager and a supervisor, with similar representation in 1911. There were six bank managers or agents and five bank clerks in 1901; a decade later, fourteen Americans were employed in banks. Bookkeeping occupied eight Americans in 1901 and ten in 1911, including Florence E. Stewart, a Congregationalist from Canada who kept books for a provisions merchant. Her Canadian younger sister, Belfast father (a shop-man plumber), and mother from Antrim occupied eight rooms in Willowfield Gardens in Ormeau ward.

Joseph Alphonsus D. Henderson, clerk to a surveyor of taxes in 1901, also catered to the growing demand for secretarial skills by teaching shorthand. A Catholic living with his widowed mother from Waterford in Belfast, he was returned simply as a civil servant in 1911. William Little, a 51-year-old Methodist auctioneer, lived with his wife and six children in an eight-roomed house in Newry. Though returned as a local man in 1901, he declared his Canadian birth in 1911. A few Americans worked in real estate. John J. Conboy, a Catholic, worked as an accountant in an estate office in Midleton, Co. Cork, where he lived with relatives from the county. Walter A. McCaffrey, a Catholic real estate broker, was staying in Shankill ward with relatives from Down. Aged 17 in 1911, the Episcopalian Canadian George Albert Cass, apprentice in an estate agency, lived in his English mother's confectionery and bakery shop. Another Episcopalian was John Randolph Hamilton, an auditor and inspector in the car and cycle trade who lodged in the Grenville Hotel, Lower Sackville Street.

Though widely despised, pawnbrokers provided an essential service for poor urbanites that might never have entered a bank or taken out insurance. Three Americans were pawnbrokers in 1901: Delia Gildea, an Irish-speaking Catholic in Galway; John McConnell, a 16-year-old 'Prespiterian' on the Shankill in Belfast; and Joseph O'Flaherty, a Catholic, one of four assistants living in a pawn shop in Thomas Street, Cork. Only Delia Gildea remained in Ireland in 1911.

Management

In 1901, the small managerial class (18 members in 1901, 24 in 1911) ranked high for the proportion of matches with the other census and of household heads, and extremely low for the proportions of members who were Catholic and unmarried. The sector included four bank managers: an unmarried Catholic (John Towers in Kilkenny); two Episcopalians with Irish wives and children (the Canadian Francis H. Walker in Kinsale, Co. Cork, and Francis Purcell Woods in Castlederg, Co. Tyrone); and a Presbyterian Canadian with an Irish wife (William John McMurray in Coleraine, Co. Londonderry). Of these, only Walker and McMurray remained in 1911, McMurray having been transferred to Portrush, Co. Antrim. McMurray's brother Charles James, an insurance agent in 1901, appeared as a retired bank manager living in Cliftonville, Belfast (his wife was a Scot). Other Americans in 1901 were managers for a restaurant, wine merchant, hydropathic establishment, gas works, manufacturing jeweller, and cement works. Businesses managed by American newcomers in 1911 included a hotel, a laundry company, a fish factory, and a cold-storage business.

Gerard O'Callaghan, a Catholic Canadian, managed a creamery in 1901. Along with his father, a local farmer, mother from Carlow, four brothers or half-brothers from America and one from Kerry, he lived in a substantial farmhouse with eleven rooms and eight windows near Listowel, Co. Kerry. Charles Bosworth, an Episcopalian currently 'not employed' in managing a condensed milk factory and creamery, lived with his English wife and sons (born in England and Cork) in eight rooms in Midleton, Co. Cork. As shown below under manufacturing, the Canadian Cleeves had a major impact on the Irish creamery industry.

The Episcopalian Charles H. Gwynn managed a flour mill in Bellmount, King's County. Joseph Newman Hall, a Methodist graduate of Trinity College whose wife was also Canadian, managed a Belfast damask factory and lived in Ashley Avenue, Windsor. By 1911, Hall was managing a linen factory and had upgraded to a nine-roomed house in Eglantine Avenue. An Episcopalian railway director from Cincinnati, Eugene Zimmerman, was staying in 1901 with the family of his daughter Helena Montagu, Duchess of Manchester, in Tanderagee, Co. Armagh. Thomas W. McClughan, an Episcopalian Canadian, was a commercial clerk in 1901, who advanced to managing a sack and bag business in Belfast's Pottinger ward. His father from Antrim, who had married a woman from Bangor, was a retired carpenter who, in 1901, had proudly returned himself as a 'joiner on strike'.

Commercial

The other sub-sector of white-collar workers comprised 32 commercial travellers, agents, and buyers in 1901, rising to 48 in 1911. Its collective profile displayed no extreme values for any variable. Though now obsolescent in an age dominated by major wholesalers supplying vast chains of retail stores (material or virtual), this itinerant army long remained essential to Ireland's disaggregated economy. It ensured that small rural suppliers could find buyers in Ireland, Britain, and beyond for their primary produce, and that large suppliers of manufactured goods, typically British, could find retail outlets even in remote Irish villages. In 1901, there were American agents dealing in insurance, land, houses, rent, underclothing, sewing machines, and shipping; commercial travellers offering paper, butter, oils, wines and spirits, and whiskey; and a butter buyer. Additional sectors for agents in 1911 included tea, margarine, cork, the theatre, furniture, and building construction, with travellers promoting building materials, grocery, and provisions. There were buyers in pursuit of drapery, pigs, art, and millinery.

Patrick Dunlop was a Catholic cycle agent from California who settled in Thurles, Co. Tipperary (his mother's birth county), extending his business to the motor trade by 1911 after marrying a local woman. Despite a similar trajectory, he had no known connection with John Boyd Dunlop, the Scottish immigrant celebrated for inventing the pneumatic tyre. Frederick William Armstrong was a prosperous Episcopalian shipping agent in Londonderry, where he lived in 1901 with his wife from Co. Down, two daughters from Dublin, and a young Methodist visitor born in India. By 1911, he had moved to a slightly larger house in the same city, returning himself as a shipbroker's manager. Charles Reid in Tralee (another Episcopalian) and Maurice Patrick Riordan in Limerick (an Irish-speaking Catholic from Pittsburgh) both followed the stereotypically American occupation of advertising agent. Like many agents and travellers, Reid was a boarder in 1901, whereas Riordan was sharing two rooms with his widowed father from Tipperary. Reid was no longer in Ireland by 1911, but Riordan had married a Limerick woman, appearing as a shipping and general agent with a twelve-roomed house in George Street, Limerick. Alban Butler Donovan, a Philadelphia Catholic married to a native of Merrion, Co. Dublin, was a traveller for Guinness's brewery. They lived in some comfort (with a servant in both census years) in Summerhill Road, Glasthule.[3]

III   Official

The 'official' category comprises three mutually exclusive sub-sectors (civil service, postal service, and the forces). The number so classified rose from 113 in 1901 to 120 in 1911. Apart from having the largest proportion of Canadians, the category was devoid of extreme values. The unifying criterion for inclusion is employment by the various arms of the state operating at all levels, including a few in the services of the United States. The growth of the state sector was at once an agent and a symptom of modernisation, accelerated by massive government investment in reforms designed to mitigate Irish hostility to British rule. What were the political and cultural consequences of transforming thousands of Irish people, increasingly Catholics of humble origins, into officials trained along British lines to serve the United Kingdom or the empire? Though much debated, the outcome was more complex than mere 'Anglicisation' or 'assimilation'. Public service, whether within Ireland or beyond, often fostered strong feelings of Irish patriotism and solidarity that could assume covert political expression (despite sanctions against 'disloyalty') because of the extreme difficulty of dismissing tenured officers, and the growing influence of liberal Irishmen in the highest offices ('the greening of Dublin Castle').[4] But public service also counteracted insularity by bringing bureaucrats into contact with colleagues of cosmopolitan origins and with Irish people of all backgrounds and religions. For those in the armed and imperial services, the cosmopolitan influence was even stronger. Apart from contributing in a minor way to that cosmopolitan influence, the presence of North Americans also exposed them to a key element of Ireland's modernisation.

Civil Service

The collective profile of those performing civil services (49 in 1901 and 50 in 1911) betrayed no extreme characteristics, as one might expect of so respectable a sector. Within this sector, the most visible manifestations of Americanism were the consular officials who dealt with trade connections, passport applications, and problems arising for American citizens in Ireland. Canada's sole official representative in 1901 was its commissioner in Dublin, Charles R. Devlin, a Catholic who had brought over his family. Though the honorary consular agents representing the United States in Irish towns were typically Irish-born merchants or businessmen with connections in the United States, most senior officers were American natives on fairly brief assignments in Ireland. Four American-born consuls appear in the 1901 census: Malcolm Brice and William

W. Touvelle (Belfast), Arthur Donn Piatt (Dublin), and his presumed brother Cecil Piatt (deputy-consul in Queenstown, Co. Cork). Apart from Brice, an Episcopalian, all refused to give information about their religious denomination, a rarity for the period and perhaps a token of American modernity. Arthur Piatt (whose wife was an Irish-speaking Dubliner) was the only consular officer still in Ireland in 1911, having moved from Sandymount to Highfield Road, Rathgar. His American-born colleagues in that year were Edward L. Adams (Leeson Park, Dublin), John S. Armstrong, Jr (Queenstown), and George E. Chamberlain (Queenstown). Piatt again withheld his religion, but Adams and Armstrong were returned as Episcopalians and Chamberlain as a Presbyterian.

Though not qualifying for my American-born 'elite', the larger group of American consuls and consular agents born in the United Kingdom deserves separate discussion as public embodiments of the American–Irish connection. Only two such consular officers were so returned in the 1901 census, but ten others have been identified from the annual lists of consuls, deputy-consuls, vice-consuls, and consular agents published under town entries in *Thom's Official Directory*. Four lived in Queenstown, the main Irish port of departure for emigrants. They were Daniel Swiney, James William Scott, Walter James Cummins, and George Brown Dawson, all Episcopalians. Apart from Swiney (a native of Donegal but a professional consul), all were Corkonian shipping agents, living in substantial houses ranging from eleven to twenty rooms. Two other shipbrokers acted as consular agents in Munster: William H. Farrell in Waterford and Edmund Ludlow (an Englishman) in Limerick.

The remaining consular officers who were not of American birth were all located in Ulster, with none listed in either Leinster or Connaught. Wilson McKeown (a Presbyterian apprentice solicitor) and George Ballentine (an Episcopalian ex-clerk of petty sessions) both lived in Ballymena, Co. Antrim. Philip O'Hagan (Catholic solicitor, born in Donegal) and Peter Taylor Rodger (Catholic, born in Scotland) were both regular consular officers, based respectively in Londonderry and Buncrana, Co. Donegal. Episcopalians Edward Harvey (a goods clerk from Down) and Frederick William Magahan (a clerk of petty sessions from Donegal) acted for the United States in Belfast and Lurgan, Co. Armagh. All lived in substantial houses, four of which had at least twelve rooms. Apart from Ballentine, Rodger, and Swiney, all of these consuls and agents reappeared in the 1911 census.[5]

In addition to numerous national school staff, who will be considered under education, the public service category spanned a medley of workers in local or central administration, ranging from boy copyists to senior officers. O'Connell Shaw, a 63-year-old Methodist widower from New Brunswick, was computer of rates for Belfast Harbour (he had retired by 1911). With his extended family, including his Canadian sister Adelaide (a retired teacher) and a niece from Hong Kong, he occupied eleven rooms in Mountcharles, Windsor. The Canadian Edward Downes Martin, proprietor of Shrigley Mills near Killyleagh, Co. Down, was a magistrate. A 32-year-old Episcopalian, he shared his nineteen rooms and thirteen windows in 1901 with a servant (his wife was absent).

Among the more arresting official descriptions returned in 1911 were a surveyor of ships and three officers in the Department of Agriculture and Technical Instruction for Ireland: a tobacco expert, an inspector of sheep-dipping, and a senior geologist. The ship surveyor was William A. Wallace, a Canadian Episcopalian, who lived in an eleven-roomed house in Princetown Avenue, Bangor, with his German wife and her family along with two children born in Scotland. The tobacco expert was George N. Keller, a Presbyterian living in Marlborough Road, Pembroke, with his wife from King's County and daughter born in Dublin. Theobald Larkin, a Catholic with Irish-speaking parents from Galway and Wicklow, attended to the sheep in Kiltomer, Co. Galway. The geologist was another Canadian Episcopalian, Sidney Berdoe Wilkinson, a 61-year-old living in his mother-in-law's sixteen-roomed mansion in Killiney, Co. Dublin. This 93-year-old 'lady of means' hailed from Tyrone, her daughter from Londonderry; the houseful was completed by four servants and three hospital nurses.

The Department of Agriculture (formed in 1899) was one of several bodies recently established to tackle endemic social problems arising from archaic systems of farming and land tenure, which were widely blamed for Irish poverty and under-development. Robert Wilson Brown, an Episcopalian American listed simply as a government clerk in 1901, was a staff officer of the Irish Land Commission (established in 1881), living with his Dubliner family and a servant in seven rooms in Sandymount. At the opposite end of the hierarchy was 16-year-old George Green (an Episcopalian whose mother was from Westmeath), who worked as a boy clerk in the Commission's office in Dublin. John Patrick Dorman, a 25-year-old Catholic living in his uncle's drapery in Carrickmacross, Co. Monaghan, was clerk of the local Old Age Pension sub-committee (appointed to implement a momentous statute enacted in 1908). The increasing enrolment of Catholics in the colonies was exemplified by Willie Leonard Farini, a 37-year-old Canadian who had already retired from the 'colonial service' and described himself as a 'general servant', yet occupying six rooms in Grange, Co. Kilkenny.

Farini's wife and two sons were from Wicklow, along with a daughter from Kilkenny.

Postal Service

The humblest and largest sector of public servants worked for the post office, mainly as postmen, telegraphists, and messengers (31 members in 1901, 34 in 1911). This sector was one of extremes, with very high proportions of its members being Catholics, matched in the other census, co-resident with kin, and with other Americans. It also had extremely low proportions of Canadians and applicants unrelated to household heads, and exceptionally low median age.

Though not a recent creation, the postal service was expanding rapidly, not least through the recent extension of the imperial penny post (in 1905 for outgoing mail) and the introduction of cheap postcards (1890). Maurice O'Brien, a Catholic second-division clerk at the GPO in Dublin, shared a five-roomed house in Elmwood Avenue, Pembroke, with his Dublin wife. A decade later, still in the second division, he had acquired seven children, an additional forename proclaiming aristocratic connections (Lucius), and an eight-roomed house nearby in Park Avenue. James Winter, an Episcopalian Canadian described as a 'postal lineman', had married a woman from Armagh and lived in a ten-roomed house in Coleraine, Co. Londonderry. By 1911, he was an inspector of postal telegraphs in Londonderry (he had evidently had several intercensal postings, with children born in Louth and Armagh).

Three postmistresses, all American Catholics with local connections, were returned in 1901: Ellen Doran (Old Leighlin, Co. Carlow), Mary McNulty (Stranorlar, Co. Donegal), and Kate Moloney (Ballyclough, Co. Cork). Doran lived in her father's grocery; McNulty had taken over the business from her widowed father; and Moloney's husband (the postmaster) and daughters were all born locally in Co. Cork. Mary McNulty remained as the sub-postmistress of Stranorlar in 1911, but Kate Moloney (as the wife of a farmer and shopkeeper) was no longer assigned a separate occupation. Several women were employed as telegraphists, and there was one 'rural post girl'. She was Emily J. Foster, an 18-year-old Presbyterian living with her grandfather (the sub-postmaster) in Ballyrotton, an evocatively named townland in Co. Donegal.

Senior postal workers in 1911 included James Bannon, a Catholic American 'telegraph linesman' living with local parents in their ten-roomed house in Athlone; and Margaret Treacy, a Catholic telegraphist turned assistant postmistress in Churchtown, Co. Cork, likewise living with her locally born widowed mother. Margaret Adelaide Collins, a Canadian Episcopalian telegraph supervisor in Cork, was an unmarried 47-year-old who shared eight rooms with her widowed mother and spinster sister. The most intriguing entry was for James Hurley, a Catholic married to an Irish-speaking American, returned as a 'United States Postman' inhabiting a two-roomed hovel in Dunmanway, Co. Cork.

The Forces

The most controversial instruments of the state in Ireland, and among the most expensive, were the armed services. These included not only the army, the Royal Navy, and the coastguard, but the United Kingdom's only fully armed police force, the highly centralised Royal Irish Constabulary. When interpreting the presence of Americans in the army, it is essential to realise that Ireland was at once a major recruiting ground and a major location for non-Irish units. These were deployed to Ireland to 'assist the civil power' in emergency and, in the absence of emergency, to act as a deterrent against potential rebels. The presence of thousands of mainly British troops in Irish barracks (including some of the Canadian-born officers discussed below) was welcomed by many local people because of the undeniable economic benefit of military demand for goods and services, ranging from food and transport to drink, bets, and prostitutes. By the end of the nineteenth century, fears of disloyalty and wasteful expenditure had led to the winding up of the county militias and locally raised volunteer units ('yeomanry'), vastly reducing the number of Irishmen under arms. When the Territorial Force was created in 1908, Irish counties were excluded.

Yet Irish enlistment in the regular army and special reserve remained a significant source of employment, especially for southern Catholics living in towns. Most joined Irish units and were trained initially in Ireland, that number being multiplied at the period of the 1901 census by the raising of additional temporary units for the South African War. The North American presence was therefore a combination of men who had joined Irish units, and members of British units who happened to have been stationed in Ireland. The American police presence was restricted to the former category, as Ireland was self-sufficient in this sector and the great majority of the ordinary constabulary were Irish-born Catholics. The officer corps was more cosmopolitan in its origins, but still largely Irish with a growing Catholic minority.

American-born members of the forces (including numerous pensioners) amounted to 34 in 1901 and 36 in 1911. This was another sector characterised by extremes, with high median age, a high proportion of Canadians, and low proportions of females, who were unmarried, co-resident with other Americans, and matched in the other census. The North American military contingent ranged from privates and gunners to senior officers. Some belonged to units only temporarily assigned to Irish barracks, while two were incarcerated in Irish prisons in 1901. 'T. L.', an Episcopalian army bandmaster from Canada, was in Kilmainham Jail awaiting trial for false pretences. 'W. I. S.', a Presbyterian Canadian identified only as a 'soldier', was in Belfast's Crumlin Road Jail serving 56 days' hard labour for a military offence. Americans also served as prison warders: Owen Thomas Lloyd, an Episcopalian Canadian living in Belfast but married to a Corkonian, and Jeremiah O'Mahony, a Catholic American warding convicts in Mountjoy. By 1911, Lloyd was serving as a prison warder in Waterford, whereas O'Mahony (though only 37) had retired on a pension to Dundalk, where he lived with his Irish-speaking father (also a pensioner) and younger brother (a solicitor's managing clerk born in Limerick).

A few Canadians of high military rank have also been identified. Alexander Anderson, a 57-year-old Episcopalian retired lieutenant-colonel in the Royal Army Medical Corps, occupied a mansion in Galway with twenty rooms and sixteen windows. His imperial service was betokened by the birthplaces of his wife (Cape Colony) and six children (four born in India and two in England). Three were serving officers. Arthur Keogh, a 26-year-old Catholic lieutenant in the Connaught Rangers, lived in Co. Kildare with his Canadian mother, English sister, and Carlovian father (a retired major). William H. O. Kemmis was a 37-year-old captain in the Royal Artillery, living with his family in an eleven-roomed house in Tivoli Gardens, Cork (his wife and son were natives of Down and England, respectively). The most celebrated Canadian officer was Henry Worsley Gough, then a 26-year-old Episcopalian second lieutenant in the Connaught Rangers living in barracks in Rinmore, Co. Galway. In 1911, he was already a retired captain in the Reserve of Officers, living with his Galwegian wife and extended family, and four servants in a twenty-five-roomed house in Laurencetown, Co. Galway. Gough subsequently marched on to military celebrity as a major in the Irish Guards, staff officer, leader of the 'Curragh mutiny' in 1914, and winner of the Military Cross in the First World War. Gough's reputation was irrevocably tarnished by his removal as commander of the Fifth Army at Ypres in 1918.

The other Canadian officers enumerated in 1911 were George Deane Bourke, still serving aged 58 as a surgeon-general in the RAMC and principal medical officer in the Irish command; George French, a staff colonel in the Army Service Corps living in Wexford with a local wife and extended family; and James C. Lang, a serving captain in the King's

Own Scottish Borderers located with his English wife in Holywood, Co. Down. L. J. B. Lloyd, a lieutenant in the King's Shropshire Light Infantry, was in barracks in Fermoy, Co. Cork; David West was a lieutenant in the Royal Artillery living on 'Bear' (Bere) Island, Co. Cork, with his English-born family; and J. W. [West], was a lieutenant in the Army Ordnance Department stationed at Haulbowline, Co. Cork. William Ernest Date was a cavalry major in the Canadian militia, staying without his wife in Jury Brothers' Prince of Wales Hotel in Lower Sackville Street. Lang, West, and Date were Presbyterians, the rest Episcopalians.

It is noteworthy that all identified army officers in both census years were subjects of the monarch, having been born in Canada rather than the United States. This also applied to George Usborne, a retired Royal Navy captain turned harbour master, living in Queenstown with his Corkonian wife.[6] William Lillico, a 55-year-old Episcopalian Canadian, serving in 1911 with the Coastguard service in Mullaghmore, Co. Sligo, would also have been a naval veteran. His wife and four of their five children were English. A few natives of the United States were, however, enumerated among the military rank and file, both as serving personnel and as pensioners. In addition, John Costello was returned in 1901 as a widowed Catholic pensioner of the United States navy, living on King's Island, Limerick; in 1911, he was living with a niece and grandson in Moneyglass, Co. Antrim. Another Catholic 'American pensioner' was Marshal Bailey, living outside Longford in 1911 with his wife from Limerick and three Dublin step-daughters.

About one-quarter of North Americans in the forces were policemen, ranging from pensioners and constables to senior officers. Two pensioned district inspectors of the Royal Irish Constabulary, both Canadians in their early sixties with Irish wives, were enumerated in 1901. Joseph Saville Hoare Hume, an Episcopalian, lived in a ten-roomed house in Mallow, Co. Cork, with his recently acquired Carlovian wife and three children born in different counties. This reflected the policy of periodically relocating policemen of all ranks in order to minimise the corruptive effects of integration with local communities. By 1911, the Humes were living in a slightly smaller house in Bushy Park, Terenure, and Joseph proudly described himself as an 'armiger', a touchingly archaic assertion of his pedigree signifying an esquire entitled to bear heraldic arms. His father had owned over one thousand acres of inferior land in Wicklow, enough to secure inclusion in *Walford's County Families*.[7] William Henry McArdle, one of the expanding minority of Catholic officers so much resented in Ulster, shared a thirteen-roomed house in Duncairn, Belfast, with his wife from Wicklow and four children from three counties. There they remained in 1911.[8] William J. Burke, identified only as a retired police officer, was boarding in Harrington Street, Dublin in 1911.

IV   Professional

The professions constituted the apex of the hierarchy of service providers in terms of training required, social esteem, and (in varying degree) potential income. The 'professional' category comprised 165 North Americans in 1901 and 203 in 1911. It ranked highest among the four major categories for median age and for the proportion unmarried. It was also the category with the lowest proportion of household heads and of members with co-resident kin. The professions have been classified in five sectors (education, health, law, engineering, and religion). The extensive presence of Americans in the Irish professions did not simply reflect broader patterns of transatlantic migration, being critically influenced by the recruiting strategies and international alliances of professional bodies and institutions.

By 1900, many professions (including medicine, pharmacy, law, engineering, architecture, and surveying) had developed independent colleges and institutions to provide or approve qualifications, regulate conduct, disseminate knowledge, promote corporate interests, accredit competent practitioners, and side-line impostors. In some cases, the universities also offered recognised professional degrees. Then, as now, such bodies often actively recruited students from abroad to train for Irish qualifications, in order to compensate for inadequate supply at home and to raise income. They also admitted professionals with qualifications acquired outside Ireland, usually in Britain or the empire but sometimes in the United States. Some professional bodies catered for the entire United Kingdom or empire rather than Ireland alone, further diminishing the insularity of the professional elite. These factors tended to augment the American-born element of Irish professions.

Education

Though far more centralised and state-influenced than in Britain, Ireland's vast educational profession had stubbornly defied attempts to remould it as a cultural monolith along the lines of the Royal Irish Constabulary. It is true that, by 1900, the majority of school teachers relied on state qualifications under government-appointed boards of control (the commissioners of National Education and of Intermediate Education). Yet national teachers were also subject to clerical managers, either Catholic or Protestant, who could hire or fire them and controlled religious instruction (almost universally studied though not to be taken within 'school hours'). Seventy years had passed since the inauguration of the national system in 1831, with a common curriculum, designed to integrate pupils of all religious faiths, in schools transferred from numerous church organisations and private masters or mistresses ('hedge schools'). Yet hundreds of elementary schools refused to co-operate, including major networks run by the Christian Brothers, the Sisters of Mercy, other Catholic religious orders, and the (Protestant) Church Education Society.

Most school pupils never passed beyond the lower grades of national and elementary education, but more advanced classes were available to those wishing to qualify as 'monitors' (apprentice teachers) or for civil service examinations (for which enrolment in a 'crammer' was also normal). In 1878, however, the Intermediate Education Act had introduced centralised examinations at several levels leading towards university entrance, also based on a common curriculum, but without establishing any state-run schools. Schools run by religious institutions thus continued to monopolise the secondary sector, but their teaching programme was largely moulded by the intermediate programme. Many ambitious pupils prepared for university as well as intermediate examinations by hiring private tutors or attending private colleges and crammers, which were often large and profitable enterprises skilfully promoted like their contemporary equivalents.

The universities, though far more autonomous than today, were not free from state control and political interference. Trinity College (the University of Dublin), Ireland's only university until the creation in 1845 of Queen's ('Godless') Colleges in Cork, Galway, and Belfast, was governed under royal charter by a cabal of mainly 'senior fellows' who elected the provost (vice-chancellor), but the office of chancellor remained in government patronage. Only about one-fifth of pupils were Catholics, and 50 years earlier Trinity had been a major force in evangelical proselytism. Persistent attempts by Liberal administrations had so far failed to reform Trinity with a view to rendering it acceptable to the Catholic hierarchy. The 'Godless Colleges', at first equally obnoxious to the hierarchy, and the Royal University of Ireland (discussed below) had achieved a *modus vivendi* with Catholic intermediate schools; but effective Catholic control was not achieved until the National University of Ireland Act of 1908.

Such was the convoluted and ever more sectarian Irish educational system which employed 68 North Americans in 1901 and 87 in 1911. University and professional students are included, but not 'scholars' (school children). The education sector was noteworthy for its extremely high female and unmarried components, the rarity of co-residence with fellow Americans, and (in 1911) an exceptionally low median age. Teaching was a poorly paid profession, often providing for upward social mobility for children of humble rural origins, and many American-born teachers worked in remote districts. In 1901, 25 North Americans (mostly female) were returned as national school teachers, and others returned simply as 'teachers' may also have received state salaries. Four American nuns were resident teachers in convents, in addition to a Franciscan friar teaching in a monastery in Achill, Co. Mayo. The sector also embraced governesses, teachers in private schools, independent tutors or 'professors', and college students.

Educators in senior official positions included two Canadians: William Bartley, an unmarried Presbyterian university graduate and inspector of national schools in Cork (1901) and Kilkenny (1911); and Charles W. McDermott, a Catholic superintendent for the Board of Trade and examiner of masters and mates in 1901. With his Corkonian family, including a son studying medicine with the Royal University of Ireland, McDermott lived in a twelve-roomed house in Blackrock, Co. Cork. The Royal University conducted examinations and conferred degrees but offered no teaching, which was instead provided by associated colleges, schools, and private tutors. Philip Merry was the educational equivalent of a prison warder, a Catholic American school attendance officer living in Clontarf in both years, with his Dubliner wife and children born in Dublin and Wexford. Another native of the United States, Swift-Paine Johnston, was professor of moral philosophy at Trinity College from 1898 to 1901, when he became assistant commissioner of Intermediate Education. Johnston's house in Terenure had eight rooms and twelve windows.

Well-heeled teachers included Ebenezer Walter Todd, a 26-year-old American Methodist heading a household with ten rooms in Victoria ward, Belfast, who described himself as a teacher, Royal University undergraduate, and beneficiary of interest on money. Simply a 'teacher' by 1911, he had moved to a house of the same size in Cyprus Park, Pottinger ward. Harman Cloak was an assistant master and Royal University undergraduate, living in the nine-roomed rectory at Drum-harken, Cloone, Co. Leitrim, with his Monaghan-born father, English mother, and a servant. The Royal University catered for women, including Agnes Eva Robb, a Presbyterian Canadian undergraduate. In 1901, she shared a ten-roomed house in University Street, Belfast, with her widowed mother from Co. Tyrone and siblings from Galway and Tyrone (including the barrister John Hanna Robb). Another Canadian

Presbyterian, Arthur Williamson, a graduate of the Queen's University of Belfast (formerly one of the colleges preparing students for Royal University examinations), had married a woman from Co. Down. Simply a Belfast 'schoolmaster' in 1901, a decade later he had become principal of Dublin's Municipal School of Commerce in Rathmines.

Several American-born college students were enumerated in 1911, including an aspirant national teacher at Marlborough Street Training College, a veterinary student, and five medical students. Of these, all but one (a Canadian and three Americans) were boarding together in Pembroke Street, Dublin, betokening the cosmopolitan intake of institutions such as the Royal College of Surgeons for Ireland. George van Beneveld Gilmour, a Canadian Presbyterian, lived in both census years with his farmer uncle in Lisboy, Co. Tyrone. In 1911, he was proudly returned as an undergraduate at the University of London, which already offered external degrees. Another Canadian Presbyterian, Roy Leitch, was an Oxford undergraduate staying in a hotel in Killarney, Co. Kerry.

Health

The health sector had long been dominated by the Royal Colleges of Surgeons and of Physicians in Ireland, whose training regulations sidelined those regarded as 'quacks' or, in today's terms, practitioners of 'alternative medicine' such as osteopathy. Admission to the medical register, in Ireland as in Britain, had been regulated since 1858 by the General Medical Council, which had a subsidiary Irish branch with its own executive.[9] Nurses were also aspiring to claim professional status through the introduction of college degrees, though the term also applied to untrained servants looking after young children (excluded from my database). The health sector accounted for 39 North Americans in 1901 and 52 in 1911, and was notable only for the extreme infrequency of co-residence with kin.

About half of the sector were nurses (including four nuns in 1901). In both years, Mary Forde, a Catholic whose Corkonian husband derived his living from dividends, was lady superintendent or proprietress of a small private hospital in Baggot Street, Dublin. Apart from a dental mechanic in Mountpleasant Place, Pembroke (Ranelagh), the only dentist was Gustavus Haas, an Episcopalian American staying on St Stephen's Green in 1901. American dentists had multiplied by 1911: John Blakey was boarding in Grand Parade, Cork, with Abraham Goldfoot, a 'Hebrew' dentist born in Russia; Eugene Lincoln, another Episcopalian American unmarried at 45, lived in a nine-roomed house in Eglantine Avenue in Belfast's Windsor ward;

Roy Stuart, a Catholic, was living in Charleville, Co. Cork, with his violinist wife and son from Edinburgh.

The emergence of nursing as a recognised profession was proclaimed by two North American women in each census. Agnes Sloan, a 30-year-old Catholic living with an Irish-speaking uncle in two rooms in Creggan Lower, Co. Armagh, was proudly returned as a 'trained' nurse in 1901. Katherine Horne, a 'trained maternity nurse' in 1911 like her widowed mother from Co. Dublin, was an Episcopalian Canadian. Belle Jackson, a 34-year-old Presbyterian Canadian, was a 'professional nurse' visiting rural Antrim in 1901. Mary Anne E. Burns, a Catholic first described as a mere 'nurse and domestic servant' in Holywood, Co. Down, was recognised as a 'professional' nurse by 1911, though still in service in plush Malone Park in Belfast's Windsor ward.

A few Americans on the fringe of professional medicine practised as druggists or 'apothecaries', a venerable guild regulated by the Apothecaries' Hall of Ireland. Until the creation of the General Medical Council, there had been no generally recognised demarcation between medical practitioners and apothecaries. Michael Francis O'Donnell (a Catholic from New York) exhibited the recent professionalisation of this occupation, being a licentiate of the Pharmaceutical Institute of Ireland (1875), yet occupied just two rooms in Phibsborough Road, Dublin. Still unmarried, he remained there in 1911 as a mere 'apothecary'. William Pemberton (an Episcopalian), also unmarried in middle age, was a 'manufacturing chemist' living with his widowed mother from Dublin in an eight-roomed house in Tate's Avenue, Belfast, headed by his brother-in-law from Down (who followed the same trade).

Seven of the twelve medical practitioners in 1901 came from the United States, along with four from Canada and one from 'South America'. Four of these, presumably working towards higher qualifications, were to be found in a student dormitory in the Rotunda Buildings. These included Mark Goldstein, the only practising Jew among American medical men in Ireland. Bond Boyce was a Canadian licentiate of the RCSI living with his Dublin wife in Lower Baggot Street. Rodolph A. C. Burnes, an Episcopalian Canadian, lived with his wife from Tyrone in Glasnevin. Charles G. Clarke, a Quaker married to another American but with two local children, was a general practitioner in Camlough, Co. Armagh. Like Boyce and Burnes, he occupied a substantial ten-roomed house. Another general practitioner, the Presbyterian William John Ross Knight from Philadelphia, had married a Londonderry woman and settled in Cookstown, Co. Tyrone. Knight's census return in 1911 proudly enumerated three medical qualifications, not to mention his chairmanship of the Cookstown urban council and the magistracy temporarily attached to that elective office. In both years, William Kidston Law, an Episcopalian Canadian with Glasgow qualifications, lived in Coleraine with his wife and seven children born in Co. Londonderry. All of these practising doctors lived in substantial houses ranging from nine to thirteen rooms. Thomas Joseph McDonald, a Presbyterian Canadian, lived on Belfast's Antrim Road but had married a Kilkenny woman. Finally, Arthur Clarence Turner, an American Catholic trained in Edinburgh, lived in Foyle Street, Londonderry, with his American sister and Welsh parents (his father was a magistrate and steamship agent for the Allan Shipping Line).

Several American doctors were enumerated only in 1911. Donald Cameron and Charles Oliver, both Presbyterian Canadians with Toronto qualifications, were returned in the Rotunda hospital; William E. Fraser, an Episcopalian Canadian, was enumerated in the Coombe Lying-In Hospital; William Symmers, an Episcopalian American doctor, was staying at the Shelbourne Hotel. Two American Methodists operated on the margins of conventional medicine as 'doctors of osteopathy'. Osteopathy (dismissively known in Ireland as 'bone-setting') was a regulated profession in Canada and the United States, but not in Ireland. Jacob Dunham lived in Shaftesbury Square, Belfast, with his wife from Armagh and son from Belfast; Harvey Ray Foote, an unmarried 30-year-old practised in Harcourt Street, Dublin. Foote proudly paraded his credentials from a college of osteopathy in Des Moines, Iowa. Both Foote and Dunham occupied ten-roomed houses, suggesting that osteopaths could make a good living. The lone South American in 1901, Thomas Gerald Fenton (a 24-year-old unmarried Episcopalian), practised in Castletown, Co. Sligo. This catalogue confirms that medicine was the most ecumenical of the major professions in its religious intake and recruiting zone, with many doctors born or trained outside Ireland.

Four medical graduates attract attention because they chose *not* to practise their skills. Philip A. McCarthy of Dangan, Co. Cork, was a 38-year-old Catholic living with his wife from Louth, English daughter, and two servants in a house with fourteen rooms and thirteen windows in Dangan, Co. Cork. Ample private means are suggested by his self-description in 1901 as 'MD, not practising'. He remained so in 1911, though his wife was absent and he had moved to a similar house in Riverstown, Co. Cork. Joseph Austin Evans, a 28-year-old Catholic Canadian, held Canadian qualifications which he also did not utilise in 1911. Presbyterian William Hanford Whyte, an 80-year-old non-practising physician from the United States with an American wife, lived with relatives in Killevan, Co. Monaghan. The sixteen-roomed house with four servants was headed by a resident magistrate from

Londonderry whose wife was a native of New York. The other non-practising American doctor, with Edinburgh qualifications, was doubly unusual in an era when female doctors remained a curiosity. Mildred Jane Croskery had married a Presbyterian minister from Londonderry and lived in a ten-roomed manse in Gortgranagh, Co. Tyrone. In 1911, the minister no longer bothered to parade her qualifications in the family census return.

Law

The legal profession was largely controlled, as today, by two autonomous professional bodies which zealously defended their institutional privileges. These were the Incorporated Law Society of Ireland and the Honorable Society of the King's Inns, catering respectively for solicitors and barristers. Along with the universities, these provided reputable training and apprenticeships, regulated their members, and side-lined impostors selling quasi-legal services to credulous folk. Only ten North Americans had legal occupations in 1901, rising to seventeen in 1911. In 1901, four were solicitors and the remainder assistants and clerks. Though too small to permit rigorous comparison with the major occupational sectors, law was notable for the extremely high proportions co-resident with kin and matched at the other census.

Aged 51, Michael William Dunne from Pittsburgh had already retired from practice as a solicitor and lived in his half-brother's eleven-roomed parochial house in Meelick, Queen's County. Ten years later, he was enumerated as a boarder in Carlow. In 1901, 33-year-old William Early lived on his parents' substantial farm in Errigal, Co. Tyrone; by 1911, he shared an eleven-roomed house in Aughnacloy with his Longford wife and locally born children. Both Dunne and Early were Catholics. Matthew Henry Jackson, a 33-year-old Episcopalian Canadian with a university degree, lived in Newgrove Avenue, Pembroke, with his parents (a retired surgeon-general from King's County who had married a Londoner). He was still in the parental home in 1911. In 1901, the Presbyterian American Robert Henry Parke was living in Loughgall, Co. Armagh, in the thirteen-roomed house of his brother-in-law, a general practitioner from Co. Armagh. He subsequently married a woman from Reading and moved to a slightly larger house in Monaghan town.

It is noteworthy that all four North American solicitors in 1901 had clearly found secure and settled livings in Ireland. Three others were first returned as solicitors in 1911. George Cunningham, senior, a 32-year-old Catholic, had married an Irish-speaker from Tyrone and lived modestly in a five-roomed house in Omagh. John E. Smyth-Edwards, a 33-year-old Canadian Presbyterian, lived in the parental home in Hawthornden Road, Victoria ward, Belfast, with his mother, father (a retired farmer) from Londonderry, and twin brother (a secretary and bookkeeper). Charles Andrew MacKenzie, a Presbyterian whose birthplace was given as Belfast in 1901 but America in 1911, was a solicitor's apprentice in Belfast in 1901, living in the home of his father, a Belfast-born blacksmith. By 1911, he had married a woman from Bradford and occupied an eight-roomed house in Kincora Avenue. The only North American barrister enumerated in either census was a 46-year-old retired barrister from a prominent Episcopalian family of Huguenot origin, Benjamin St George Lefroy. Scarcely a year earlier, he had married a much younger namesake born in England, with whom he shared an eleven-roomed house in Derrycashel, Co. Roscommon.[10] As in 1901, the remainder of the legal sector were clerks and assistants, including five Episcopalians and four Catholics.

Engineering

Engineering was another fairly minor sector for North Americans, with 15 engineers of all varieties in 1901 and 19 in 1911. Like law, the sector is too small to be included in my formal rankings; but it was noteworthy for the rarity of women and matches with the other census, and for its very low median age. Most of these 'engineers' were not qualified professionals in the modern sense, as the term remained notably ambiguous and wide-ranging. Engineering had recently become a major university subject, as the technical demands of many engineering sectors became ever more sophisticated. An Institution of Civil Engineers of Ireland had been established in 1835, and attempts were made to professionalise surveying and architecture. In 1901, the 'engineering' sector embraced civil, electrical, mining, railway, and ship engineers, along with a factory engineer and fitter, an architect's assistant, and draughtsmen. Additional entries in 1911 included an engineer and millwright, a lance-corporal in the Royal Engineers, and motor and mechanical engineers.[11]

Most of those listed in 1901 were young unmarried men living as dependants of relatives. The married exceptions were Matthew Fortescue (Episcopalian Canadian, civil engineer), Henry Sherlock ('Protestant' Canadian, mining engineer), and John O'Donnell (Episcopalian American, railway engineer). Fortescue had married a Dublin nurse and lived in a seven-roomed house in Grosvenor Road, Rathmines; Sherlock and his English wife had six rooms in Cushkillery, Co. Galway; and O'Donnell and his wife (a Catholic) lived in the grocery of his

Catholic father-in-law in Kilrush, Co. Clare. He was presumably partly responsible for the erratic mechanical performance of the West Clare Railway, memorably parodied by Percy French.

Only Fortescue remained in Ireland in 1911, when he had acquired a university degree, two professional qualifications as a civil engineer, and three extra rooms in Grosvenor Road. Thomas George Beattie from Toronto, an unmarried 'gass' (gas) manager in Queen's County in 1901, returned himself in 1911 as a 'resident engineer' in Belfast. He had meanwhile changed affiliation from the 'Irish Church' to Wesleyan Methodism, married a woman from King's County, and roamed about (their two children were born in Rangoon). Along with his mother-in-law from Killarney, they lived in an eight-roomed house in Duncairn, Belfast. Robert Graham Glendinning, an American engineering contractor and Baptist, had married a Belfast Methodist and lived in a nine-roomed house in Wellington Park, Belfast. Ten years earlier, he was returned as an electrical engineer living in the fourteen-roomed parental home in nearby Windsor Avenue. An American brother was working as a linen merchant. Edward G. Hope Johnstone, an Episcopalian Canadian mechanical engineer with a wife from Fermanagh, occupied twelve rooms in Kilcooley, Co. Meath. The only American-born architect was Richard Neely, a Presbyterian boarding in Belfast.

Religion

A different professional model, strongly encouraging cosmopolitanism, applied to the various churches which exercised so powerful an influence in education and health as well as pastoral care and social control. The most global religious institution was undeniably the Roman Catholic Church, whose structures of government, training, and ordination made it relatively easy for Americans to qualify for Irish appointments (even if the partial autonomy of the Irish hierarchy and local loyalties obstructed some foreign aspirants). International transfers to Ireland were particularly straightforward within the self-governing religious orders, unrestrained by diocesan administrators, and often originated outside Ireland in countries such as France, Britain, and occasionally the United States.

Most Protestant churches had strong international links over a narrower terrain. Between 1801 and 1869, the Episcopalian Church of Ireland had been formally united with the Church of England, which in turn governed (rather haphazardly) kindred churches throughout the empire. As *Crockford's Clerical Directory* attested, there was no perceptible impediment to ordination for imperial subjects of any origin, and a

substantial minority of the Irish clergy were natives of Britain, Australasia, or Canada. The Presbyterian and Methodist churches had equally
strong British and imperial connections, and much closer links with
'sister' churches in the United States. Theological qualifications from
approved North American institutions were recognised by all major
Protestant churches in Ireland. Likewise, thousands of Irish-trained religious personnel of all denominations served abroad, often in North
America. The missionary trade worked in both directions, with an
increasing flow of American evangelists visiting Ireland to propagate their
doctrines and, if possible, establish local missions. We should therefore
not be surprised by the diverse array of American priests, nuns, ministers, and missionaries revealed by Irish census returns.

The religious profession accounted for 42 North Americans in
1901 and 46 in 1911. The sector's collective profile was remarkable,
with exceptionally high median age and a very small component with
co-resident kin. It also ranked top in both years for the proportion
with co-resident Americans, with a very large unmarried component.
Very high proportions of Catholics and women were recorded in both
years, though the scores just fell short of those required for the accolade
of 'extreme' values.[12]

About half of the sector were nuns, often serving as teachers or nurses,
and living in convents established by numerous religious orders. There
were Sisters of Mercy, St Brigid, Charity, the Cross and Passion, Loreto,
Presentation, the Sacred Heart, Reparation, and St Louis; Little Sisters
of the Poor and of the Assumption; as well as Dominicans, Faithful
Companions of Jesus, and Franciscan Missionaries of Mary.[13] Of these,
only three in 1901 and four in 1911 were Canadians. Since nuns had
chosen a job for life, many were traced in both censuses (despite inconsistent use of original and religious names). These included (among
others) Mary Corcoran from Chicago, a Loreto teaching nun in North
Great Georges Street, Dublin, in 1901, and Balbriggan, Co. Dublin, in
1911. She was evidently the mother superior in Dublin, as she signed the
institutional return. In both years, Nellie (Ellen) Cunningham from
Chicago taught at the Loreto convent in Rathfarnham, Co. Dublin;
Mary Berchmans O'Neill from New York continued to teach at
St Brigid's convent in Abbeyleix, Queen's County; and Julia Curtin
from Jersey City remained an *hospitalière* with the Little Sisters of the
Poor, at the Manor Hill home for the aged in Waterford. Though North
Americans accounted for only a tiny fraction of Ireland's mighty and
multiplying army of brides of Christ, their presence exemplified the
impressively cosmopolitan background of this highly influential (yet
widely underrated) element of Irish social history.

American priests were less numerous than nuns. Nicholas Landy, a 40-year-old Irish-speaking priest in Dungarvan, Co. Waterford, living with three servants and relatives from four counties, was recorded only in 1901. Benedict Joe Tully from New York was a Franciscan monk of the Third Order teaching in Achill, Co. Mayo, in 1901. Disguised as an 'agriculturist', he had moved to Kilkeeran, Co. Galway, by 1911. His fellow American Andrew Tully, perhaps his brother, was parish priest of St Peter's, Belfast, in 1901, and Rossconor, Co. Down, in 1911. The Canadian John Joseph Farrell ministered in Roosky, Co. Leitrim, and later Mullanaghta, Co. Longford. John Nugent was enumerated in both years at a monastery in Mountheaton, King's County, where he followed the discipline of the 'Order of Cistercians of the Strict Observance'.

Though the religious sector was dominated by Catholics, about two-fifths belonged to other denominations. With one exception, the Church of Ireland ministers were Canadians. Edward Albert Boulter, with a Dublin wife, was rector of Holywood, Co. Down, throughout the period. Robert Forsyth Clarke, aged 75, was rector in Brinny, Co. Cork, where in 1901 he shared fourteen rooms and thirteen windows with his five spinster daughters and two servants. William Sherlock, aged 74, had a similar profile, living in both years in Sherlockstown near Bodenstown, Co. Kildare with three spinster daughters from Wicklow and England and three servants. His house featured twenty-five rooms and nineteen windows. Sherlock owned a substantial estate of superior land in Co. Kildare.[14] In 1901, as incumbent of Knockbreda, Belfast, 66-year-old Henry William Stewart (the only American in this group) shared a sixteen-roomed house with his American wife, children born in Westmeath and Down, daughter-in-law, family from Belfast, and the usual three servants. The only Church of Ireland clergyman enumerated solely in 1911 was Francis Henry Archbold in Clontarf, a 58-year-old who had married a Corkonian. Alleged to have been born in Sydney rather than Canada in the published clergy list for Dublin, he died in Toronto in 1928. Though the Archbolds and their two servants occupied only ten rooms with five windows, these returns confirm the material benefits (in living space rather than income or assets) of taking Holy Orders in 'the formerly established church'.

Americans ministered in other Protestant churches in less pampered circumstances, though most churches provided fairly substantial tied accommodation. The two Presbyterian ministers were both Americans. David Boyd was a city missionary in Duncairn, Belfast, where he lived in 1901 with his widowed mother and American-born elder sister (a mere 'factory girl'). In 1911, newly married to a Belfast woman at the age of

47, he had moved house locally and upgraded from five to eight rooms. Henry Patterson Glenn, who married a Scot in about 1907, ministered in Bray, Co. Wicklow (where his manse in Quinsborough Road apparently shrank from nine to five rooms, and from five to three windows, between 1901 and 1911).

Being 'itinerants' who were expected to move circuit every 3 years, Methodist ministers often worked (and accumulated children) in several Irish counties. Charles Henry Crookshank, a 65-year-old widower, ministered in Londonderry in 1901, but married a woman from Bandon and moved to Palmerstown Road, Belfast, where the couple and a servant shared fourteen rooms and thirteen windows. Henry James Munton, a 37-year-old with a wife was from Cork and sons from Wicklow and Galway, was stationed in a ten-roomed house in Ballinasloe, Co. Galway in 1901. A third Methodist minister, 22-year-old Canadian William Wright, was enumerated as a visitor in Crumlin, Co. Antrim. All three ministers were Canadians.

Other Canadians belonged to more obscure religious movements. There were also two emissaries of the 'Holiness Movement'. Lydia Bradley, a 29-year-old 'evangelist' in 1901, was visiting a family in Duncairn, Belfast which included two children also born in Canada. In 1911, John C. Black, a 33-year-old 'clergyman' who had recently married another Canadian, was living in Belfast in 1911 in a seven-roomed house in Old Park Road, along with a fellow clergyman born in Down and an evangelist from Belfast returned as boarders. John James Sims was a 59-year-old evangelist, described as 'Protestant undenominational', who was living in 1911 with his wife and son (both 'singers' from Canada) in Haddington Road, Pembroke.[15] Another group of evangelical missionaries was sufficiently exotic and idiosyncratic to deserve closer examination in the next chapter. These were the parties of Mormons or 'Latter Day Saints' who worked so hard and so fruitlessly for the conversion of sinners in pre-war Ireland.

V   Miscellaneous

Miscellaneous sectors in which visitors could be viewed as exhibits of American modernity account for 182 members of the North American elite in 1901 and 179 in 1911. Collectively, the miscellaneous category had the highest median age in both years and the lowest proportion matched with the other census. Manufacturers included several wealthy Americans, notably the Cleeve family. Most Americans grouped under transport were employed by railway companies. Hospitality, a sector increasingly permeated with American practices and preferences, incorporates those providing food, drink, and accommodation. With the partial exception of manufacturers, these sectors may also be classified as service providers.

Manufacturing

The North American elite included a few manufacturers (6 in 1901, 10 in 1911), mostly living in substantial houses in Ulster or Dublin. This sector, like law and engineering, was too small to allow rigorous comparison with the fourteen major occupational categories. But, such as they were, manufacturers had the highest median age, no women in either year, extremely low Catholic and unmarried components, and a small proportion with co-resident Americans.

Benjamin Courtney Hobson was a Quaker linen manufacturer, born in Canada with a wife from Armagh, who occupied a fourteen-roomed house in Old Warren, Lisburn in 1901. By 1911, he had moved to a house of thirty-two rooms in nearby Drumbeg, Co. Down.[16] His namesake and presumed kinsman John Bulmer Hobson (son of another Benjamin) helped to reorganise the Irish Republic Brotherhood and became secretary of the Irish Volunteers before the 1916 rebellion, during which he was 'kidnapped' by a more militant rival faction. Frederick C. Cleeve, a 49-year-old Canadian-born condensed milk manufacturer, belonged to an Episcopalian family which controlled the largest network of private 'creameries' in Ireland. Along with his Limerick-born wife and two sons, he occupied a first-class house with eighteen rooms, fourteen windows, and four servants in Limerick in both census years. By 1911, his unmarried brother Edward, a manufacturer of butter and condensed milk, had also moved to Ireland, where he occupied a house with eleven rooms, twelve windows, and three servants in Tipperary town. The Condensed Milk Company of Ireland had been established by their eldest brother (Sir) Thomas Henry Cleeve, who started out in business with a maternal uncle in Limerick dealing in agricultural machinery.[17] Though the parent company went into liquidation in 1923 following sustained attacks on its factories by the Crown forces as well as the IRA, a subsidiary famous for its toffee survives as a brand-name.[18]

Another prosperous manufacturer (of clothing) was Robert Bell Walkington, with his fifteen-roomed house in Ballygrott, Bangor. Walkington was remarkable for the fact that his Unitarian wife from Lancashire was returned as head of household, the only such case that I have come across in the Irish census. By 1911, however, she had reverted to being a mere wife, Walkington had redescribed his nativity as Co. Down rather than the United States, and the family had moved to a twenty-roomed house in Belfast's Malone Road. Other goods manufactured by Americans included colours, soap, boots, fancy goods, jewellery, and organs, indicating the ambiguity of a term incorporating both humble tradesmen and rich investors.

Transport

Transport occupied 22 North Americans in 1901 and 18 in 1911. In 1901, almost all of these also qualified for the elite as clerks or engineers. The sector's collective profile was unexceptional, apart from extremely small female and unmarried components. The most important sub-groups were the railways and the marine (in which foreigners such as Americans were obviously over-represented). The flourishing railway system had for more than half a century been essential to Irish economic growth, internal mobility of goods and people, and access to ports of commerce and emigration. It remained in private hands, with many small local operators as well as major networks such as the Great Northern, Great Southern and Western, and Midland Great Western railway companies.

One of the most visible functionaries in pre-war Ireland was the stationmaster, whose potential to acquire local knowledge and gossip was surely exceeded only by the policeman and the postmistress. George Miller Allely, an Episcopalian aged 25, shared a house in Six Mile Cross, Co. Tyrone, with his wife from Down, their infant daughter born in Louth, and his wife's Presbyterian sister. In 1911, he had risen to the rank of railway inspector in Letterkenny, Co. Donegal. Daniel Lee, a Catholic railway clerk in Killarney, Co. Kerry, in 1901, had become stationmaster in Adare, Co. Limerick, by 1911. His wife was from Cork and the three younger children were from Cork and Limerick, but two daughters were natives of the United States. George Mulcahy, another American Catholic, had followed the same career trajectory between 1901 and 1911 from Cappoquin, Co. Waterford, to Manserghs Hill, Graystown, Co. Tipperary, where his landlord was the Great Southern and Western Railway Company. An aunt with whom he lived in 1901 was from Waterford and his wife from Galway. Alexander Morrison, an Episcopalian married to a Down woman, was a mere railway porter in Ballyclare, Co. Antrim, in 1901. By 1911, he had risen to the rank of stationmaster at Red Bay in the same county.

Three Canadians were returned as master mariners in 1911. Apart from Oliver King, a Baptist, whose fishing boat from Barrow-in-Furness merely happened to be in the port of Waterford on census night, all were settled in Ireland. Horace MacCully, a Catholic recently married to an Armagh woman, lived in a twelve-roomed house in Warrenpoint, Co. Down. Charles Edward McNutt, another Catholic, lived more modestly with his wife and five children in a three-roomed cottage in Tullyratty, Strangford. In 1901, he was temporarily absent from the seven-roomed family home in Irish Street, Downpatrick, leaving behind his wife and three younger children from Down, the others being natives of Liverpool and Canada. His Canadian-born son, Bernard John McNutt, a schoolboy in 1901, was also a mariner but not yet a master in 1911, when he remained with his parental family at the age of 23.

Hospitality

Hospitality, a sector dominated by the drink trade, engaged 34 North Americans in 1901, rising to 52 in 1911. The sector was notable for extremely high proportions of Catholics and household heads, low median age, and its small Canadian component. Rural towns in Ireland were until recently remarkable for the high proportion of occupiers holding liquor licences (apart from those that evaded them), and most public houses were family businesses without hired labour which also sold basic groceries. New York or Boston accents could be heard from hotel and restaurant managers and numerous publicans, as well as bar-maids and barmen.[19] John Murnin, for example, was returned in 1911 as a 16-year-old Catholic 'vintner's apprentice', working at the Capstan Bar in Ann Street, Belfast. His employer was Owen McMahon, notoriously murdered with his family in March 1922.[20]

Ernest Everest, an Episcopalian, managed a restaurant in Belfast in 1901, living with his Welsh wife and son-in-law in a six-roomed house in Stranmillis. By 1911, he had become resident manager of the Avenue hotel with sixty-five rooms in Royal Avenue. His wife, now described as English, was the manageress. Herman Henssler, an unmarried American Lutheran, had been proprietor of the same hotel in 1901. William Martin, a Presbyterian Canadian, managed an immense 'hydropathic establishment' in Blarney, Co. Cork, featuring 101 rooms and 123 windows. He remained there as 'secretary' in 1911, his Roscommon-born wife having become a sub-postmistress. Andrew James Rowand, a Presbyterian American with wife and children from Limerick city, was a wine merchant's manager in Pery Square, Limerick. By 1911, he had moved to a larger house in Ennis Road (with twelve as against eight rooms), which also accommodated his widowed mother-in-law from Kerry. Sarah Ann Baxter, also Presbyterian, did business on a more modest scale as an hotel-keeper and farmer in Milford, Co. Donegal.

In 1901, her six-roomed hotel had ten inhabitants including her 27-year-old American daughter, a son and grand-daughter from Donegal, aunt from Tyrone, three servants, but only one 'visitor'. Ten years later, there were two servants and no guests.

A precociously successful American entrant to the sector in 1911 was Jennie Acres, a 27-year-old Episcopalian who managed the 120-roomed Metropole Hotel in Cork. Alice Morgan, a Catholic widow with children from Belfast and Down and an unmarried American sister, kept a twenty-five-roomed hotel in Main Street, Bangor, Co. Down. Her circumstances had improved notably since 1901, when she and her horse-dealing husband from Armagh had lived in seven rooms on the Falls Road, Belfast. Robert Alexander Patterson had also risen in the world since 1901, when he was a newly married 25-year-old, working as a sewing-machine agent with two rooms in Saintfield, Co. Down. By 1911, he had overcome any Methodist scruples to become the manager of a ten-roomed public house in Donaghadee. There he lived with his wife, three children, and mother-in-law, all natives of Down. By contrast, the widowed Catholic Mary Anne Little shared her ten-roomed 'hotel' in Blackrock, Co. Louth, with an 80-year-old barman from Louth (an unmarried uncle), a servant, and no guests.

Though most public houses and 'spirit dealers' were small, doubtless doubling as groceries in accordance with Irish custom, several larger premises licensed to Americans were returned in 1901. All but one of these belonged to Catholics from the United States. William Haughey was an Irish-speaking grocer and spirit merchant, living with his locally born wife and children in a ten-roomed public house in Glencolumbkille, Co. Donegal. Maggie Slimmand and her husband from Greenock were both returned as Presbyterian publicans occupying a ten-roomed shop in Coleraine, but untraced in 1911. Likewise, Margaret McArdle and her husband from Keady, Co. Armagh, were both described as spirit merchants in a thirteen-roomed pub in Newry (only his occupation was returned in 1911). Patrick McShane and his wife from Sligo occupied eighteen rooms in Dee Street, Victoria ward, Belfast. His spirit business evidently failed to prosper, as he occupied only five rooms in Mountpottinger in 1911, having become a crane driver and spent time in Londonderry.

William Pope, aged 41, from Iowa, more grandly returned as a 'wine and spirit merchant', lived in a sixteen-roomed private house in Mountsion, Co. Kilkenny, attended by a governess and two servants. His cosmopolitan past was reflected in the birthplaces of his wife (Melbourne, Australia) and seven children (born in Waterford, Dublin, and Co. Dublin). Pope wittily declared his religious profession as

'Roman Catholic or Idolater according to H. M. Edward VII'. By 1911, he was living alone in a single room in his vast wine store (with ten windows) in Waterford. He had lost his sacred fire, declaring that he had 'no religion' and refusing further information when pressed by the enumerating constable. After her husband's death, the Presbyterian Canadian Mary Sands remained in her husband's seven-roomed farm-house in Glaskermore, Co. Down, now occupied as a 'publican and farmer'. Her only boarder was a female missionary from Fermanagh.

Many of these personal chronicles remind us of the vagaries of the drink trade, notorious for its pitfalls and the uncertainty of retaining customers in an overcrowded sector. The same insecurity applied to those involved in the performing arts. By contrast, the clerks, officials, and professionals who formed the majority of American service providers could look forward to fairly secure careers, often with protection of tenure and pensions. In this respect they resembled the annuitants and ladies and gentlemen of 'private means' who, along with the 'performers', provide material for the following chapter. One important attribute present in all groups was genuine cosmopolitanism, often stretching well beyond the boundaries of North America and the place of residence in Ireland. Through specifying the nativity of parents, spouses, children, relatives, and visitors, I have shown how common it was for members of the American elite to have personal connections with several Irish counties, as well as with Britain and the empire. An American accent was often inflected by myriad cultural echoes, greatly complicating our perception of what it meant to be an 'American' in Ireland. And, by extension, what it meant to be 'Irish'.

5   America on Show: Special Cases

I   Independent Means

Two loosely defined groups of elite Americans, 'independents' and 'performers', stand out from those previously surveyed because of their idiosyncrasies and, in many cases, their public profile. Independents such as annuitants, persons of 'private means', those reliant on interest or dividends, landed proprietors, and self-designated ladies or gentlemen numbered 74 in 1901 and 49 in 1911. The sector's collective profile was predictably extreme, with the highest female component in both years, extremely high median age, a large component with co-resident Americans, and a very small Catholic component.[1]

Though fuzzy and subjective, this sector captures an important element of the social elite virtually invisible in the published occupational returns: those without gainful occupation, yet not without wealth and social status. In many cases, those named in census returns may be identified in published genealogies and reference works relating to the aristocracy and 'gentry', enabling us to compare self-descriptions with recognised indicators of wealth and social status. Because the occupation of wives was seldom stated, most American heiresses who married into the Irish gentry have probably escaped identification in my search for women of independent means. Even so, the category gives some sense of the extent to which Americans penetrated Ireland's most exalted social circles.

Three Canadians (all Episcopalians) are known from the census of 1901 to have married into the Irish aristocracy.[2] Helena, Duchess of Manchester, presided over the sixty rooms and forty windows of Tanderagee Castle, Co. Armagh.[3] The household included the duke (a 24-year-old Irish-speaking Londoner), her father (an American railway director), and two other American visitors.[4] Below stairs there was an Irish housemaid, a French cook, and eight servants from England. The 9th Duke of Manchester was an egregious example of the profligate aristocrat vainly trying to save his heavily encumbered estates by marrying well-endowed North Americans. His marriage to the daughter of a major shareholder in Standard Oil in November 1900 coincided with prolonged bankruptcy proceedings and legal actions from creditors, and an action for breach of promise. At one court hearing, it was stated that 'the duke had recently married and gone to America. In consequence of the illness of his wife it was said that the duke was unable at present to return to this country.'[5] Such embarrassments in no way diminished the duke's reputation in his own circle, and before departing for America he accompanied the lord lieutenant and other notables to Rossmore, Co. Monaghan, for some 'excellent shooting', after which the party moved on to Tanderagee Castle and elsewhere in pursuit of yet more birds.[6] The gay young blade withered into a notorious *roué*, leading to an uncontested divorce in 1931 'on the ground of his adultery at the Felix Hotel, Jermyn-street' (Helena now resided in Paris on the Quai d'Orsay). Less than a fortnight later, the duke married Miss Kathleen Dawes in Greenwich, Connecticut, his new life again being disturbed by court actions from creditors.[7] The pinnacle of his service to the public as a Liberal peer was appointment as Captain of the Yeomen of the Guard (1905–7).

Victoria Alexandrine, Lady Plunket, a Canadian-born 'peeress', shared twenty-six rooms and twenty windows at Old Connaught House near Bray, with the baron (a Dubliner) and their five children born in Dublin and England.[8] All four servants were English. Victoria's father was an illustrious former governor-general of Canada, the Marquis of Dufferin and Ava, owner of a large estate at Clandeboye in Co. Down.[9] By 1911, their seven children included a New Zealander, a product of Plunket's tenure as governor of New Zealand (1904–10). Another product was the Plunket Society, founded in 1907 to advance maternal and child welfare under the directorship of Sir Frederic Truby King. The swollen servant body at Old Connaught House had been thoroughly democratised by 1911, with five Irish Catholics, three Irish Episcopalians, two from England, and an Australian nurse. Plunket also donated the Plunket cricket shield, and was elected grand master of New Zealand's Freemasons (Irish jurisdiction). Plunket, the Irish-born son of an evangelical archbishop and an inveterate doer of good works, was the antithesis of the Duke of Manchester as a specimen of the aristocracy.[10]

A few months after her marriage in 1900, Mabel, Viscountess Avonmore, was staying in Dungannon, Co. Tyrone, with her mother and sister (also born in Canada), father, and French daughter. Her father (George Evans) was a 'gentleman' of 'private income' living in ten rooms in William Street; he had once served as aide-de-camp to one of the Marquis of Dufferin's predecessors as governor-general of Canada. The Evans family connection with Canada persisted after his death, as the eldest son remained in Toronto as a barrister.[11] Mabel's absent husband, Algernon William Yelverton (the 6th viscount), had seats at Belle Isle, Roscrea, Co. Tipperary and Hazle Rock, Westport, Co. Mayo. Shortly after his marriage, he was commissioned as a captain in the Royal Garrison Artillery (Dublin district). The title became extinct upon his death in 1910.[12]

In 1911, Beatrice Lichtenstein Macnaghten was a 'lady' guest of Richard Arthur Grove Annesley, 'gentleman farmer', of Annesgrove, Castletownroche, Co. Cork, a house with twenty-five rooms and fifteen windows.[13] In contrast to so many big houses, the majority of the servants at Annesgrove were Catholic and all were Irish. Beatrice's father had been chief justice of the Canadian Supreme Court, and her middle name (omitted from *Burke's Peerage*) suggests additional sources of wealth. Though returned as an unrelated 'visitor', her husband (Francis Alexander, aged 48 and 20 years older than Beatrice) was in fact a first cousin of Grove Annesley's wife. The latter was a daughter of the 2nd Baronet Macnaghten of Dundarave, Co. Antrim, while Beatrice's husband unpredictably became the 8th baronet after the death of two nephews at the Somme in 1916.[14] The household in 1911 included two other 'lady' visitors, one of whom (a relative from Co. Cork) was only 11 years old. The other was Mabel Louis Findlay, a 26-year-old Episcopalian American, who was visiting with her husband, an English 'gentleman'.

Though not used in census returns, the term 'landed gentry' cannot be avoided in my attempt to identify the 'independents', because it generated vital contemporary documentation. This subjective category, representing only a small fraction of landowning families, was effectively defined by inclusion in various editions of *Burke's Landed Gentry*. The last Irish edition appeared in 1958, long after almost all of the listed families had lost their estates, yet many of these resurfaced in *Burke's Irish Family Records* in 1976.[15] The self-styled 'gentry' overlapped heavily with the 'county families' catalogued in other manuals.[16] The same was true of those families whose 'stake in the country' was traditionally recognised by commission as a justice of the peace (unpaid magistrate), appointment to the inner circle as a deputy lieutenant, or selection for the grand juries that dominated local government until 1898. Once again, the cachet (or obloquy) associated with official appointments under the *ancien régime* long outlasted the abolition of grand juries, the appointment of thousands of Catholics of humble origins as magistrates, the diminished importance of those magistrates in the court system, and the confinement of deputy lieutenants to ceremonial functions.

The 'landed gentry' had at least two representatives in 1901, both Episcopalian Canadians. Mervyn Montgomery Archdall had 'settled in

America', where his livelihood was derived from 'ranch (stock)'. His Canadian birth was perhaps attributable to his father's peripatetic military career. He and his Swedish wife were staying with a maiden aunt, Richmal Magnall Archdall of Drumcullion, Co. Fermanagh, whose income was derived from investments.[17] John Thomas Rashleigh Lucas was a 'landed proprietor' living in the nine-roomed Manor House near Dunmanway, Co. Cork.[18] This he shared in 1901 with his newly wed Indian-born wife and two Catholic servants. By 1911, when his wife's Indian-born sister was also present, he modestly returned himself as a 'retired farmer'. Lucas, a magistrate educated at St Columba's College in Dublin, had married Grace Ellen Donovan, daughter of a Corkonian officer in the Bengal civil service whose pedigree intersected with that of 'the O'Donovan', head of an ancient Irish clan revived to the satisfaction of the Ulster King-at-Arms and *Burke's* in the nineteenth century.[19]

At this point, let me look more closely at the meaning of terms such as 'landowner' and 'landed proprietor' (the pejorative term 'landlord' was seldom used). Until the 'revolution' in the law of land tenure initiated by Gladstone in 1870, there was a generally recognised if blurred distinction between 'landholders' (occupiers), usually farmers (those who actually worked properties and were responsible for paying local rates), and 'landowners' (usually the 'immediate lessors' who were entitled to rental or leasehold payments from landholders). When the only comprehensive inventory of Irish 'landowners' was drawn up in 1876 (dubbed 'the Modern Domesday Book'), an attempt was made to exclude 'middlemen' by restricting landowners to those holding land in 'fee simple', or on long or perpetually renewable leases. These computations embraced not only tenanted lands but tracts farmed directly by the landowner, often including extensive demesnes, woods, gardens, and pasturage.[20]

The distinction between landholders and landowners became obsolete with the implementation of 'land purchase', whereby owners were induced to sell part or all of their estates to state agencies, which in turn made most tenements over to the sitting tenants in 'fee simple', subject to long-term mortgage repayments ('annuities'). As a result, former 'landowners' who retained only their country seats and demesnes became farmer-occupiers, while their former tenants (farmer-occupiers) became landowners.[21] This role-reversal had staggering social effects, but did not eliminate the cachet attached to the old nomenclature. Though incomplete (about one-third of property qualified for purchase remained unsold when the Union was effectively dissolved in 1922), the dissolution of landed estates was mainly achieved under acts assented in 1903 and 1909. As a result, the objective meaning of all terms relating to land ownership changed fundamentally between the censuses of

1901 and 1911. One might therefore expect a multiplication of 'land-owners' and beneficiaries of 'landed property' unconnected with the former gentry. The fact that this did *not* occur confirms the lingering power of long-prevailing social and class distinctions, even after their material and legal foundations have been shattered.

Two other factors had long since eroded the conventional equation between 'landowners' and 'gentry'. Thousands of Irish proprietors were insolvent by the 1840s, especially through loss of rental income during the Great Famine, and this had led to the creation of courts charged with auctioning 'encumbered estates'. Though many buyers were kinsmen of expropriated landlords, others were 'parvenus' or 'speculators' who found it difficult to gain acceptance as 'gentry'. The second factor, less widely discussed, was a long-term consequence of massive emigration, which gradually attenuated the value placed on land occupation by those staying at home. As it became more difficult to find successors within families for incumbent occupiers, farms were amalgamated or assigned to unrelated occupiers. Though this process was delayed in remote and poor regions such as Connaught, even there it was apparent by 1900 that long-established succession practices were faltering. This opened up attractive opportunities for Americans and Canadians with some liquid-ity not merely to acquire 'the home place' or 'family farm', but to invest in larger Irish properties. As shown in Chapter 9, gaining control of property in rural Ireland was a central preoccupation for naturalised emigrants from Leitrim who applied for passports between 1914 and 1925. To what extent does my census study suggest that those born in North America, especially children of emigrants, chose to invest their wealth in Irish land?

Two 'gentlemen' in 1911 were prosperous Americans without Irish-born relatives in the household, occupying Irish 'big houses' with their American families. Paul D. Mills, an Episcopalian, shared a twenty-four-roomed house with ten windows in Killeen Glebe, Co. Meath, with his American-born wife and children. The house belonged to the Earl of Fingall of Killeen Castle, and appears to have been rented out in 1901.[22] Arthur V. Willcox, an 81-year-old who refused information on his reli-gion, lived in a house with twenty-five rooms and thirteen windows in Ballinafadd, Co. Galway. Willcox and his wife and children were all irregularly returned not as American-born but as 'American citizens'. The fact that his wife Marion and the children were Catholics suggests Irish origins, and she may have acquired her American citizenship through naturalisation or marriage. The Willcox family also had strong English connections: the only house visitor was an English magistrate and estate manager, and six of the seven servants were English.[23]

Lisnabrucka House was a fishing lodge ('a fine example of Edwardian architecture') built in 1910 for Willcox, reportedly a Philadelphia banker.[24] It is possible, but not certain, that Mills and Willcox had been lured from America by the prospect of acquiring an Irish mansion at a bargain price. Willcox may have used Lisnabrucka only as an occasional retreat, and Mills may have been one of a sequence of short-term tenants of Killeen Glebe house.

Several Americans with landed interests did not belong to lines whose membership of the 'gentry' was affirmed by *Burke's*, but three owned estates that can be traced in other sources. A widowed 'landowner' and American Catholic, Mary Devereux, resided in 1901 in a fourteen-roomed house in George's Street, Wexford. She was evidently the widow of John T. Devereux of the same street, who owned almost 400 acres in the county and town in 1876.[25] William L. Scanlan, a 33-year-old unmarried Episcopalian, was a 'landowner' sharing fourteen rooms at Ballyknockane, Ballingarry, Co. Limerick with his aunt from Kerry, American niece, and two servants. In 1876, this was the seat of Michael Scanlan, owner of over 1,000 acres in the county.[26] George Ramsay, a 78-year-old Presbyterian, described himself as a 'landowner' in 1911, but magistrate and farmer in 1901. Ramsay shared ten rooms in Claggan, Co. Londonderry, with his wife and two unmarried children in their fifties, all born in Canada. His small estate in 1876 comprised just under 400 acres of poor land.[27]

Otherwise, I have yet to firmly link North American beneficiaries of landed property to particular estates. An Episcopalian Canadian, Julia Cunning, a widowed 'landed proprietor' with a daughter born in Aldershot, had a seventeen-roomed house in Ballymachugh, Co. Cavan. Sisters Letitia and Joanna Lane, Episcopalian Americans dependent on 'landed property', lived in the twelve-roomed house of a widowed sister in Bray, Co. Wicklow. She and their widowed mother were born in India. Another set of siblings, unmarried Episcopalian Canadians in their thirties and forties, lived with their widowed mother in six rooms at Courtmacsherry, Co. Cork. Like their mother, Henrietta Alice, Ida Wigmore, and Nicholas Alfred Howell were all occupied in 'land, house property'. None of these reappeared in the census of 1911. Two 'land-owners' were first returned in that year. Mary Kennedy, a 45-year-old widowed Catholic American, lived with her two Galwegian children in a six-roomed house near Tuam. The only landowner of that surname in Tuam in 1876 was Patrick Kennedy, whose property occupied less than 60 acres (suggesting a snug farm rather than a landed estate).[28]

Most terms and euphemisms chosen by those I have called 'independ-ents' are redolent of social aspiration as much as social status (after all, even 'landowner' had no single or fixed meaning). Some, however, were neutral (private or independent means, shares, annuities, interest on money, and income from dividends, land, house, rents, or property). In one case in 1911, the source of such income was specifically American. Louisa Egan, a 70-year-old unmarried Catholic living in twelve rooms in Orwell Road, Rathgar, gave her profession as 'real estate USA, independent'. She applied the same description to her American niece, also unmarried at 37 (in pre-modern straight talk, she was a spinster living with her maiden aunt).

Subjective descriptions such as gentleman, 'gentleman farmer', gentle-woman, lady, and 'private lady' laid claims to gentility that are often impossible to verify, except by applying the crude (and cruel) test of house size. Ella J. Whiteside was a 26-year-old Episcopalian married to a 47-year-old English banker working in Omagh. Widowed by 1911 and no longer described as a 'lady', she was living in eleven rooms with two aunts in Cookstown. In 1911, Sophia Elizabeth Fayle, an American Methodist widow living with two servants in five rooms in Clonmel, Co. Tipperary, described herself as a 'lady living on annuity'. Likewise, Hannah Owen, an Episcopalian Canadian, aged 63, who had never married and lived alone in six rooms near Kinsale, Co. Cork, described herself as a 'lady, living from dividends'. The family return for 1901 listed her father as a retired quartermaster in the Artillery Militia. None of these ladies have been traced as landowners or gentry. A counter-example was Alicia F. Maunsell, an Episcopalian Canadian 'lady' with children born in Meath, Tipperary, and Co. Dublin, who was living in seventeen rooms within Kildare barracks. Despite this martial address, she was a 'clergy widow' who had married a younger son of Richard Maunsell of Oakley Park, Celbridge. The rector's elder brothers both acquired large properties in Limerick, but the Kildare estate amounted to only 700 acres.[29] Alicia's peripatetic Scottish father was in Jamaica at the time of her marriage, having formerly lived in Orkney and England.[30]

The majority of purported 'ladies' were visitors or boarders so returned by their indulgent hosts, such as (in 1901) Geneva Barclay, Episcopalian wife of an English boot merchant boarding in Glasnevin; Jane Berry, a Catholic 'private lady' visiting Rathgar Road, Rathmines; Maggie Bucknor, a young unmarried Catholic visiting relatives with a fourteen-roomed house in Bandon, Co. Cork; Rosanna Johnson, a Catholic Canadian staying with her step-brother, a farmer, in Dun-shaughlin, Co. Meath; Lydia Jane Martin, an Episcopalian Canadian boarding in Ballinasloe, Co. Galway; and Theresa O'Cahill, an Irish-speaking Catholic visiting a four-roomed house in Tralee. Ellen Roddy, a

Catholic American 'lady' married to a 'gentleman' from Donegal, was staying at the Central Hotel in Banbridge, Co. Down.

In 1911, Mary Early Davison (an Episcopalian American 'lady') was staying with Sir Richard John Musgrave, Bt, at Tourin, Co. Waterford, in a house with twenty-three rooms and sixteen windows. Musgrave's wife was a Canadian, his two daughters were English, and a variety of English accents would have been audible below stairs and in the guest rooms. Apart from Sir Richard, the Irish minority on census night comprised four of the ten servants (including the butler), and three of the seven visitors (including a 'gentleman' and 'lady' from Co. Cork).[31] Mary Davison's host was a great-grandson of the 1st baronet, execrated by nationalists for his partisan but stunningly circumstantial histories of the rebellion of 1798, still invaluable as a repository of contemporary testimony collected, analysed, and published by Musgrave during and immediately after the event.[32] Mary Davison's fellow visitors included a major-general and a captain in the Rifle Brigade. Yet only a decade earlier, aged 13, she had been working as a domestic servant in Co. Londonderry.

Two pairs of Episcopalian American sisters in 1901 were coyly identified as 'gentlewomen'. Anna and Jane Eliza Jackson and a servant shared ten rooms in Bray. They were probably related to two minor landowners named Jackson, with urban estates in Co. Wicklow and addresses in Bray in 1876.[33] Nancy and Caroline Irwin, along with another 'gentlewoman, no trade' born in India, lived in an eight-roomed house in Garville Avenue, Rathmines. Only Nancy remained in 1911, subsisting in the same suburb on an 'investment annuity'. Another Episcopalian gentlewoman, Almeda J. Lloyd, lived with her children born in Sligo, Louth, and Dublin in a ten-roomed house in Clontarf; and Stella Smith, an unmarried Presbyterian, was returned as a visiting gentlewoman in Rugby Road, Belfast. Apart from the Jackson sisters, these gentlewomen have eluded further documentation.[34]

The term 'gentleman' is notoriously ambiguous, being variously understood to signify one entitled to bear arms, a person of wealth or consequence, or simply 'one of nature's gentlemen' as betokened by integrity or good manners. Terms such as 'gentleman famer' implied not unusual wealth, but a claim to social esteem not normally conferred on even the wealthiest common-or-garden farmer. 'True' gentlemen, however, were inclined to abhor the description as an affectation, unlike 'lady'.

An extreme personification of the 'little gentleman' immortalised by Hilaire Belloc was 6-year-old Hugo Graham de Burgh of the 'Irish Church', a native of America (an origin not stated in *Irish Family Records*). He lived in 1901 with his widowed English mother, younger

Welsh siblings, and widowed aunt from Kildare (all gentlemen or gentle-women) in a fifteen-roomed house with seven windows at Ballynapierce near Enniscorthy, Co. Wexford. Even Hugo's Episcopalian governess from Co. Down was a gentlewoman. Apart from a French cook, the other three servants were Catholics from three Irish counties. Hugo was to become a much decorated hero of both world wars, who escaped from a prisoner-of-war camp and received the French Order of Liberation. His father, recently killed in the South African War at Jammersburg Drift in the Orange River Colony, had married Mabel Patty Beaumont from St Albans in 1893, and Hugo was born in America just a year later. Mabel's excessive use of genteel phraseology suggests a desire to live up to the cachet of the de Burghs, once headed by the 9th Earl of Clanrick-arde (celebrated in nationalist history for leading his regiment in support of James II at the battle of Aughrim in 1689).[35]

George R. Bissell, a Congregationalist 'gentleman', was staying in Dromore, Co. Down, with a Unitarian linen manufacturer and his American wife. John Regan, a Catholic boarder in Cork city, was returned as a 'gentleman no occupation'. In 1911, when living with relatives headed by an Irish-speaking pig buyer, he was identified as a rent agent. The Episcopalian Harry Hawe, an unmarried boarder in Glasnevin in both years, was returned as a 'gentleman' in 1901 but a 'victular' (victualler or publican) in 1911. William Reid, a Catholic 'gentleman' from Brooklyn, lived in six rooms in Dolphin's Barn with his wife from Wicklow and Dubliner children. His occupation in 1911 was police pensioner.

The American 'gentleman farmer' was well represented in 1911. Walter Keely Grehan, a Catholic American with a Galwegian wife, lived in a thirteen-roomed house with three servants in Lisbride, Roscommon. Henry Lloyd Meadows, a 33-year-old Episcopalian from Toronto, lived alone in a nine-roomed house with seven windows near Killinick, Co. Wexford. In 1901, his father Joseph (a retired civil engineer from Wexford living in a much larger house nearby) had returned him simply as a farmer. Joseph Meadows of Cahereen owned about 400 acres in the county in 1876.[36]

The most intriguing example of this sub-species is Robert Marshall, a 21-year-old American Catholic newly wed to a girl named Binty from King's County, who returned himself and his younger brother (also American) as gentlemen farmers. This case presents formidable chal-lenges. Their house in Mountshannon, Co. Limerick, had no less than 110 rooms with a retinue of nine servants (horse-trainer, jockey, two grooms, kitchen and parlour maids, housekeeper, and cook). The forty-three out-offices included twelve stables, two coach houses, three harness rooms, and (a category not allowed for on the printed form) a kennel. What is the explanation for the precocious Robert's occupation of one of Ireland's great houses? The insolvent Mountshannon estate of over 10,000 acres, formerly the seat of John FitzGibbon, 1st Earl of Clare, had been put up for auction in 1890. Three years later it was bought by Thomas Nevins, a contractor and quarry-owner of Irish birth who had made his fortune in the United States. After his death from a riding accident, it remained with his widow Esther until 1907. It was subsequently acquired and divided by the Irish Land Commission before being torched by the IRA in 1920. It was during this period of flux that Marshall had somehow secured occupancy of Mountshannon House.[37]

In 1901, the Marshall brothers had been 'scholars' (schoolboys) living with 20-year-old Henry Vincent Jackson, who brazenly described himself as a 'Land Lord'. Jackson's house in Inane outside Roscrea, Co. Tipperary, had only sixty-five rooms but forty-six out-offices. Young Jackson's father was presumably the Henry Vincent Jackson returned in 1876 as the owner of almost 3,000 acres in King's County and Tipperary, though his address was politely mis-transcribed as 'Junne' rather than the correct but risible 'Inane'.[38] Robert Marshall and his three siblings were puzzlingly returned as Jackson's children, despite the fact that Robert was only 9 years younger than Jackson and had a different surname. They were evidently his wife's children by a previous marriage, though Mary Celia Jackson (another American) was allegedly just 25 in 1901 (her true age was 32).[39] All four Marshalls and the Jackson's elder boy were American-born, the only native son of Roscrea being 6 months old. The American presence was ubiquitous at Inane: the wife of Nicholas Doyle, a visiting Catholic 'Land Lord' from Wexford, was also American.

The other 'visitors' present in 1901 were Thomas and Esther Nevins, Thomas also being returned as a Catholic 'land lord' aged 51 from Kildare. The fact that the future and current owners of Mountshannon coincided in Inane suggests that some personal connection enabled Robert Marshall to acquire the estate after Esther Nevins's departure. The connection is confirmed by the certificate of Robert's marriage to Marie Binty Caroline Stoney in June 1910, at Castleconnell Catholic church. His full name was Robert Nevins Marshall, son of Robert Marshall, a medical doctor, his bride being the daughter of a surgeon-general in the army.[40] On this basis, I inferred that Robert Marshall had inherited the property from Esther Nevins because of kinship ties. I am relieved to report that an exhaustive family tree confirms this. A daughter of Thomas A. Nevins married Robert J. Marshall in Philadelphia in 1889, subsequently marrying William Henry Vincent Jackson in Orange,

New Jersey, in about 1898. Robert Marshall was therefore a grandson of Thomas Nevins of Mountshannon; Jackson and Robert the younger were indeed half-brothers. Robert Marshall returned to America and died at the age of 41 in Bryn Mawr, Montgomery, Pennsylvania; Henry Vincent Jackson died in Tipperary in 1913.[41]

II   Performers

Artists and performers of North American birth were, in many cases, agents of Americanisation, exhibiting American cultures and values, and diffusing facts and fantasies about American life. I have therefore looked closely at this diverse and intriguing sector, occasionally contextualising the census returns from other sources. The artistic elite numbered 45 in 1901 and 51 in 1911, incorporating writers and journalists, graphic artists and photographers, actors, and musicians. The sector was notable only for the extremely low proportion matched with the other census.

Writers

Adela Elizabeth Orpen from Virginia was returned as a 'farmer and author' in 1901 and 'writer of novels' in 1911. Described as 'Protestant' in 1901 but 'agnostic' by 1911, she was married to the Dublin-born, Irish-speaking medieval historian Goddard Henry Orpen, initially a 'theist' who likewise became 'agnostic'. Doubtless infected by the growing scepticism of her husband and children, Adela's religious views had been transformed since 1893, when the Religious Tract Society published *The Chronicles of the Sid; or, the Life and Travels of Adelia Gates*. Goddard described himself as a 'retired barrister, farmer' in 1901, and as a 'barrister (not now in practice), writer of history, J.P., B.A. Dublin' in 1911. The Orpens lived with their two London-born children and three servants at Monksgrange, a house with thirteen windows and about twenty rooms in Killann, Co. Wexford. Adela had inherited the house and estate in 1899 from her father, Edward Moore Richards, 19 years after her marriage to Goddard Orpen.[42] Her mother, Sarah Elizabeth Tisdale, was from Virginia. Her varied output up to 1900 included *Stories about Famous Precious Stones*, *Perfection City*, *Corrageen in '98: A Story of the Irish Rebellion*, and *The Joy Hawkers: A Story of Free Soil and Ruffian Days*. At least four of her works appeared in American editions. *The Downfall of Grabbum: An Ulster Fable* by 'An Ulster Clergyman', which features 'Uncle Sam' as a stereotypical character, has been dubiously attributed to Adela Orpen.[43]

Two 'authoresses' who emerged in 1911 have defied my attempts to trace their writings. Ellen Jane Clarke, a 30-year-old Canadian Wesleyan Methodist, was living with her uncle, an insurance manager occupying a mansion with fourteen rooms and eighteen windows in Malone Park, Belfast. Her aunt and brother (a clerk) were also natives of Canada. Annie Evans, a 45-year-old Episcopalian, was the daughter of a magistrate, farmer, and land valuer living in similar opulence (with sixteen rooms and fifteen windows) in Skahanagh, Co. Cork. Her widowed father was from Limerick and her mother from Cork.[44] Was she the 'Miss Annie Evans' who performed in Strindberg's *The Spook Sonata* for the Dublin Drama League in 1925, along with celebrated Abbey actors such as Shelah Richards, Gabriel J. Fallon, Arthur Shields, and F. J. McCormick?[45]

Journalism was represented in 1901 by Effie Evans, an Episcopalian guest of the Duke of Manchester in Tanderagee, Co. Armagh; Patrick Begadon, a Catholic junior reporter living in Athlone with his mother from Queen's County; and Henry Beatty Vint, an Episcopalian reporter living with his uncle, an English-born 'newspaper proprietor' listed as a stationer in Lurgan. Begadon went on to marry a Westmeath woman and by 1911 was living in Portarlington, Queen's County. The Episcopalian Charles W. Frith, a 35-year-old widower without occupation, was living with his widowed Corkonian mother in 1901. By 1911, he was a journalist, sharing eight rooms in Eccles Street North with his three Dublin children and an unmarried Canadian sister.[46] Two journalists present only in 1911 were Catholic Americans: Edward T. Moran, who lived alone in Bruff, Co. Limerick; and Patrick J. O'Connell, a reporter boarding in Tralee.

Artists

Four North American graphic artists were living with parents in 1901. Julianne Finn, a local shopkeeper's daughter, was an Irish-speaking Catholic art-class teacher in Kinsale, Co. Cork. She remained at home in 1911, described more impressively as a technical instructress in lace, drawing, and design. William Gibson Corr, a Methodist artist's apprentice born in New York, was the son of a Belfast general merchant from Tyrone whose wife was from New Jersey. By 1911, the 'lithographer' had moved with his family to a larger nearby house in Cyprus Gardens, his father now trading as a paint merchant. John Andrew Fee, an Episcopalian sculptor, came from a family of stone-cutters near Corboy, Co. Longford. He too remained at home in 1911, now described as a stonemason.

Charlotte E. Irvine, a Canadian Presbyterian practising as a 'litho' artist, was the daughter of a Tyrone draper and his wife (a grocer), living in Disraeli Street in the Shankill. William Joseph Reynolds, an Irish-speaking Catholic American living with Meath cousins in Charleville Avenue, Dublin, followed the same avocation. Two Catholic artists, Frank Riley and Thomas J. Ritchie (a portrait artist), were boarding in Belfast. John Riley, an Episcopalian photographer, was living in Fermoy, Co. Cork, with his English wife, an 'artist retoucher', and their children born in Mayo and Listowel, Co. Kerry. The artists' catalogue for 1901 is completed by Harold and Hessie Anderson, both portrait artists (though Hessie's occupational entry was erased) who professed an 'independent Christian religion' and lived with their two American-born sons in Gresham Street, Belfast.

Newcomers in 1911 included Allen Coon, an agnostic 'photographer and theatrical showman' married to a Belfast woman and living in Londonderry; Harvey Clay Everts, a Catholic 'artist enlarging photographs etc.' from Michigan, lodging in Ballymahon, Co. Longford; Nicholas Faithfull, an Episcopalian 'photographic artist' living with a wife from Wicklow in Castlereagh, Co. Roscommon; Francis O'Connor, a Catholic photographer lodging at a temperance hotel in Kilkenny; and 'W. R.', a widowed Catholic artist incarcerated in the North Dublin workhouse, following amputation of both legs in 1905. Mary Moran, a 22-year-old Catholic photographer's assistant, lived in Dorset Street Lower, Dublin with her three American sisters (a dressmaker and two milliners) and widowed mother from Roscommon (the family had also been returned in 1901). William Morris, a Methodist photographer, lived in Grosvenor Road, Belfast, with his parents from Cavan, two sisters and a pawnbroker brother from America, and other siblings born in Cavan and Belfast. His father was a plumber.

These cameos show that many American-born 'artists' and photographers (overlapping categories) were the children of Irish tradesmen and shopkeepers rather than emerging from the educated elite. They were probably in many cases artisans rather than creative artists, admittedly a blurred distinction. The finer side of art may have provided a living for Jane Elizabeth Flynn, an Episcopalian Canadian lodging in Bray, Co. Wicklow. She was returned as a 'buyer of art', her Canadian sister as a buyer of millinery. And the conservation of works of art was possibly in the remit of Samuel A. Stewart, a 75-year-old Methodist 'curator' at the Belfast Museum in College Square North, where he shared two rooms with a widowed American sister.[47]

Actors

Bertha Leslie, a 36-year-old Catholic actress married to an Episcopalian English artist, lived in three rooms in northside Dublin, along with her American son (a printer) from a previous marriage. Alix Lukas, a 'dramatic actor', was Ireland's only non-missionary, American-born Mormon. Several were clearly on the move, perhaps touring with a theatre company. Lilian Nash and her English husband, Episcopalians in the 'theatrical' profession, were staying at the Central Hotel in Belfast's Royal Avenue. Jack Warren, a 30-year-old 'Protestant' in the 'stage profession', was boarding in Fermoy, Co. Cork, in the company of three barmaids, one of whom presided as head of household. In 1911, Jack (now John Warren of the Church of Ireland) was boarding at a public house in Midleton, Co. Cork, his fellow boarders being three other actors from England and Co. Down. Joseph George Woodword, a Canadian Baptist, was boarding with his English wife (also of the 'theatrical profession') in a shop in Great Brunswick Street near Trinity College. He topped the Easter bill at the Empire Palace Theatre, which announced 'Startling Engagement of Prof. Woodword's SEA LIONS AND SEALS, From London Hippodrome. An Astonishing Attraction.' His performing mammals were backed up by the Chicago Ladies' Quartette.[48]

Performers not present in 1901 included two 'theatrical' Catholic Americans visiting Belfast: 37-year-old Charles J. Carter, staying with his American wife at the Avenue Hotel in Royal Avenue; and Anna Lehmann, aged 24, visiting a house in Brunswick Street. Two 'comedy artists' were boarding together in Dublin's Great Brunswick Street: Francis F. Morton, a 40-year-old Catholic from Canada; and Edward P. Whaley, a 30-year-old Methodist travelling without his wife. Whaley spoke French and German, and a German music hall artist was among his fellow boarders. Eugene Swords, a New York Catholic, aged 20 in 1911, was proudly returned as a 'theatrical agent' by his father, a house painter from Monaghan who occupied three rooms in Liffey Street Upper.

Others enumerated in 1901 worked on the theatrical fringe. Like her Episcopalian husband from Dublin, Esther Farrell (a 30-year-old Catholic) belonged to a 'travelling circus'. Their five children were divided on religious lines, Catholic girls versus Episcopalian boys. Along with their five children from five different Irish birthplaces, their dwelling in Clogheen, Co. Tipperary, was a 'waggon' (a term never before encountered in an Irish 'house and building' return). Frederick Tinare of the 'Irish Church' was a 65-year-old widowed circus labourer boarding in Trillick, Co. Tyrone. If liberally defined, the performing arts also embraced 'M. A. L.', a 35-year-old Catholic 'prostitute' in Mount-joy Female Prison, serving a 10-month sentence for drunk and violent conduct (her customary residence was Tyrone Street, North Dock ward).

Musicians

Among the most interesting American performers were musicians, some of whom (as music hall artists) were also actors; others were teachers as well as practitioners. In 1901, no less than three North Americans in Ireland were organists, reflecting the heavy demand for church musicians of all persuasions. Annie Campion, a 22-year-old Catholic Canadian, was an organist and music teacher living in her widowed mother's delph shop in Waterford. John Delaney, a 49-year-old Catholic organist and 'professor of music' from Massachusetts, was a 'paying guest' boarding along with a priest in Palmerston Park, Rathmines. By 1911, still an unmarried boarder, he had moved to Sligo. Marion Arnold-Jackson, a 24-year-old Episcopalian organist, lived in her aunt's fifteen-roomed shop in Ahoghill, Co. Antrim. She subsequently married an Antrim mechanical engineer, but remained in Ahoghill following the same occupation. Several others worked as music teachers. The importance of military bands as popular entertainers was confirmed by the presence of various American-born performers: a trumpeter in the Royal Artillery, an army bandmaster, a drummer, and two army sergeants who were or had been musicians.

Travelling 'musicians' in 1901 (all American Catholics) included Maurice Brennan, an Irish-speaking 27-year-old boarding in Galway; Thomas Jaxon, a 20-year-old boarding in Cork; Charles Ryan, a 38-year-old 'itinerant musician' staying in Dungarvan, Co. Waterford; and two 'unemployed musicians', 25-year-old John Shalley and (in 1911) 27-year-old Albert Macardle, respectively, visitors in Tober-adosh, Co. Galway and Newtownhamilton, Co. Armagh. Arthur Herbert Fitzgerald-Thomas, a 28-year-old Episcopalian 'professional musician' married to a Dubliner, occupied a modest five-roomed house in Tavanagh Street, Belfast in 1911. Arthur Meredyth, a 31-year-old Episcopalian Canadian 'musician', shared just three rooms in Carlisle Road, Londonderry, with his Irish wife (an actress) and English daughters (all Catholics). Charles Fixott, a Catholic 'professional singer' boarding in 1901 with his English wife on St Stephen's Green, would doubtless have looked down on the touring entertainers who performed in public houses and halls throughout the provinces.

Music played a central part in missionary religion, appealing to a much wider audience than today by catering to popular tastes, in the hope of warbling the masses towards salvation. In 1911, a small family of enterprising gospellers was occupying three rooms in a house in Haddington Road, Dublin. Describing themselves as 'Protestant, undenominational', John James Sims and his family were Canadians. Sims was an 'evangelist', while his wife K. Alice and his son C. Whitfield Sims were both simply 'singers'. On Good Friday, eleven days after the census of 1911, Sims conducted the last of a series of 'picture services' in the Round Room of the Rotunda in Dublin, twice necessitating overflow lantern services. These multimedia extravaganzas presented 'beautiful scenes of nature and pictures from the Great Masters and the Royal Academy to illustrate the truths of Christianity', with separate lanterns displaying the words and the pictures. The *Irish Times* stated that Sims was 'well known both in America and in the British Isles', appealing 'to the intelligence rather than the emotions'. The services also featured 'the singing of Mrs. Sims and Mr. Whitfield Sims', and the pictorial presentation was impressively adapted to match pieces such as '"The Crucifixion Hymn" of the Jubilee Singers'.[49]

Meanwhile, a substantial party of American 'professional singers' were boarding together in Botanic Avenue, Belfast: Annie Brown Achlen, a Baptist; Samuel Collins, an Episcopalian from South America; and two Methodists, Ellenette Hamilton and Hattie Winrow. These were the American Jubilee Singers, touring with their manager, Daniel W. Brown. Apart from 25-year-old Collins, all were mature performers aged around 40. In November 1910, a large crowd in Dublin's Sackville Hall had been entertained by 'the American Jubilee Singers, a band of talented coloured vocalists who are carrying on the great work that their predecessors, the Fisk Company, set before them some thirty years ago, to provide funds for the University established at Nashville for the higher education of the freed slaves'. By 'singing the old negro melodies', the company had raised £20,000 for university funds. Among those present in Dublin was Daniel Brown, 'one of the tenors in the old company'. The programme included 'familiar songs' such as 'Steal Way', 'My Old Kentucky Home', 'Massa's in the Cold Ground', and 'The Old Folks at Home'.[50] The American Jubilee Singers moved on for the Christmas season to Belfast's Assembly Hall, where their songs were juxtaposed with 'cinematograph displays'.[51] The troupe was already famous when it visited Dublin in 1875, and made frequent tours thereafter to Irish cities and provincial towns as remote as Ballina, Co. Mayo.[52]

The American Jubilee Singers had not introduced this kind of spectacle to Ireland, with 'blackface minstrel shows' recorded in Dublin from

1836, annual visits from Christy's Minstrels between 1859 and 1868, and a performance in 1852 by the 'Southern Troupes of Sable Harmonists' (genuine Negroes rather than 'blackfaces').[53] The tone of these shows was increasingly secular, though the evangelical strand never lost its appeal. Reports in the Belfast press from the 1870s suggest that the blackface was an irresistible source of titillation for Ulster audiences, not only in music halls but in amateur entertainments. An 'amateur negro troupe' under various names performed regularly in Carrickfergus between 1879 and 1889.[54]

At the Maze races near Lisburn in July 1883, 'a military officer, the son of a clergyman residing in Belfast', put on a convincing impersonation of an Ethiopian 'negro minstrel' with cornet, being advised by 'unpatriotic boys' to 'wash his face'. It is noteworthy that Africa as well as America was often given as the origin of the impersonated 'negro minstrel'. At the Willowfield Star Flute Band's annual concert in 1885, a 'negro troupe' caused 'great merriment' and 'kept the audience in roars of laughter'. At the Rosemary Street Lecture Hall in 1891, the 'phonetic dancing class' put on 'a very laughable negro sketch' titled 'Tickle Me', featuring the eccentric Sam, 'a travelling negro minstrel'. Two years later, in Brough-shane, Co. Antrim, 'a very fine Christy Minstrel entertainment was given in full darky costume by a local negro troupe', in the presence of local notabilities and gentry. In the same year, 'Mr. Charles Harrington's negro troupe' appeared in *Uncle Tom's Cabin* in Belfast's Theatre Royal.[55] There was no end to the enjoyment that Irish audiences derived from seeing people of one race pretending to belong to another.

The most popular forum for light entertainment was neither the band-stand nor the gospel hall, but the music hall with its enticing 'variety' shows combining music, recitations, and dance. Two American hus-band-and-wife teams of youthful 'music hall artists' have been traced in the census. Anna and Robert Alden (who belonged to 'no church') occupied a hotel room on Eden Quay, Dublin, in 1911. Fanny and James Howard (both Catholics) were boarders in Gloucester Street, Belfast, in 1901. James may have been the 'Howard' who performed at Belfast's Empire Theatre of Varieties on the eve of the census, along with 'the famous Leggetts' and three acrobats on silver chains.[56]

The most celebrated American-born music hall artist in my catalogue was the Episcopalian William John Ashcroft. In 1901, he described himself as a 55-year-old 'stage professional' (like his English wife and her brother), occupying a six-roomed house in Lincoln Avenue, Clifton ward, Belfast. Ashcroft, born in Pawntucket, Rhode Island, to Belfast parents, had run away to join a band of minstrels that roamed across the Canadian provinces, moving on to several of the United States with another troupe. Having opened the Théâtre Comique in New York in 1870, he brought his troupe to London, achieving a 'huge success' in 1876 with his comic ballad, 'Muldoon the Solid Man'.[57] Along with seven other Ashcroft favourites, preceded by nine from Percy French, this featured in a collection of *Famous Irish Songs* advertised by Pigott & Co. in July 1901.[58] Himself known as 'the Solid Man' because of his 'frock-coat, mutton chops and tall hat', Ashcroft became increasingly unstable with several spells in asylums. Ashcroft had acquired the Belfast Alhambra for £2,000 from Dan Lowrey in 1879, but lost it when declared bankrupt in 1900. He performed regularly in Dublin at Lowrey's Star of Erin Music Hall (and its successor, the Empire Palace) from the 1880s up to Christmas 1908.[59]

A few weeks after his appearance in the 1901 census, Ashcroft displayed his dramatic flair in a Dublin police court:

Mr. W. J. Ashcroft, the well-known music hall artist, and who performed in the Empire Palace Theatre on the previous night, was charged with having thrown a water jug through the window of Moran's Hotel … Defendant was rather excited in manner, and sprang from the dock to the solicitors' table, and from that he rapidly moved to the desk of the Court Clerk, with the intention apparently of making towards the Bench.

Moran's solicitor observed 'that he was completely off his head', and 'that unfortunately, it was not the first time. In his day he was a great artist, and commanded a tremendous salary.' Ashcroft escaped punishment and was committed to a lunatic asylum.[60] He reappeared in 1911 as 'W. J. A.', a 65-year-old married Episcopalian inmate of the Purdysburn asylum in Ballydollagh, Co. Down. This 'music hall artist' had been committed from Belfast in summer 1909, suffering from 'mania acute'. Ashcroft died in Purdysburn in 1918. At his funeral in St George's, Belfast, the rector (Dr Hugh Davis Murphy) affirmed that he had been 'an upright and a thoroughly religious man'.[61]

III   Latter Day Saints

By way of a coda, an additional group of idiosyncratic and utterly unrepresentative Americans has been chosen for special scrutiny. Of particular interest to students of proselytism in Ireland is the inflated presence of the Church of Jesus Christ of the Latter Day Saints, otherwise simply Latter Day Saints or Mormons.[62] Five American Mormons were enumerated in 1901 and ten in 1911, remarkable for a country with only 58 resident Mormons of all appellations in 1901 and 97 in 1911 (including these American visitors).[63] As mentioned above, the only

American Mormon not identified as a missionary was Alix Lukas, the 23-year-old 'dramatic actor' enumerated in 1901 (along with two music hall artists) as a boarder in Cromac Street, Belfast. The four Mormon missionaries listed in that year were boarding together in My Lady's Road in Ormeau ward. Two were married men of 38 and 40, travelling without wives, and two were youths aged 21 and 24. The mission was more diffused in 1911, with ten men aged between 21 and 38 (including three unaccompanied husbands) staying in five separate locations. A delegation of three American Mormons, described as president and secretary of the 'conference' and a travelling elder (along with an English elder), occupied a house in Rugby Avenue, Cromac ward. The president of the Irish conference was 'Will' (William Wallace) Osborn from Salt Lake City, and the secretary was his younger brother Isaac Melvin Osborn. Pairs of missionaries were boarders in Baltic Avenue, Duncairn, Campsie Road, Omagh, and South Terrace, Cork, along with a lone Mormon in Railway Street, Armagh.

These clean-cut proselytes with their dark suits would have remained obscure but for the meticulously transparent record-keeping of the Latter Day Saints, whose missionary registers and other nominal documents are now digitally accessible. All but one of the fourteen American emissaries identified in the census have been matched with Mormon records, offering insight into their background, education, and church careers. Eight were natives of Utah, four of Idaho, and one of Arizona. Born between 1862 and 1890, most were baptised at the age of 8. All had been invited to join the British mission, which covered the United Kingdom and oversaw an 'Irish conference' with its own officers. Missionaries received some training in Utah, paid their own travel expenses, and had to demonstrate their fitness to the president of the church. After about 2 years' service, they returned to the United States.

In seven cases, letters have been preserved in which the future visitors to Ireland accepted the president's call to join the British mission, typically signing off as 'your brother in the Gospel'. Though some were educated men, including three products of Brigham Young University, others were conspicuously unlettered. The college men included William Clifton Davidson from Salt Lake City, who boasted of having been 'brought up in a family that have the right ideas of Our religion', including two brothers who had already returned from missions. He asked to be excused from missionary classes that clashed with his 'Vocal & Piano lessons', having already made a close study of 'the Book of Mormon and the other Books of the Church'. Thatcher T. Jones showed a touch of arrogance by using the letterhead of the university's weekly newspaper, *The White and Blue*, an impression confirmed by a laconic, rather moody photograph depicting the young Jones in a formal suit with embroidered white waistcoat and wing collar.[64]

Hermon Leroy Pierson was less polished: 'I am willing to respond to the call but if possible I would prefure to go to Europe.' The most ingenuous letter was from William Benjamin Baker, who was appointed president of the Irish conference in mid-1900. Baker admitted that he had felt inhibited in taking the call 'as i have not hade mutch schooling'. On the other hand, 'My circumstances are prety fair i feel that with the bessing of god my hevenly father that my family will not sufer i have a prety good farm and some few cattle.' His common touch might have struck chords in rural Ireland, if only deeply ingrained dread of proselytes had not thwarted Baker's determination 'to do the very best I can for the spread of truth in the nations of the earth and the building up of the kingdom of god at home'.[65]

Despite their endemic failure to embed Latter Day Saints in Ireland, the missionaries remained an object of fascination and fear for both Catholic and Protestant commentators.[66] In 1877, the *Irish Times* noted that 'a sharp and clever Yankee' elder had 'lamented that as yet no Mormon congregation had been established in Ireland, and that no sacred missionary had been able to obtain a footing in that country. We would not recommend Mr William Pasman to open "a temple" here.'[67] Both clergy and laity took a prurient interest in the practice of polygamy (officially condemned in the 1880s because of its illegality), while impressed by the martial efficiency of the church's government and its heroic missionary endeavours. Press reports from the late nineteenth century show that Mormons were regarded, like Red Indians, as American exotica, amusing and alarming in equal measure. A Presbyterian minister in Bangor raised funds for his church by lecturing on 'A Trip to Salt Lake City and the Mormons'. The chief engineer for the Belfast and Northern Counties Railway Company, at a social evening in the Permanent Way Carpenters' Shop, lamented that he had been unable to combine a visit to the World's Fair in Chicago with admission to the Mormon temple in Salt Lake City, 'which no Gentile is ever allowed to enter'. Addressing a similar topic in the YWCA hall, he recounted 'an express tour by rail' including a 'peep … at the Indian tribes and at the Mormons'. Patrons of Belfast's New Theatre Royal were urged to attend *The Danites*, which offered 'a graphic illustration of the life among the miners and the Mormons in the "glorious climate of California"'. A concert in the Church of Ireland schoolhouse in Finvoy, Co. Louth, juxtaposed a 'Lecture on the Mormons' with a performance of 'The Enchanted Wood'.[68]

Scare stories about Mormon proselytism were particularly common around 1911, when the tiny Mormon census population peaked at 97.

A few weeks after the census, the *Irish Times* cited the 'Mormon official returns of the British mission', which hyperbolically recorded 295 adherents including infants in Ireland, adding 'that during the year 12 persons left Ireland for Salt Lake City'. This revived the old belief that the missionaries' primary purpose was to entice Irish girls to cater for the needs of polygamous male Mormons in Utah. Missionary activity had recently been extended from Belfast to the Dublin district, where agents would 'get into conversation with servant girls', leave leaflets, and issue invitations to meetings. In Swords, Co. Dublin, 'the people of the place had indignantly disturbed their meetings, and the Protestant and Roman Catholic pastors co-operated in securing the withdrawal of the unacceptable propagandists'. Polygamy was far from extinct among rich Mormons requiring 'concubines' to expand their electoral influence.[69] Another report, published on the same day, quoted a Dominican priest confirming the secret Mormon practice of polygamy, and claiming that missionaries carried revolvers for self-defence because of popular outrage at their machinations.

Both Protestant and Catholic leaders believed that the campaign would win few adherents, at least in Dublin.[70] Yet, in May 1912, the *Irish Times* ridiculed suggestions that 'Mormonism in Ireland is dead', following interviews with seven of the twenty-six missionaries currently in Ireland ('mainly sons of Utah farmers'). The Dublin president had declared defensively that 'we do not pose as missionaries with University degrees', and claimed that the church was 'gaining in members, slowly … but surely'. Several elders noted that hostility was mainly exhibited by Protestants, who had on occasion 'attacked and chased' missionaries in 'the North of Ireland'.[71]

This digression confirms the gulf between expectation and achievement so characteristic of proselytism, and the unshakable optimism which drove so many Americans of many denominations to pursue salvation for stubborn Irish souls. Of all concerted attempts to export a version of American values to Ireland, the Mormon mission was perhaps the most spectacular in its failure as well as the least 'modern'.

The foregoing parade of the North American elite in pre-war Ireland has exhibited, if nothing else, its diversity. Using little more than census snapshots in most cases, we have surveyed a broad range of occupations, material and family circumstances, and personal connections with Ireland. Occupational categories that initially seem homogeneous, such as 'lady' or 'artist', turn out to conceal a cauldron of ambiguities, aspirations, and subjective judgements. In many cases, comparison of the returns for 1901 and 1911 has revealed sharp changes in circumstances or social status, as well as distinguishing between temporary visitors and longer-term settlers. This approach cannot, however, illuminate the 'returned Yank', a far more familiar type in literature and folklore than the American-born. An attempt is made below to identify and depict some of these reverse migrants, hitherto a shadowy presence in studies of the Irish diaspora. The focus is on Co. Leitrim, treated as an epitome (to the point of caricature) of rural Ireland. Chapter 6 examines both the American-born and their emigrant parents in Leitrim, where the great majority of American visitors and settlers lived in humble circumstances, far removed from the comfortable homes of the elite.

I   Sources

The idiosyncrasies of Ireland's American-born elite, though a fascinating facet of the American presence, probably differed little from those of American expatriates in Britain and elsewhere. What made Ireland unique as a site for American settlement was the far larger population of American-born children, sometimes accompanied by Irish-born parents, who found refuge in Irish cottages or farmhouses throughout the poor and backward regions that had nurtured the post-Famine 'diaspora'. As shown in Chapter 2, the predominance of children was already evident in 1861, when at least three-fifths of the American-born in every province had yet to reach 20 years (Table 2.12). In Connaught, that proportion fluctuated by about four-fifths throughout the subsequent half-century, whereas it declined somewhat in the other provinces as short-term adult visitors multiplied in the cities and towns. The even sex-balance of Ireland's American-born population, recorded in every province from 1841 onwards, provided further evidence that their presence was a by-product of the Irish diaspora, rather than being a mere overflow of American settlement in Britain and Europe.

In order to generate an intricate and intimate profile of rural Ireland's American-born residents and their families, I have chosen to examine one county in depth rather than skimming over the entire country. Once again, the most important accessible source is the digital index of 'family' census returns for 1901 and 1911. It has been possible to identify almost every American recorded in a single 'backward' county characterised by abnormally heavy emigration, predominance of farming, and ubiquity of small farms: Leitrim. By 1911, it was also the county with the highest concentration of American residents, an indirect reflection of its exceptionally high rates of net outward migration over the previous four decades. Close study of Leitrim in 1901 and 1911 reveals a widely dispersed population rising to almost 300 American settlers, most of whom were evidently children of emigrants from Leitrim who had struggled to make ends meet in America ('losers'). Because about half of Leitrim's Americans were co-resident with parents, typically born in Leitrim, this study also clarifies the characteristics and circumstances of the 'returned Yank' of rural folklore (discussed in Chapter 1).

II   A County of Extremes

This hub of American settlement was, in outward aspect, perhaps the least 'modern' of all Irish counties. Virtually land-locked, arid and mountainous in the northern districts abutting Sligo, Donegal, and Fermanagh, Leitrim was almost untouched by industrial development outside the Arigna coalfield that straddled the Roscommon border near Drumshanbo. Leitrim was the only county without a single town qualifying for a measure of local government. In 1911, less than one-tenth of the population were living in its fifteen separately enumerated towns, the largest of which (Manorhamilton and Carrick-on-Shannon) each had only about one thousand inhabitants (Map 6.1). While Leitrim's town population had declined continuously since 1841, the rural population had fallen even faster.[1] In 1911, over nine-tenths of Leitrim's population lived on agricultural holdings, the highest proportion for any county, just ahead of neighbouring Roscommon.[2] Only Mayo exceeded rural-Leitrim's level of poverty, here measured by the proportion of agricultural residents on holdings valued below £15 per annum (84%).[3] Leitrim's abnormal concentration of rural poverty had long made it prone to social unrest and to mass enrolment in political organisations with agrarian agendas, such as the United Irish League and later Sinn Féin. The Irish Volunteers, later known as the IRA, were relatively sparse and ineffectual during the revolutionary conflict.[4]

    Leitrim's demographic regime was an advanced example of the remarkable amalgam of practices that made post-Famine Ireland so anomalous in pre-war Europe. The most obvious Irish aberration was continuous depopulation after 1841, while virtually all other European populations grew despite tightening constraints on nuptiality and fertility. Leitrim's census population declined by over one-quarter over the Famine decade (1841–51), and by a further 43% between 1851 and 1911. Though its Famine losses were among the heaviest recorded, Leitrim's subsequent depopulation was unremarkable by Irish standards.[5] What were the demographic factors contributing to Leitrim's continuous loss of population? Apart from heavy emigration, did these include either diminishing fertility and nuptiality or severe mortality?

    While marital fertility declined steadily in most European countries, Leitrim stayed fairly close to the Hutterite standard for uninhibited

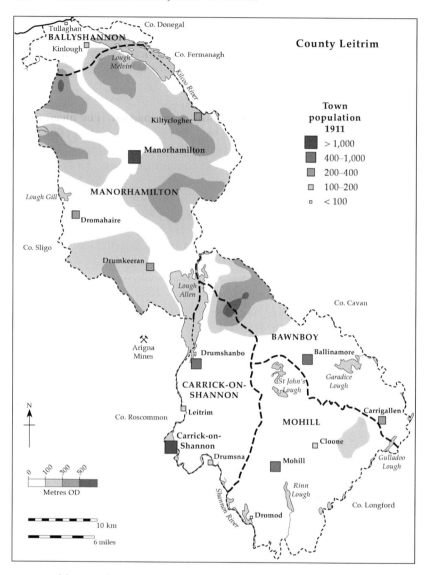

Map 6.1 Leitrim, showing administrative boundaries and towns, 1911

procreation within marriage, with no downward trend between the 1870s and the 1910s.[6] Procreation outside marriage remained exceptionally rare. As in most of the country, fertility was increasingly restricted not by contraception or abstinence within marriage, but by postponing or avoiding matrimony. Throughout north-western Europe, women typically married about a decade after menarche, while a significant proportion of each cohort (around one-tenth) never married. The mean age at marriage for the cohorts born between 1821 and 1851 changed little in Leitrim, the typical bride being about 25 and the typical groom 5 years older. Leitrim was not exceptional in these respects, though only a few counties had younger bridal cohorts. The first sign of a nuptial crisis arose for the cohort born in 1861, whose mean age at marriage rose to 28 for brides and 32 for grooms.[7]

Leitrim also conformed to the aberrant Irish trend towards increased 'celibacy' (a demographer's euphemism for the proportion of 50-year-olds who had never married). Male 'celibacy' increased steadily from less than one-fifteenth of 50-year-olds in 1841 to over one-quarter in 1911, the proportion already being far in excess of the north-western European norm by the 1890s. Female celibacy, a much more formidable obstacle to procreation, hovered around one-tenth until 1891, before also rising sharply to one-sixth in the early twentieth century.[8] By comparison with most Irish counties, Leitrim had few 'celibates' as well as relatively few who married early; yet, by 1900, it was clear that even Leitrim could no longer provide marriage opportunities for an alarmingly large proportion of each new cohort.

Except perhaps during the Great Famine, mortality losses were never sufficient to account for depopulation through 'natural decrease', since births always greatly outnumbered deaths. One of Ireland's demographic paradoxes is the fact that the poorest counties also tended to have the lowest mortality rates, as reflected in survivorship ratios for the cohorts born in 1846 and 1856. These indicate that about three-quarters of 15-year-olds who remained in Leitrim would have survived to the age of 55, an exceptionally high survivorship ratio by comparison with Irish cities or urbanised Britain. Unusually, women were less likely to endure than men, and the prospects for both sexes were better for the cohort of 1846 than for their successors of 1856.[9] This apparent retrogression was, at least in part, a by-product of improved death registration, which had been notoriously inadequate for a decade or so after its introduction in 1864.

In any case, mortality was unusually low in Leitrim, reflecting the benefits of a well-ventilated and sparsely populated environment ('plenty of fresh air') in restricting the spread of the infectious diseases that endemically ravaged urban quagmires such as Dublin.[10] Leitrim's advantage was even more pronounced for reported infant mortality, which declined steadily for both sexes between the 1870s and the 1910s. In the final decade, less than fifty infant deaths were registered for every 1,000 births, one-third of the ratio in Dublin. Leitrim was almost always the safest or second-safest county in which to be born.[11] It also offered a much more salubrious environment than the putrid American cities in which so many Leitrimonians had settled, a factor that encouraged return migration in search of better health.

The primary source of depopulation was undoubtedly massive and sustained net outward migration, kick-started during the Famine but reaching comparable peaks during subsequent periods of less life-threatening privation. Even in phases of relative agricultural prosperity, counties like Leitrim continued to supply emigrants on a scale seldom matched in any European country. The predominance of long-distance movement in post-Famine Irish migration, discussed in Chapter 1, was particularly marked in the case of Leitrim. Admittedly, birthplace returns show steadily increasing net outward movement between Leitrim and other Irish counties between 1841 and 1911; yet, even in 1911, net displacement out of Leitrim amounted to less than 6% of the county's population. The majority of inter-county migrants moved only between Leitrim and its six county neighbours, often making a short border-crossing as a result of marriage or acquisition of land.[12] Leitrim was also part of the north-western recruiting zone for seasonal migration, though the number of 'migratory agricultural labourers', regularly absent during the summer, never exceeded 1,000 between 1880 and 1915.

In four consecutive decades from the 1870s to the 1900s, Leitrim experienced the highest rate of 'cohort depletion' for any Irish county, losing up to 41% of its people initially aged 5–24 in the course of the following decade. Despite various technical flaws, this proxy is the most reliable indicator of net outward migration. Though a few other counties had slightly heavier cohort depletion in earlier decades, the proportion of young adults who 'disappeared' from Leitrim never fell below one-third between the Famine and the First World War.[13] These findings are broadly confirmed by police returns of the number of Leitrim residents leaving Irish ports with the intention of settling abroad 'permanently' (for a year or more). These admittedly defective annual returns indicate that few counties had heavier gross out-migration than Leitrim between the 1870s and the First World War, though its outflow during the quarter-century immediately after the Famine was unexceptional.[14] Nine-tenths of the reported outflow was bound for the United States, but many emigrants to Britain were probably missed by official enumerators.[15] In several decades, as in most Connaught counties, the majority of recorded emigrants were female. Around the turn of the century, no less than 138 women were leaving Leitrim for every 100 male emigrants. Except in the immediate aftermath of the Famine, Leitrim ranked high among Irish counties as a relative exporter of women.[16]

These returns also reveal that most of Leitrim's emigrants were young unmarried adults: no county had so small a proportion of married or widowed emigrants, and few counties sent out so few children as Leitrim.[17] Emigration was increasingly concentrated in the age group 20–24, people who in less dysfunctional societies would have been entering employment and marriage markets nearer home. At its peak in 1886–95, the annual outflow from this age group amounted to almost one-tenth of the entire population aged 20–24 in 1891, the fourth highest county ratio.[18] Had this rate of outflow been sustained, it would obviously have left only a tiny rump of young adults to cope with later life in Leitrim. It is easy to understand why so many contemporaries and historians depicted emigration from rural Ireland as an unstaunchable 'haemorrhage' or a malign 'exodus', even if most recent studies have emphasised the social and economic benefits rather than costs of mass emigration.

So far, we have treated Leitrim as a unit, ignoring the regional disparities to be found within any administrative territory such as a county. By comparing the regions north and south of Lough Allen, which bisects the county with only a narrow land passage connecting the two portions, we may capture some of those disparities.[19] The two regions experienced similar rates of depopulation (one-third in each case between 1871 and 1911). North Leitrim had an even higher proportion resident on agricultural holdings, and a greater proportion of agricultural residents living on smaller holdings.[20] Far more northerners than southerners lived in dwellings of only one or two rooms, yet southerners were slightly more likely to reside in electoral divisions officially designated as 'congested'.[21] These symptoms of rural poverty were particularly pronounced in the Kinlough district in the extreme north-west, which also far exceeded any other district in the proportion of its people living in congested divisions (Map 6.2).[22] Irish-speakers were rare but less uncommon in the North; both districts contributed equally to seasonal migration, but northerners were much more likely to make for Scotland rather than England.[23]

There was little regional difference in the intensity of emigration, as measured by cohort depletion, though the richer South was slightly

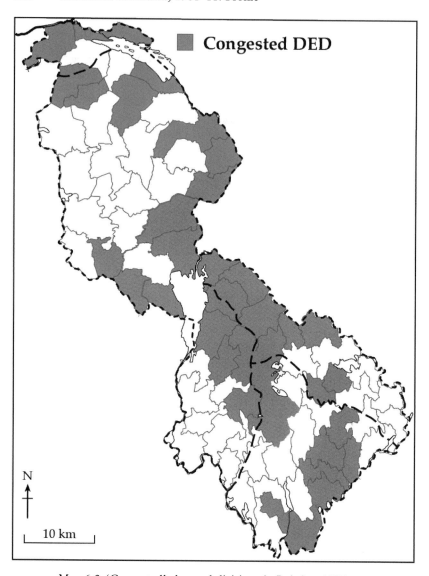

Map 6.2 'Congested' electoral divisions in Leitrim, 1907

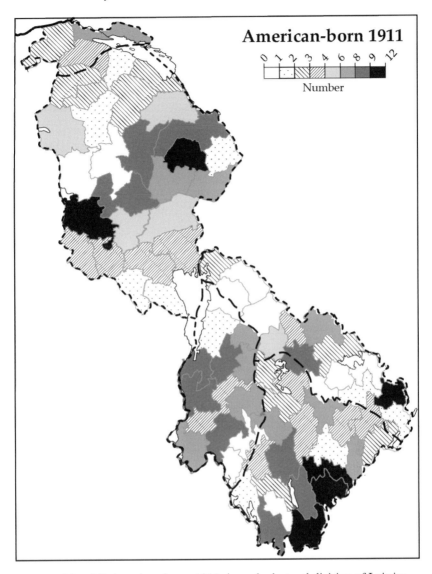

Map 6.3 American-born, 1911, in each electoral division of Leitrim

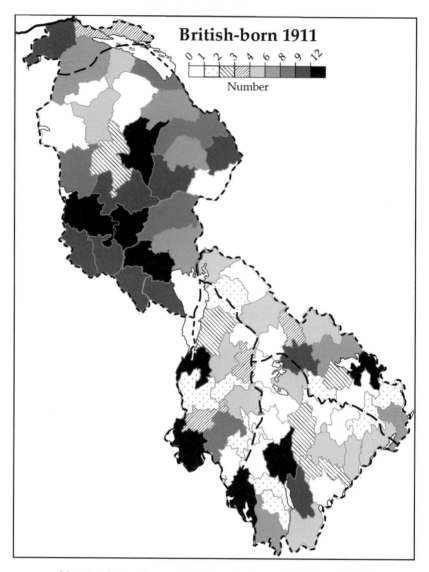

Map 6.4 British-born, 1911, in each electoral division of Leitrim

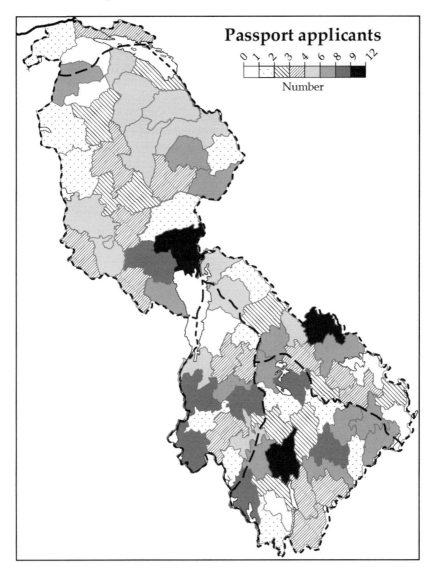

Map 6.5 Electoral divisions of origin of passport applicants from
Leitrim, 1914–25

more prone to net out-migration.[24] In this respect Kinlough, despite its extreme poverty, lagged somewhat behind the rest of the county until the Edwardian decade.[25] As for recorded inward movement, Britons were clustered in the North, whereas foreigners (almost all American) were equally inclined to settle in each region.[26] The contrast between the distributions of British and American settlers is displayed in Maps 6.3 and 6.4, which depict their presence in each electoral division in 1911. In general, it appears that regional economic disparities within the county only marginally affected the patterns of migration, which were shaped by social strategies and norms that pervaded most of rural Ireland (Map 6.5).

Those who moved from America to Leitrim around 1900 faced a formidable cultural challenge. Leitrim was one of the poorest and least industrial counties of Ireland, recurrently wracked by agrarian unrest, doggedly reproducing far more children than its society and economy could provide for. This strategy reflected the widespread belief that long-distance migration would continue to offer its surplus population a better livelihood elsewhere, overwhelmingly in the United States, and that emigrants would provide essential social insurance for those who stayed at home. Returning emigrants and their children entered a community whose physical and social environment was as unlike urban America as any European place of origin. Yet the home population, however 'backward' and primitive it might seem, was also deeply if vicariously soaked in Americanism, almost every Leitrim family having been stretched across the Atlantic. The ultimate imaginative challenge for those returning 'home' was to match their hosts by straddling two apparently incompatible worlds.

III   Leitrim Americans

By 1911, Leitrim's 300 Americans outnumbered both Scottish and English residents, with an intriguing sprinkling of colonials and Europeans.[27] The American-born population had doubled since 1901 and octupled since 1871. In a sparsely populated county this amounted to 47 Americans for every 10,000 inhabitants, the highest proportion for any Irish county (Galway, Longford, and Donegal were runners-up). How did the profile of Leitrim's Americans compare with other parts of the country? Published tabulations for 1911 indicate that almost half of Leitrim's Americans were female, while less than one-quarter were adults.[28] Leitrim's conspicuous American presence was a novelty. The belated expansion of its American population has already been traced in Table 2.11, which shows that Leitrim (and Connaught) had lagged behind Ireland as a whole at every census between 1851 and 1901. Over the same period the American presence in Ulster and Leinster (up to 1891) consistently exceeded the recorded density for Connaught and Leitrim. Table 2.12 shows that up to 1871 the majority of Leitrim's tiny American population was female, the male component being consistently smaller than for Ireland as a whole. That pattern was reversed between 1881 and 1911, though Leitrim's female component seldom fell far below the overall level. In one important respect, Leitrim's Americans were exceptional from 1891 onwards. Whereas two-thirds of Americans in Ireland were aged less than 20 in both 1891 and 1901, the proportion in Leitrim exceeded four-fifths. The peculiar character of American settlement in Leitrim (and Connaught in general) was shaped largely by the astonishing predominance of children.

In order to reconstruct a collective profile of Leitrim's Americans, I have abstracted the census returns for all Leitrim households containing any American member in 1901 and 1911.[29] A handful of Canadians (individually introduced in the next chapter) have been excluded from the statistical analysis that follows, as there were too few to allow useful comparison with those born in the United States.[30] Table 6.2 depicts Leitrim's 294 Americans in 1911, distinguishing between households with 'solitary' or 'multiple' American-born members. Almost half of the group (46%) were solitaries, surrounded by non-Americans almost always born in Leitrim. Most solitary Americans were in households headed by an uncle or aunt (26%) or a grandparent (27%), while one-tenth had no stated family connection with the householder. Only one-fifth were children of the household head. Though the bare majority of 'multiple' Americans were children of the householder, 30% were living in a grandparent's household.

The analysis also separates Americans with at least one co-resident parent (51%) from the remainder, whose parents were either absent or dead. Even among the Americans with a co-resident parent, over one-fifth were living in grandparental households, reinforcing the impression that most returning Americans were taking advantage of home charity. For Americans without parents present, no less than 36% were grandchildren of the householder and 30% were nieces or nephews. All but one of the thirteen Americans described as visitors, boarders, lodgers, or servants were solitaries without accompanying parents.

As already indicated, the published census returns for 1911 revealed that the majority of American residents were minors, with an unusually even balance of the sexes. My Leitrim analysis amplifies these broad findings, recording a small male excess and a very youthful population: its 'upper-quartile' age was 18 years, indicating that only one-quarter would be viewed as adults today. Since the median age was 12, most were returned as 'scholars' without gainful occupation. It also followed that the vast majority (92%) of Americans were unmarried. Though solitaries and parentless Americans tended to be slightly older, even for these groups the median age was only 13 or 14. In other respects, the American profile closely resembled that of the local population. Virtually all Leitrim Americans (97%) were Catholics, less than one-twelfth could speak Irish, and nine-tenths of those aged 5 or more were reportedly able to read and write (implicitly in English).

Over four-fifths of the heads of 'American' households were farmers, along with a few labourers and shopkeepers, two policemen, an unemployed carpenter and an assistant, a teacher, a herdsman, a creamery man, a civil bills officer, a printer, and even a Catholic curate.[31] The great majority of Leitrim Americans lived in modest farmhouses or cottages, over three-quarters of which had thatched roofs, though only 6.5% were old-fashioned mud cabins with 'perishable' walls. The median household squashed five members into three rooms with three front windows.[32] Indeed, over two-fifths of Americans were housed in standard dwellings with three rooms, three windows, perishable roofing, and imperishable walls, suggesting remarkable uniformity in Leitrim's vernacular housing stock.[33] 'Solitaries' and Americans without co-resident parents were particularly unlikely to have the protection of slates above their heads. This profile strongly suggests that most of those looking after the children of emigrants were poor farmers who could ill afford the extra burden.

Given the rapid expansion of Leitrim's American population between 1901 (153) and 1911 (294), one might expect marked contrasts between the profiles of the two groups. In fact, as shown by comparison between Tables 6.1 and 6.2, the changes were mostly minor. There was some advance in literacy (from 77% of the group in 1901 to 89% in 1911), and a minor diffusion of Irish-speakers (from 4% to 8%). In 1901, as in 1911, almost all Leitrim Americans were unmarried Catholics living under thatch, though the proportion in inferior housing was even higher in 1901 than a decade later. The Americans of 1901 were even younger than in 1911, the median age being 10 with an upper-quartile value of only 16. Once again, almost half were grandchildren, nieces, or nephews of household heads, with similar contrasts between solitaries and multiples, and between Americans with and without co-resident parents ('orphans'). But it is noteworthy that the multiplication of Americans over the decade was accompanied by a shift towards slightly less isolated family environments: in 1901, unlike 1911, both 'solitaries' and 'orphans' had been in the majority.

By analysing the precise addresses of Leitrim Americans, we may compare their spatial distribution with that of the general population, in order to establish if they tended to avoid particularly poor or 'congested' districts. In both census years, the Americans were somewhat under-represented in North Leitrim, the poorer zone, with high concentrations in the Carrick-on-Shannon district.[34] There was no marked tendency within either region to either choose or avoid congested divisions.[35] In all cases, the regional differences were minor, confirming the general finding that the profile of Leitrim's Americans closely mirrored that of the home population.

IV   Continuity

To what extent were Leitrim's Americans long-term residents rather than visitors? Though in general it is not feasible to trace their subsequent movements through passenger lists, a lower-bound indication of the proportion remaining after a decade may be obtained by attempting to match the names of all known Leitrim Americans in both years. Of 153 Leitrim residents returned as Americans in 1901, no less than 68 (44%) have been traced somewhere in Ireland in 1911 (Table 6.1). Five of the 'settlers' had moved to other counties, and eleven were no longer returned as American-born, though otherwise firmly identifiable with an 'American' of 1901.[36] The marked male majority among settlers probably resulted from my inability to trace girls who had married during the intervening decade and consequently changed surname. Otherwise, there was no great difference in profile between the settlers and the 'visitors'.[37] A few of the residual visitors would have died before 1911, and others with common names could not be confidently matched. We may conclude that about half of the surviving Americans of 1901 were still (or again) in Ireland a decade later.

Projecting backwards from 1911, it appears that less than one-quarter (71) of the 294 declared Americans in Leitrim had been in Ireland in 1901 (Table 6.2). The settlers included thirteen who had previously been returned as both born and resident in Leitrim, along with one whose nativity as well as residence in 1901 was given as Westmeath. The lower proportion of settlers for 1911 is an arithmetical by-product of the sharp increase in Leitrim's American population, including many children too young to have been alive in 1901. The 'settlers' of 1911 were self-evidently a decade older than those of 1901, more likely to be married, and less likely to be relatives (other than children) of the household head.[38] Until the household census forms for 1926 are released as half-promised, we have no means of estimating what proportion remained in

Ireland after 1911. But these calculations confirm that many Leitrim Americans were would-be settlers rather than tourists, even if some who lingered in Leitrim over the intercensal decade later moved on.[39]

Table 6.2 indicates that 'solitaries' and 'orphans' were markedly *more* likely to have been in the country a decade earlier than those co-resident with other Americans or with parents, probably because of the recent trend towards the reverse migration of entire families. This reversed the pattern for 1901 (Table 6.1), but in this case the differences in the proportions still present in Ireland in 1911 were insignificant.

Comparison of the returns for 1901 and 1911 allows us to chart the domestic mobility of the 'settlers'.[40] Incidentally, this exercise confirms the imprecision of census returns, not just in the attribution of birthplace. Less than half of the settlers had aged by exactly 10 years between 31 March 1901 and 2 April 1911, with a pronounced upward shift even among the young.[41] Only three settlers were married or widowed over the decade, but one-third were either promoted or demoted within the household pecking-order in almost equal numbers.[42] Among those who had a co-resident parent in either census year, a substantial minority lost a parent over the decade.[43] The three reported Irish-speakers all acquired that skill between 1901 and 1911, probably because of the expansion of state-subsidised Irish classes in national schools. Perhaps the most interesting finding is the residential continuity of Americans in a rural environment, so unlike the extensive intercensal mobility of elite Americans. Only one-fifth of matched Americans moved to a different townland between 1901 and 1911, reflecting the fact that most were tied to family farms.[44] For those who stayed in Ireland, there is little evidence of either upward or lateral mobility over the course of the decade.

An equally revealing signifier of long-term reverse movement is the presence of non-American siblings of those born in America. In both census years, this applied to almost one-quarter of all Americans in Leitrim. The proportion was much higher for 'multiples' (32% in 1911) than 'solitaries' (17%), and negligible for Americans without co-resident parents (6%). These contrasts closely replicated those for 1901. Table 6.3 looks more closely at the character of these mixed sibling groups. In 1911, over one-quarter of the non-Americans were singular, meaning that the American had only one co-resident sibling born elsewhere. Almost one-third were in groups of two, and one-quarter were in groups of five indicating long-term resettlement in Leitrim. In 1901, the proportion of non-American siblings in groups of one or two had been substantially smaller.

Very few non-Americans were older than their American brother or sister (6 in 1901 and 10 in 1911, or 7% in both years).[45] Equally few non-

Americans were born outside Leitrim (10 in 1901 and 8 in 1911).[46] Of
the 10 older non-Americans in 1911, 7 were 'singular' and the remainder
belonged to the Scanlon family, discussed below. Of all non-American
siblings in 1901, 6 came from Scotland, 3 from Roscommon, and 1 from
Dublin. Of those enumerated in 1911, 5 came from Scotland, 2 from
Fermanagh, and 1 from Cavan. The relative prominence of Scottish
children reminds us that the migratory trajectory of many Irish emigrants
incorporated both Britain and America, not always in that order.

The census returns for 1911 may also be deployed to measure cosmopolitanism within individual families including a co-resident parent. Few
of these parents were themselves born in America, and most had married
Leitrimonians. Only 18 Americans had co-resident spouses in 1911, of
those 13 were natives of Leitrim, along with 1 each from Cavan,
Donegal, Roscommon, Tyrone, and Scotland.[47] In 63 cases, it is possible to establish the origin or whereabouts of all the siblings in families
with an American child in 1911 (Table 6.4). One-eighth of all children
born alive in these families had since died, and 8% were absent on census
night. Of the remaining 201 children, 134 were natives of America and
67 had been born elsewhere, all but one in Leitrim. With six exceptions,
these locally born children were younger siblings of Americans. All told,
35 of the 63 families incorporated both nationalities, showing that it had
become commonplace for parents to return home from America,
midway through the child-bearing phase, to rear their children in Ireland.
By 1911, the human traffic between Ireland and America was undeniably
two-way.

V   Returned Yanks

America's human presence in Ireland was not restricted to those born
overseas. Even more important was that elusive figure, the returned
Yank, who left no direct trace on census schedules. A valuable by-
product of my analysis of Leitrim Americans is information about their
co-resident parents, most of whom were natives of Leitrim who had
returned home. Table 6.5 presents a profile of 70 mothers and 51 fathers,
all Catholics, living in 73 households in 1911 (the matching profile of
parents in 44 households in 1901 is similar). Almost all fathers were
accompanied by their wives, but 29% of mothers were either widowed or
separated from their husbands. In 1901, no less than 12 mothers out of
41 were returned as married without a co-resident husband, suggesting
that the male breadwinner had remained in America while consigning his
family to relatives in Leitrim, in an effort to make ends meet. Though less
common in 1911, one-tenth of mothers were still in this awkward

situation. By contrast, only one father of an American (in 1901) was recorded without a co-resident wife.[48]

Whereas nine-tenths of the fathers were from Leitrim, one-quarter of the mothers had been born elsewhere in Ireland (only one mother was American-born). Most returned parents headed their own households, but 23% of the mothers were living in a grandparental household. The median age for returned fathers was 45, 5 years older than the median mother. No less than 88% of the fathers were farmers, along with a shopkeeper, a farmer–shopkeeper, a printer, and four labourers or farm servants. Their houses were just as modest as those for Leitrim Americans in general.[49] It is clear that very few returned Americans in Leitrim were the swaggering figures of fiction, investing their ill-gotten foreign gold in an Irish pub or bringing home a Yankee bride.

Examination of the 44 families with a co-resident parent in 1901 demonstrates that most had returned to Leitrim as settlers rather than visitors. In no less than 31 cases (70%), at least one parent was still in Ireland in 1911. Three-quarters (23) of these settled families had both parents present in each year, while 5 had only a mother in 1911 as in 1901.[50] Apart from 5 sets of parents who moved household within Leitrim, all remained at the same address. The retention rate for parents was much higher than for their American-born children. Only 15 of these settled families (48%) included any Americans who could be matched in 1911, including three cases where the American children were living separately from their parents in 1911.[51]

The profile of the 13 parental families that disappeared after 1901 was very different. In all but two cases, the American children likewise disappeared from Ireland over the following decade. In 8 of these families, the sole parent present in 1901 had been a mother whose husband was absent, suggesting temporary separation while the father remained in America.[52] But the mother's death might lead to the same outcome, as perhaps in the case of three American-born siblings in Drumshanbo who were living with their mother in 1901 but formed an autonomous household in 1911. Overall, the analysis strongly suggests that the reverse migration of parental families from America to Leitrim typically entailed a long-term commitment to remain in Ireland.

The complexities of family migration are exhibited in two cases meriting close examination, each centred on a 12-year-old girl who was the lone American in her household. The first from 1901 concerns Lizzie Mahon of Effrinagh, Drumsna (also the birthplace of the highly migratory James Gralton).[53] Her father Patrick, a Leitrim-born farmer, had married a Scot, and their two eldest children aged 16 and 15 were born in Scotland. Lizzie (12) was followed by five children born in

Leitrim who ranged in age from 10 to 1. The Mahon household of ten occupied a 'standard' dwelling with three rooms and three front windows. This case implies a four-stage migration from Ireland to Britain, on to America, and back to Ireland. Ten years later, Patrick and Bridget Mahon were still living in Effrinagh with their seven Leitrim-born children, allegedly the total number ever born. Since she had been married to Patrick for 28 years by 1911, the couple had erased their three eldest children, born in Scotland and the United States, from the record. There is no civil record of Lizzie's marriage or death in Leitrim.[54] What lay behind this act of oblivion is beyond recovery from the available documents.

The second case from 1911 is a rare example of the consequences of *family* migration both to and from the United States. Annie Scanlon of Cattan, whose parents and siblings were all natives of Leitrim, had four siblings aged 19, 15, 14, and 8 (4 years younger than Annie). The household of eight members, including her widowed 84-year-old grand-mother-in-law, co-existed in two rooms with three front windows. The family's age profile suggests that the Mahons had left Ireland by 1898, returning home before 1903. This conflicts with the fact that Francis Scanlon and his two sons aged 9 and 5 were living in Cattan in 1901, whereas his wife Annie and daughters Kate and Annie (aged 14 and 12 in 1911) were both absent. The two Annies may well have remained in the United States when the male Scanlons returned to Leitrim, adding an extra twist to the family's circular migration.[55] In most cases, however, the migratory trajectory implied by sibling birthplaces consisted of three simple phases: emigration from Ireland before marriage, marriage and procreation in the United States, and resettlement in Ireland followed by further procreation. Yet even this model trajectory may be a statistical illusion, inviting challenge from family historians deploying sources other than census schedules.

These two exceptional case studies remind us that no statistical profile of Leitrim's Americans can do justice to the often complex domestic environment and migratory history of those who visited or settled in the county. The next chapter introduces a parade of particular Americans, parading significant variations within this superficially homogeneous sub-population. As Louis MacNeice remarked in *Snow*:

> World is crazier and more of it than we think,
> Incorrigibly plural.

Table 6.1 *Characteristics of Leitrim Americans, 1901*

%	Total	Solitary	Multiple	Parent	No Parent
Characteristic					
Female	46.4	47.1	45.6	44.4	48.1
Catholic	96.1	92.9	100	98.6	93.8
Literate	76.5	75.3	78.0	82.5	71.0
Irish Speech	3.9	4.7	2.9	2.8	4.9
Unmarried	90.8	83.5	100	100	82.7
Relation to Head					
Head	9.2	16.5	0	0	17.3
Child	34.0	21.2	50.0	72.2	0
Grandchild	31.4	31.8	30.9	23.6	38.3
Nephew, Niece	16.3	16.5	16.2	0	30.9
Visitor, Boarder	5.2	9.5	0	4.2	6.2
Servant	1.3	2.4	0	0	2.5
Present					
Non-American Sibling	24.2	16.5	33.8	47.2	3.7
In 1911 Census	44.4	42.4	47.1	45.8	43.2
Housing					
Inferior Class	31.4	34.1	27.9	29.2	33.3
Thatched Roof	78.4	82.4	73.5	73.6	82.7
Mud Walls	8.5	11.8	4.4	9.7	7.4
Age in Years					
Lower Quartile	6	6	6	7	6
Median	10	11	9	11	9
Upper Quartile	16	19	12	15	19
Number	*153*	*85*	*68*	*72*	*81*
% of Total	100	55.6	44.4	47.1	52.9

Note: Proportions relate to all residents of Co. Leitrim born in the USA or 'America' (located in a digital search of the family schedules, incorporating those miscategorised under 'other' birthplaces). Those living in households without others born in America are termed 'solitary', the residue being 'multiple'. Those with at least one co-resident parent are distinguished from those with no parent. 'Literate' refers to the proportion aged over 5 years who could read and write; every Irish-speaker was bilingual in English. Family schedules also record the relationship of each Leitrim American to the 'head of family' responsible for completing the form. 'Head' includes wife; 'child' includes step-child; 'visitor' includes boarder or lodger. The table also shows the presence of siblings not born in America (see Table 6.3), and of Americans matched in the other census. The accompanying house and building return for each townland records the 'class' of dwelling (3 and 4 being 'inferior' categories), and enumerates 'perishable' roofs (usually thatched) and walls (usually mud). *Source*: Census of Ireland (1901), family schedules, house and building returns.

Table 6.2 *Characteristics of Leitrim Americans, 1911*

%	Total	Solitary	Multiple	Parent	No Parent
Characteristic					
Female	46.3	39.7	51.9	51.0	41.3
Catholic	96.6	92.6	100	100	93.0
Literate	89.2	91.1	87.6	88.1	90.3
Irish Speech	8.2	5.2	10.6	8.6	7.7
Unmarried	91.8	83.1	99.4	98.7	84.6
Relation to Head					
Head	7.8	14.0	1.9	0	15.4
Child	38.7	19.9	56.3	75.5	0
Grandchild	28.9	27.2	30.4	21.9	36.4
Nephew, Niece	16.0	25.7	7.6	2.6	30.1
Visitor	2.7	6.6	0	0	6.3
Servant	1.7	3.7	0	0	3.5
Present					
Non-American Sibling	24.8	16.9	31.6	42.4	6.3
In 1901 Census	24.1	30.9	18.4	21.2	27.3
Housing					
Inferior Class	22.5	18.4	25.9	20.5	24.5
Thatched Roof	76.5	80.1	73.4	72.8	80.4
Mud Walls	6.5	8.1	5.1	6.6	6.3
Age in Years					
Lower Quartile	8	9	7	7	9
Median	12	14	11	11	13
Upper Quartile	18	23	16	16	22
Number	*294*	*136*	*158*	*151*	*143*
% of Total	100	46.3	53.7	51.4	48.6

Note: See Table 6.1. *Source:* Census of Ireland (1911), family schedules, house and building returns.

Table 6.3 *Children of parents of Leitrim Americans, 1911*

Characteristic	Number	%	Mean	Median
Status				
Ever Born	251	100	4.0	4
Dead	31	12.4	0.5	0
Living	*220*	*87.6*	*3.5*	*3*
Location				
Absent	19	7.6	0.3	0
Present: American	134	53.4	2.1	2
Present: Other	67	26.7	1.1	1
Number of Families	*63*			

Note: Statistics relate to families for whom the numbers of children ever born, living, and dead were recorded in the fertility returns introduced in 1911. Though only required for currently married mothers, the statistics include irregular returns for widows (3) and widowers (2). Fertility returns were available for 63 of the 73 families of Leitrim Americans with at least one co-resident parent. Statistics are expressed as a percentage of all children belonging to the 63 families, followed by the mean and median number of children in each category per family. *Source*: Census of Ireland (1911), family schedules.

Table 6.4 *Non-American siblings of Leitrim Americans, 1901 and 1911*

Group Size	1901: Groups	Siblings	% of Siblings	1911: Groups	Siblings	% of Siblings
1	15	15	17.2	37	37	26.8
2	11	22	25.3	22	44	31.9
3	5	15	17.2	6	18	13.0
4	2	8	9.2	1	4	2.9
5 or more	4	27	31.0	7	35	25.4
Total	*37*	*87*	*100*	*73*	*138*	*100*

Note: Statistics refer to the number of Leitrim Americans with co-resident siblings born outside America, classified by the size of each group of such siblings. For each census, the columns show the number of groups, the number of siblings in those groups, and the proportion of all siblings within each group. In 1901, the four largest groups contained 5, 6, 7, and 9 siblings each; in 1911, no group exceeded 5 siblings. *Source*: Census of Ireland (1901, 1911), family schedules.

Table 6.5 *Characteristics of parents of Leitrim Americans, 1901 and 1911*

%	Total	Solitary	Multiple	Parent	No Parent
Characteristic					
Born Leitrim		83.9	80.5	90.2	72.9
Catholic		96.8	97.6	100	100
Literate		83.9	95.1	96.1	95.7
Irish Speech		6.5	7.3	7.8	4.3
Married (Spouse Absent)		3.2	29.3	0	10.0
Widowed		6.5	2.4	3.9	18.6
Relation to Head					
Head		90.3	7.3	82.4	15.7
Spouse		0	63.4	0	60.0
Child		3.2	22.0	9.8	15.7
Child-in-Law		3.2	2.4	5.9	7.1
Occupation					
Farmer		71.0	29.4	88.2	70.6
Labourer		12.9	5.9	7.8	0
Servant		0	52.9	0	11.8
Other		16.1	11.8	3.9	17.6
Age in Years					
Lower Quartile		39	31	38	36
Median		42	37	45	40
Upper Quartile		50	42	51	50
Number		*31*	*41*	*51*	*70*
% of Families		70.5	93.2	69.9	95.9

Note: Proportions relate to parents with one or more American-born children resident in Leitrim in 1901 and 1911. Proportions for each occupation exclude unspecified cases. 'Farmer' includes relative (apart from wife) not otherwise occupied; 'labourer' includes farm servant and farm labourer; 'servant' (domestic) includes housekeeper. The bottom row gives the number of fathers and mothers as a proportion of all families of Leitrim Americans with at least one co-resident parent (44 in 1901, 73 in 1911). *Source*: Census of Ireland (1901, 1911), family schedules.

7   Americans in Leitrim: People

I   Exotic Neighbours

Before adding personal colour to the statistical profile of Leitrim's American-born, let us leaf through the family returns for both census years to identify their immigrant neighbours from beyond the United States. First, the Canadians, of whom only five have been identified.[1] Kate Kelly was a farmer's daughter, while Mary McLoughlin was married to a farm labourer. Their relations were all natives of Leitrim, and their Canadian birth was declared in only one census.[2] Kate H. Murphy (40 in 1901) was an unmarried national school teacher who reappeared as Irish-speaking Kathleen (58) in 1911. John Joseph Farrell, a Catholic curate boarding with a shopkeeper in Rooskey (1901), went on to become a parish priest living with a housekeeper in Roscommon (1911). Leitrim's only non-Catholic Canadian was Margaret Maria Storey from Quebec, a Methodist housekeeper living with her father from Cavan and an 'Irish Church' servant from Leitrim in 1901.

Australasia was more important than Canada as a source of inward migration to Leitrim. There were several groups of Australian-born offspring of farmer fathers and mothers from Leitrim (Mary and Nellie Earley; Mary Ellen, Frances May, and Francis Gerald Faughnan; and John, Francis, and Mary Gilhooly). Bessie Farrell from Queensland was living with her mother from Leitrim and step-father, a farmer from Sligo; by 1911, Thomas Faulkner (9) had spent 2 years in hospital with tonsillitis and adenoids; Mary Gilmartin, an Irish-speaker, was a farmer's wife whose husband and children were from Leitrim; Lizzie Murphy was a nurse from Melbourne who worked successively in Wicklow and Leitrim; and Maggie Prendergast (7) was boarding with her Leitrimonian widowed mother in a farming household in 1901. Of all national minorities in Leitrim, the Australians were most akin to the Americans in their youthfulness and obvious origins as offspring of emigrants.

New Zealand (which had declined to join the new Commonwealth of Australia in 1901) contributed Grace Margaret Dowling, a trained nurse living with her Irish-speaking father, an army pensioner from Dublin city. Joseph Kelly (6) was the son of a Roscommon-born grazier and his English wife, whose other children were born in Galway and Leitrim. William Austin MacReady, a Presbyterian bank official from New Zealand who was boarding in Ballinamore in 1901 and Holywood, Co. Down, in 1911, was the only non-Catholic from Australasia. Thomas George Jones, a widowed Episcopalian farmer from Trinidad, headed a household including eight children and a servant from Leitrim, and an unmarried sister-in-law from Cavan.

Imperial connections doubtless account for the noteworthy presence of Africans in Leitrim. Robert Bradshaw, a doctor in Carrick-on-Shannon with a wife from Longford, son from Northumberland, and servants from Leitrim and Wicklow, was a native of Sierra Leone who belonged to the Church of Ireland. Also from Sierra Leone was Nancy Alice Bradshaw, probably his sister, who lived in 1901 with her parents who were born in Tipperary and Sligo. Charlotte L. Darley of the same birthplace was married to a Church of Ireland magistrate and land agent from Dublin. Leo Milon, boarding in Leitrim in 1901, was a pedlar from the Orange Free State who adhered to the 'Greek Church'. Kathleen Wood (12) from 'Africa' was the adopted daughter of a Methodist grocer from Roscommon and his wife from Sligo. Leitrim's remaining Africans were Catholics. Jane Anne Carroll from Port Elizabeth, wife of a policeman serving in Leitrim in 1901, reappears as a licensed victualler in Fermanagh in 1911. Minnie Keon was married to a Leitrim farmer; 2-year-old Michael James Keon was apparently not their child and lived with his widowed grandmother; Mary and Lavinia Smyth were daughters of a Sligonian gamekeeper and his wife from Tyrone. This plethora of birthplaces testifies to the mixed Irish county origins of many families housing foreigners, an unusual feature in a county notable for the scarcity of in-migration from elsewhere in Ireland.

The largest group of colonial settlers were those born in India, the most prolific source of imperial employment for pre-war Irishmen. Half a dozen Leitrim Indians qualified for the class ironically termed 'the Protestant Ascendancy'. Muriel Annie Pearl Adamson was the daughter of an army officer, deputy-commandant of the Dublin district in 1901; in both census years, the household included a French governess, the Catholic Anna Thill. Charles W. Alleyne was a solicitor resident in Carrick-on-Shannon and born in Belgaum, India, who married a Leitrimonian. Vera and Millicent Marion Hunt, born in Ahmedabad and Poona, were daughters of a widowed army officer from Limerick, who remained in the household after his marriage to a Carlow woman; another sister was English. Edward W. McFarland, a Church of Ireland curate born in India, was boarding with a district inspector of the Royal Irish Constabulary in 1901. James Ormsby Lawder, a married civil engineer and deputy-lieutenant, shared his household in 1911 with a female servant from Cavan who also belonged to the Church of Ireland. The only Episcopalian Indians of inferior rank were Jane Cox, married to a printer and compositor variously returned as a native of Fermanagh or Tyrone; and George Cresswell, an unmarried police pensioner from India who boarded with a bachelor farmer and his spinster sister.

India had provided employment for soldiers, teachers, tradesmen, and labourers as well as surplus university graduates and gentlefolk, and almost half of Leitrim's Indians were Catholics in relatively humble situations. Rose Anne Dantzig, listed as an Indian-born servant of a Mohill doctor, was probably the same person as Rosalind Dantzig from 'Longford', a boarder in the Newtownforbes industrial school in 1901. Thomas Johnson was a fish dealer boarding in Carrick-on-Shannon in 1911. Robert Stubbings was a railway porter married to a Dubliner, who had become a stationmaster by 1911 and a professed Dubliner rather than an Indian. Another stationmaster from Cavan had married Theresa McTaggart from India, a ticket-collector. Millicent White, daughter of an Indian-born general dealer, was returned as an Irish-speaking national teacher in 1911; Maud Moran was a domestic servant working for a local farmer and his Leitrim-born family.

Leitrim's Europeans had a distinctive if variegated occupational profile. Apart from the governess Anna Thill, Leitrim's French population in 1901 consisted of three Marist teaching nuns in Carrick-on-Shannon (Sisters Mary Foi, Mary Odilon, and their superior Mary Paulinus). In 1911, Kate Nina Lauder from Brittany, a Church of Ireland widow aged 82, was looking after her unmarried son, a retired major in the Connaught Rangers, with the help of three servants from different counties. Mathew Faller was a German Catholic clockmaker and repairer, boarding in Mohill in 1901 and Londonderry a decade later. Joseph Jeiter, a hotel-keeper in Drumahaire, married to an Irish-speaker from Cavan, was another German-born Catholic. In 1901, Robert Zingg from Switzerland was a Catholic hotel manager in Manorhamilton, who married an English Anglican and moved to Enniskillen before 1911. Their two surviving children, born in Dublin and Fermanagh, both belonged to the Church of Ireland.

Sweden supplied Lettie White, a Catholic married to a 'farmer's son' from Garvagh who, having ascended to household headship by 1911, re-invented himself as a 'landlord'. Anders Grong from Norway, a Lutheran, was butler to George Charles Loftus Tottenham of Glenade, confirmed bachelor, deputy-lieutenant, and landowner. Leitrim's only

Russian Jew was Joseph Fine, an antiques dealer boarding with a publican in Carrick-on-Shannon in 1911. In 1901, he had been returned as a pedlar in Dublin, boarding with another Russian Jewish pedlar who had settled in Dublin about a decade earlier.[3] This completes the brief catalogue of Leitrim's human exotica. The only foreign accent widely heard in the county was the American drawl, mainly in its north-eastern variants.

II   Unusual Leitrim Americans

Though the vast majority of Leitrim Americans were Catholics living on farms, there were a few noteworthy exceptions. Of the ten non-Catholics in 1911, all but one belonged to the Church of Ireland. John Lowe (27) was the sole Presbyterian, a bank official boarding in Drumshanbo with a draper from Roscommon. The only Episcopalian displaying any signs of affluence was Stuart J. Gillmor (59), a general merchant in Drumahaire whose shop had ten rooms and ten front windows. Gillmor's household included his Scottish wife, four sons born in Leitrim, four servants, and two shop assistants. In 1901 he had five shop assistants (a Methodist and four Episcopalians) and a Catholic servant. Edward Murray (37) was a baker in Drumahaire who had married a local woman 5 years earlier and lived with her father, a 70-year-old unemployed carpenter from Sligo. William Armstrong (36), a farmer, lived with his unmarried uncle and aunt in Meenymore, Glenboy. His uncle had a 1st-class house with seven rooms and an imperishable roof, still a rarity in rural Leitrim. George Allen and Elliott Archie Hunter were both 'scholars' living in modest farming households with thatched roofs in Kilcoon, Drumahaire, and Cordiver, Gubacreeny. George shared two rooms with his widowed grandmother, and Elliott shared three rooms with an unmarried uncle and aunt.

Anna Jane Boles of Drumkeeran and Mary Kelly of Drumahaire were both Episcopalian American-born wives with a single child, living in fair-sized houses with imperishable roofs. Two years earlier, Anna had married a local shopkeeper, who occupied a 1st-class shop with five rooms and six front windows. Mary's husband was a police constable of local birth, but their daughter had been born in Belfast. Annie O'Brien (19) shared a house of five rooms in Hill Street, Mohill, with her widowed grandfather James Dobson (77), who described his occupation as 'private'. His two surviving children had left home. In 1901, she had been returned as a visitor in the larger shop of William Dobson, a leather merchant from Fermanagh (another visitor was James, a 'retired draper'). Leitrim's remaining female Episcopalian in 1911 was Francis (*sic*) Hassard (16), a domestic servant working for Anna Charlotte Adelaide Godley of Killygar, an unmarried 'farmer' occupying a mansion with twenty-six rooms and sixteen front windows. Anna's nephew John Arthur Godley, an eminent mandarin and twice Gladstone's private secretary, had recently been created Baron Kilbracken of Killygar.[4]

Four Protestant Americans were present only in 1901. Mary J. T. S. Taylor (64) of Ardmeenan, Garadice, was an Episcopalian farmer's wife with two Catholic servants, living in a thatched house with eight rooms and seven front windows. Harmon Cloak (19), an assistant master and undergraduate at the Royal University, lived with his English-born parents and a Catholic servant in the nine-roomed rectory in Drumharkan East, Mohill. At the opposite extreme of the Protestant spectrum were Caroline Elliott (15) of Gulladoo, Carrigallen East, and Fred Carlton (4) of Boihy, Cloonlogher. Caroline and a Dublin-born sibling were sheltered in the absence of both parents by her married uncle William Armstrong, an Episcopalian farmer occupying a thatched mud cabin with four rooms. Fred Carlton shared two rooms with his illiterate widowed maternal grandmother and two of her children.

Of Leitrim's Catholic Americans in 1911, only eleven were occupied in sectors other than farming, labour, service, and housework. Laurence Harpret, a retired police officer boarding with a farmer in Manorhamilton, was a 45-year-old widower. John McDade (48) was a married police sergeant (a former farmer) stationed in the RIC barracks in Carrick-on-Shannon. His Donegal wife and three children were returned separately in a six-roomed house with imperishable roof in Liberty Street. Ten years earlier, he had been stationed in Dromod, his two elder children being natives of Antrim. Joe Cullen of Knockmacrory, Roosky, and Patrick and Francis Rooney of Kiltyclogher were all American-born minors living with their parents, working respectively as a shop assistant, shop attendant, and telegraph messenger. Martin Cannon (55) was a carpenter's helper, living with his local wife and their seven children in five rooms in Aghatawny Lower, Ballinamore. In 1901, he had been working as a labourer in Lahard, Garadice, and living in a mud cabin with two rooms. John Joseph Kean (42), a clerk, lived in Tullylannan, Leitrim division, with a widowed uncle and his unmarried brother-in-law from Roscommon.

The four American-born women with atypical jobs were all aged between 17 and 28 and (with one exception) were living with parents. Katie Dolphin, a shop assistant, was boarding in a restaurant in Ballinamore. Alicia O'Reilly (28) from California was a post-office assistant in Main Street, Carrigallen, married but without children or a husband in the household; her widowed mother (the postmistress) was from

Tipperary. Alicia had come down in the world since 1901, when she and her new husband Joseph, a 'merchant' from Cavan, occupied a hotel and public house in Main Street with fifteen rooms, four servants, and five shop assistants. Dora McGoey and Elizabeth Dolan were both daughters of farmers, working respectively as a seamstress in Drummans, Rinn, and a dressmaker in Drumgownagh, Cloverhill. Both girls had already left America by 1901, when they were returned as scholars aged 6 and 14. Apart from Harman Cloak, introduced above, only two Americans with unusual occupations were present solely in 1901. Patrick Concannon (35) of Kinlough was an Irish-speaking police constable with a wife and baby born in Westmeath. John P. O'Hara (19) of Aughrim, Kiltubbrid, was an Irish-speaking college student living with an unmarried uncle (a national school teacher) and a cousin working as a seamstress.

III   'Multiple' Americans

The significance of being a native of America enumerated in Leitrim varied sharply between long-term residents ('settlers') and short-term visitors. The most important indicators of long-term residence, as argued in the preceding chapter, are the presence of an American in both 1901 and 1911, and the presence of non-American siblings. A third, if less definitive, indicator is the presence of several American-born siblings in the same household. A single child from America might be fostered at home for a year or so without heavy outlay on passenger tickets, but the cost of a short-term visit for several children would have been prohibitive for most emigrant families. When assembling personal examples of probable settlers, we are therefore dealing with three overlapping categories. For clarity, let us first examine the circumstances of 'multiple' Americans belonging to some of the larger clusters enumerated in Leitrim in 1911, beginning with those already present in 1901.[5]

Edward Lenehan was a more substantial farmer than most, occupying a seven-roomed house with an imperishable roof in Coraughrim, Carrick-on-Shannon. His four children, all Americans, were aged between 19 and 28. The entire Lenehan family had already been returned in Coraughrim in 1901. The only autonomous American threesome in 1911 was the Phibbs family, three unmarried siblings who shared a five-roomed house with an imperishable roof in Drumshanbo. Perhaps as a gesture to American progressive values, Lizzie Phibbs, a 26-year-old 'housekeeper', returned herself as head in preference to her younger brothers, farmers aged 24 and 22. A decade earlier, they had been living there with their mother, a dressmaker from Leitrim (whose husband was absent). The two Gallogly brothers of Carrickvoher, Aghavas, likewise formed an autonomous American household in 1911, having lived in 1901 with their crippled father born in Leitrim (the mother was absent).

Seven other twosomes were already living in the county in 1901, suggesting long-term settlement. They were the McPartlans of Mullaun, Munakill; the McWeeney sisters of Drumliffin Glebe, Leitrim; the Reillys of Drumdarkan, Riverstown; the Earlys of Drumineigh Glebe, Kiltubbrid; the Connolly brothers of Edenvella, Gubacreeny; the Bellweger sisters of Cornavad, Rowan; and the Clancys of Fearnaght, Drumod. Owen McPartland of Mullaun was clearly a prosperous farmer, living in a substantial house with eight rooms and five front windows with his wife, his two boys from Brooklyn, and five younger children born in Leitrim. By contrast, James McWeeney's family, including two younger local siblings, occupied only two rooms. That was also the space available to Mary Reilly, who in the absence of her husband was looking after five younger local children as well as her two from America. In 1901, when her husband was present, the Reillys had been living in the household of his widowed mother (who returned the birthplace of Mary and John as Leitrim rather than America as in 1911). The husband of Kate Early was absent from the household in 1901 as well as in 1911, suggesting permanent separation. The Connollys of Edenvella were sheltered, as they had been in 1901, by an illiterate unmarried uncle, who shared his three rooms with two unmarried siblings. The Bellweger sisters of Cornavad were living with their widowed grandmother in 1911 (confusingly identified as their aunt in 1901). Finally, the Clancys of Fearnaght were living in both census years with their grandfather Patrick Shanly and his wife, both natives of Leitrim.

Many groups of 'multiple' Americans were enumerated only in 1911, reflecting the recent upsurge in reverse migration to Leitrim implied by the doubling of the county's American-born population between 1901 and 1911. George Conboy (76) was an illiterate farmer in Killyvehy, Keeldra, living in the archetypical thatched house with three rooms and three front windows. This he shared with his son and daughter-in-law (born in Longford), their six American children aged between 5 and 17, and a younger child born in Leitrim. Rather than being mere visitors, they were surely relatives who had returned to take over the farm. Michael Rooney (46), a printer born in Leitrim, had returned to a house in Kiltyclogher town, with only two windows but the benefit of an imperishable roof. He lived there with his wife (born in Tipperary), their six American children aged between 6 and 18, and two more recent offspring born in Leitrim. The eldest boys (already introduced) had found work as a shop assistant and a telegraph messenger. Patrick McCartin from Leitrim and his Kerry wife lived with their five

American-born children, aged between 8 and 21, on a farm in Drum-gownagh, Cattan. Like the Rooneys and the Conboys, the McCartins were squeezed into three rooms. Ellen McMorrow and her five Irish-speaking American children, aged from 6 to 15, enjoyed the luxury of four rooms but only two front windows in Shancarrick, Cloonlogher. Ellen's husband was absent.

Bernard Conboy was a farmer in Curraun, Mohill, living with his local wife and four American sons, aged between 7 and 17. Since both parents were 50 and had been married for only 6 years, it seems likely that the children were the product of a previous marriage. Joe Cullen (17) has already been introduced as a shop assistant, who lived with his three younger American siblings and parents in Knockmacrory, Roosky. Peter Farrelly, his wife, and their four American children aged between 1 and 8, lived on a farm in Corduff North, Corriga, in a substantial thatched house with six rooms and four front windows. The two boys could speak Irish, unlike their American sisters and Leitrim-born parents. The same applied to the Keaveny family of Sradine, Munakill, whose two youngest children had been born in Leitrim (the Americans were aged between 5 and 11). Peter McPartland and his wife occupied a smaller farmhouse in Faughary, Manorhamilton, with four American children aged between 3 and 9 and a local infant aged 4 months. All of these groups of four American-born children were living with two Leitrim-born parents, and none had been present in Leitrim in 1901.

The remaining American foursomes did not belong to 'conjugal family units', as this ideal form is termed by demographers. Rose Rafferty of Aughrim North, Killarga, was a Leitrim-born widow sharing two rooms with four Bostonian children, aged between 14 and 20. We may surmise that she had returned home after the death of her husband. Mary Kilbride, a married woman from America whose husband was absent, was living with her three American-born children, aged between 8 and 11, on her father-in-law's farm in Finisklin, Drumsna. Four Gordon children, aged between 7 and 11, were living with their Leitrim-born grandparents in the Barr of Farrow, Glenboy. Patrick Gaffney and his wife harboured four American grandchildren in Mullaghgarve, Aghacashel. The youngest, 1-year-old Annie Elizabeth Brady, had no parent present, but the three Heernan children were accompanied by their mother (their father was absent).

The smaller the group of 'multiple' Americans, the less likely it was to be headed by two co-resident parents. This applied to only three of the ten threesomes in Leitrim in 1911. The Dolans of Drumgownagh, Cloverhill, the Loobys of Kilnamarve, Killygar, and the McGoeys of Drummans, Rinn, all lived on farms with two parents from Leitrim (only the McGoeys had a child born in Leitrim in addition to their American broods). Anne Dolan, a widowed grocer, shared five rooms with an imperishable roof with her three children from New York (aged 7–12) in Corramartin, Greaghglass. In two cases, the mother of three American children had remarried a small farmer and settled in Leitrim. The Foleys shared three rooms on Michael Costello's farm in Gowel, but the Flynns from Montana and William Grier, their stepfather, shared only two rooms in Drumlowan, Breandrum. Martin Kelly (46) was a Catholic curate residing in Edenevilla, Gubacreeny, in a 1st-class house with no less than seven windows and six rooms. Instead of hiring a housekeeper, he lived with his 30-year-old widowed sister (born in Dublin) and her three young children, all born in Montana. Two groups of three American children, the Clancys of Dergvone, Killarga, and the Macavoys of Bellakiltyfea, Lisgillock, lived with a widowed grandparent (Edward Rooney and Ellen Canning, respectively). The Macavoys were accompanied by their widowed mother from Leitrim, but neither Clancy parent was present.

Only thirteen of the thirty-one American twosomes were living in households headed by a parent, including six where both parents were present, three headed by widowed mothers, two by mothers with absent husbands, one by a widowed father, and the last by a father who had remarried. Six were living with married grandparents, seven with widowed grandmothers, and three with uncles. Instead of itemising each family in detail, I shall confine myself to cases with unusual features. These include three sibling groups living autonomously: the Gallogly brothers (discussed above), the McCabes of Tullyskeherny, Manorhamilton, and the Short sisters of Lissagarvan, Lisgillock. William and Elizabeth McCabe from America shared their three rooms with an elder sister from Fermanagh. At 16, Cecelia Short was already a self-described farmer, whose household dominion consisted of 8-year-old May. But the girls had plenty of potential family support, as Lissagarvan had no less than five other Short households including Cecelia's two immediate neighbours.[6]

In addition to three cases already discussed (the McCabes, McWeeneys, and Reillys), eight American twosomes were co-resident with siblings born outside America, a strong indicator of long-term settlement. Those born locally were almost always younger, an exception being the Stanfords of Fearglass South, Beihy, who were living with their widowed grandmother. The Logan sisters lived in two rooms in Cornafostra, Fenagh, with their farmer father from Leitrim, mother from Cavan, and two younger siblings born in Glasgow and Leitrim. Another pair of Logan sisters in Tomloskan, Ballinamore, though the daughters of an agricultural labourer, shared four rooms with their parents and three younger siblings, all born in Leitrim. The Irish-speaking Dolans of Garvagh shared three rooms catering for a household of eleven, headed by their uncle farmer John Kelly and including their three younger locally born siblings. The McGartys of Drumgrania, Rinn, the McGuires of Carrickaport, Moher, and the Shanley sisters of Toomans, Gortnagullion, were all living with grandparents in the presence of one or two younger siblings. Though none of these families were enumerated in 1901, they too seemed likely to remain in Leitrim.

This survey of households containing several American-born children confirms the generosity of small farmers and even labourers in the rural recesses of Leitrim, who shared their cramped houses with children from America that could not be provided for in the United States. As shown in the preceding chapter, about half of all 'multiple' Americans were living in households headed by relatives other than a parent. We may surmise that those living with a parent were more likely to remain in Leitrim for the long term. Many individual case studies have revealed additional indicators of permanence (the presence of locally born siblings and continuity of residence from 1901 to 1911). By contrast, only one-fifth of 'solitary' American children without a co-resident American were living in parental households in 1911, suggesting that they were more likely to be short-term visitors being fostered by relatives. Let us explore a selection of particular cases.

IV   'Solitary' Americans

In 1911, 136 'solitary' Americans were enumerated in Leitrim households without any fellow-American for company. Eight of these were particularly strong candidates for classification as long-term settlers, being enumerated in both census years and having non-American siblings as well. Almost all were children of the householder and lived in 'standard' dwellings with three rooms and three front windows. No less than four of these eight 'Americans' were returned in 1901 as natives of Leitrim, yet the matches are otherwise indisputable. Whether this resulted from shame at having failed in the United States or simply carelessness cannot be determined.

Thomas Cullen (28) of Crumpaun, Agahalateeve, was a farmer whose Irish-speaking parents had been married for 39 years. Of their six children, only Thomas and a younger sibling born in Leitrim were alive in 1911. The remainder, two from America and two from Leitrim, were all living with Thomas in the household in 1901. The other seven Americans were solitary in both census years. Three households were headed in each year by both parents, all born in Leitrim. The American children of these farming couples were Irish-speaking Bernard O'Connor (21 in 1911) of Buggaun, Cloonlogher; Mary Anne Mahon (36) of Drumineigh, Kiltubbrid; and Francis Bernard Sweeney (14) of Killaneen, Ballinamore. Bernard O'Connor, plain Connor in 1901 when he and his family had yet to learn Irish, had two local siblings in 1901, one younger and one older, but the latter had left the household by 1911. Mahon also had one non-American sibling in 1911, but Sweeney had no fewer than five. The nine Sweeneys, including Francis's widowed, illiterate grandmother, shared the usual three rooms. Apart from the addition of two children, the household was unchanged since 1901.

Mark Gallagher (13) of Carrickeeny, Glenade and Thomas Holohan (17) of Fallacarra, Glenaniff, were both New Yorkers with a single local sibling in 1911. Gallagher was unusual in being the son of a labourer, whose abode had only two rooms; his sibling was 5 years younger and therefore unlisted in 1901. Though both were co-resident with their parents in 1901, the Gallaghers were visitors in the household of Bessie Rooney, a widowed farmer. Oddly, she returned Mark (then 3) as a girl, firmly inscribing 'F' rather than 'M', perhaps because he was in petticoats. In 1901, Thomas Holahan was living in the same townland with his Irish-speaking maternal grandfather along with his parents and three local siblings, two older and one younger than Thomas. We may infer that the farm passed to Thomas Holohan senior over the course of the decade.

In 1911, Anna Maria Quinn (15) from Providence, Rhode Island, was living with both parents and five younger siblings born in Leitrim on her father's farm in Drumshanbo South, Beihy. In 1901, however, she was the solitary American in the house of her widowed grandmother Anne Dunne (80), an illiterate farmer, along with an unhusbanded married aunt. This house was in the same townland and had the same features, suggesting another case of intercensal succession. The eighth and last American in this group was Rose M. Keany (13), who lived in both years with her mother and two local siblings in Brockagh Lower, Cloonclare. By 1911, her mother was widowed, as was the householder Mary Keany, Rose's grandmother. The four-roomed house also found space for a boarder from Sligo. The Keany family had been severely fractured since 1901, when Rose's father and grandfather were still living, though her father like so many others was elsewhere.

Fifteen solitary Americans who were present only in 1911 had Leitrimonian siblings, sometimes in clusters. In addition to Annie Scanlon, whose complex case was discussed in the preceding chapter, these included Kate Kelly (22) of Drumkeel, Belhavel; James Reynolds (9) of

Lisdromafarna, Drumsna; and Ellen Travers (16) of Killarga, Belhavel. Apart from Anne Reynolds, whose father was another absentee, they all lived on farms with both parents. Kate Kelly had five local siblings, the others three each. Six other American solitaries were living in parental households with a single local sibling. Anne Walsh (10) of Cornavan-noge, Munakill, was exceptional in being 8 years younger than her sibling; the family shared four rooms with an unmarried farmer uncle. William F. Mulligan (3) of Aghamore, Rooskey and John Joseph Creegan (6) of Cloone lived in unusually large houses of twelve and six rooms, respectively, with imperishable roofs (a public house in Creegan's case, though his father described himself as a farmer).

In five other cases, a solitary American with one local sibling was living with relatives. Rose A. Kane (4) of Drumkeelan, Leitrim division, was housed by her grandfather along with her mother, step-father, a younger step-sibling, and two cousins. John McWeeney (9) of Gortnagullion lived with his widowed grandmother along with his parents and a younger sibling born in Leitrim. Vincent Paul Smith (2) of Drumbreanlis, Gor-termone, and Maggie Ellen Stanford (13) of Conaghil, Drumahaire, came from particularly migratory families: Vincent had an elder sibling born in Cavan, and Maggie's younger sibling was a Scot. In the absence of their parents, Vincent was sheltered by his 90-year-old widowed grandfather, and Maggie by an illiterate unmarried aunt. Mary Ellen Cleary (11) of Derryduff, Tullaghan, and her older local sibling lived with another such aunt, an Irish-speaker.

Leitrim's seventy-nine American solitaries without any co-resident siblings in 1911 were mainly dependants of relatives in the absence of their parents. Apart from seven householders or wives and six children, there were twenty-eight grandchildren, twenty-five nieces or nephews, three unspecified relatives, three servants, and seven visitors, boarders, or lodgers. All eight American householders were married, including two farmers, two labourers, and the wives of a farmer, a shopkeeper, and a police constable. Two Episcopalian solitaries, Anna Jane Boles of Drum-keeran and Mary Kelly of Drumahaire, were introduced in section II. John Nolan (32), a labourer in Moher Smith, Roosky, lived alone with his childless wife from Roscommon, whereas John Cullen (42), a farmer in Loughmuirren, Belhavel, was well settled with a local wife and four children. John H. Thurrett (63) from Savannah, a farmer in Killarga, Belavel, had been married for 34 years but had no children or co-resident wife; his three rooms were shared with a nephew from Sligo and a widowed boarder occupied as a servant.

Four solitary American children without siblings were living with both parents on farms, while two adult solitaries were sheltered by fathers-in-law. Edward Murray (37) of Drumahaire, a baker, lived with his childless wife in the house of her father, an unemployed carpenter, and her mother from Sligo. Charles E. Benson (45) and his childless wife, both Irish-speakers, lived with her father or step-father John McManus in Cloonaghmore, Cloonclare.[7]

Four solitaries living with other relatives also had a co-resident parent, and merit further discussion. James McGuinness (10) of Boleyboy, Kiltyclogher, lived with his widowed father (a farmer) in the household of an illiterate widowed aunt and her widowed brother (indeed a much bereaved family). John Meehan (7) and his widowed mother lived in Gorteendarragh, Kinlough, with her father Terence McGowan, an Irish-speaking farmer, along with his wife and two other children. John Patrick Skea (7) of Druminargid, Ballaghameehan, and Mamie McGuire (18) of Boggaun, Greaghglass, each lived with both parents and both grandparents. The three solitary servants were the Episcopalian Francis Hassard (discussed in section II), Nellie Pollet (16) of Drumshanbo, and Peter McPartlan (22) of Corloughcahill, Drumkeeran. Nellie's employer was a merchant occupying a public house with thirteen rooms and nine front windows, whereas Peter served a farmer named Mary Rogan, whose husband of 42 years was absent from their standard three-roomed dwelling.

V   The Disappeared

So far, we have introduced numerous individual Americans who appear likely to have become long-term settlers, having spanned the intercensal decade or belonged to substantial sibling groups, often including younger brothers and sisters born in Leitrim. As shown in the preceding chapter (section V), three-quarters of the forty-four American households with co-resident parents in 1901 persisted up to 1911, usually with both parents still living at the same address. Yet we cannot ignore the presence in 1901 of potential 'settlers' who in fact disappeared from the county, and from Ireland, in the course of the next decade. In just over half of those thirty-one incontestably resettled families, no American offspring have been traced in 1901, whether as a result of further migration, the marriage of a daughter, or death.

Though most 'multiple' Americans were matched in 1911, eighteen others had disappeared, including seven from families with non-American siblings.[8] These included four American Mulveys (aged 2–9) in Liscallyroan, Drumsna, who lived with their grandparents along with their mother and a baby born in Leitrim (the father was absent). Neither parent remained in Ireland in 1911. Three Clarkes (aged 9–13) were living with their father, Cavan-born mother, and three local siblings in five rooms in Stranagarvanagh, Drumreilly East. Thomas Hamilton (12) and his brother Martin (10) had two younger siblings, their father being a local farmer married to an Irish-speaker from Sligo and living in Doorybrisk, Killanummery. Both the Clarkes and the Hamiltons remained on the same farms in 1911, but their American children had disappeared.

Seven other groups of multiple Americans living in the households of relatives also disappeared over the decade. The Irish-speaking Kelly sisters (aged 5 and 6) of the Barr of Farrow, Glenboy, and their mother were housed as 'visitors' by her parents in the father's absence. Neither mother nor children remained in Ireland in 1911. The three Winters of Cashel (aged 3–7) lived with a farmer uncle along with a lodger, an elderly widow. The O'Brien brothers of Kiltyclogher (aged 3 and 7) lived in a lodging house run by their Irish-speaking widowed aunt from Fermanagh. The Coyle brothers (aged 8 and 11) were looked after by a married uncle with two rooms in Lugmeeltan, Drumkeeran, while Ellen Ferguson (9) and her brother William (8) lived with a widowed aunt, a dealer in Hyde Street Mohill. Willie Lofein (10) and his sister Lizzie (8) were housed by Irish-speaking grandparents in Stranagarvanagh, Drum- reilly East. Finally, the McDonald sisters (aged 2 and 4) of Gourteena- guinn, Glencar, were looked after by an Irish-speaking great-uncle and his wife. None of these American twosomes remained in Ireland 10 years later.

Before leaving the Americans of Leitrim to disappear in peace, we must explore the larger group of thirty-nine 'solitary' Americans who were unmatched in 1911. Most of these were living with relatives or unrelated householders (sixteen were grandchildren, seven nieces or nephews, five visitors or boarders, along with a sister, cousin, and servant). Only four were in parental households, though four of those in grandparental households were accompanied by mothers in the absence of a father. There were also three Irish-speaking American-born house- holders worthy of mention. New Yorker William Grimes (45) of Carnoona, Aghanlish, was a widower with five local children. Patrick Concannon of Kinlough was a police constable, already introduced, with a wife and baby born in Westmeath. Susan McGinley (27) lived with her husband and five locally born children in Geaglom, Mahanagh.

Nine solitary American children (one aged 28) were living in 1901 with both parents and with younger local siblings, in groups ranging from two to nine. None of those nine Americans has been traced in Ireland in 1911. The complex case of Lizzie Mahon, whose sibling group of seven included older as well as younger siblings, was discussed in the preceding chapter. Thomas J. McGorty (14) lived in Larkfield, Cloonlogher, with his parents, nine younger siblings, and widowed maternal grandfather. Mary Treacy (8) lived with both parents in the grandparental household in Leamanish, Castlefore. With one exception, both parents remained at the same address in 1911 in the absence of their American offspring.[9] Their families had indeed resettled in Ireland, but the Americans had flown from the nest.

Finally, let us consider the seven cases of solitary Americans living with parents in 1901, in which neither the American nor the parent(s) could be traced in the next census. We have already introduced Harmon Cloak, whose disappearance is attributable to the death in 1910 of his father, the rector of Mohill. Paternal death may also explain the departure of the Californian John Paul Ward (16) of Cartronbeg, St Patrick's division, who shared two rooms with his 54-year-old widowed father in 1901. Mary Ellen Kerrigan (5) of Glebe Street, Mohill, was an only child sharing a ten-roomed public house with her 50-year-old father and much younger mother (an 'assistant' aged 30), and the disappearance of the Kerrigans may have resulted from business failure.

The other four cases all involved an American living with a married mother in the absence of the father, suggesting the possibility of temporary separation impelled by economic necessity. James Kerrigan (1) and his mother (a housekeeper) were mere 'visitors' on the farm of Locky Feely in Edenvella, Gubacreeny, in which the household of eleven shared the usual three rooms. The remainder were all living in grandparental households: Albert La Mothe (3) of Lissinagroagh, Drumkeeran; Mary Teresa Hartigan (2) of Derrinvoher, Munakill; and Mary McMahon (9) of Carrownoona, Aghanlish. Their Leitrim-born mothers were Bridget La Mothe (whose illiterate parents described her as a housekeeper); Catherine Hartigan (housekeeper to her widowed mother, an Irish-speaking Sligonian); and Fanny McMahon (a 'visitor' in the home of her illiterate widowed mother).

Such were the Americans to be found in Leitrim in the early twentieth century. Their profile and regional distribution were almost indistinguishable from those of the home population. They were seldom living embodiments of the benefits of emigration, being in many cases surplus children of the Irish-American urban poor who were looked after, for varying periods, by families belonging to the Irish rural poor.

Since many Leitrim Americans were short-term residents, census snapshots capture only a small proportion of those who visited Ireland from America in the early twentieth century (whether born in America or in Leitrim). The gap cannot be filled from passenger lists of transatlantic shipping, which typically provide scanty information on the origins of travellers from the British Isles and even less on the background of those leaving American ports. A less familiar source, explored in Chapters 8, 9, and 10, is the vast database of American passport applications relating to those born outside the United States who had subsequently become 'naturalised' American citizens. By analysing over five hundred such applications by natives of Leitrim, we may document an important group of emigrants who returned for short-term visits during the revolutionary period. To the extent that they had the means and leisure to contemplate a round trip across the Atlantic, they may be viewed as 'winners'.

8   Visitors from America, 1914–25: Profile

I   Sources

Before the First World War, American passports were not required for international travel and were usually procured only by travellers expecting to make use of diplomatic or consular services. Fears of infiltration led to tighter surveillance of inward passengers from 1914, and foreign-born American citizens proposing to travel overseas were strongly advised to procure short-term passports to ensure their readmission on return to the United States. Between 1918 and 1921, for the first time since the American civil war, passports for such travellers became mandatory.[1] In order to secure re-entry, applicants were required to renew the oath required for naturalisation as an American citizen:

> Further, I do solemnly swear that I will support and defend the Constitution of the United States against all enemies, foreign and domestic; that I will bear true faith and allegiance to the same; and that I take this obligation freely, without any mental reservation or purpose of evasion: So help me God.[2]

The wartime disruption of international shipping and trade, as well as administrative restrictions to exclude inessential travel by missionaries, students, and unaccredited journalists, severely restricted demand for passports. These were not required for military and naval personnel when the United States belatedly joined the conflict in 1917. The abolition of compulsion in 1921 had little practical impact, because passports had become indispensable for wartime and post-war travellers seeking admission to European countries.

The vast majority of digitally accessible passports were issued during the 6 years following the Armistice, coinciding with the restoration of peace in Europe and the intensification of political and military unrest in Ireland. Passport records therefore have little value in documenting reverse movement before 1914, and limited value even for the war years.[3] The passport dossier excludes two even more elusive strands of reverse migration: British subjects travelling home after brief or prolonged spells in the United States, and American citizens proposing to change their country of permanent residence. Nevertheless, passport applications illuminate the trajectories of thousands of emigrants who had left Europe in preceding decades, and who desired to inspect what remained of their homelands and families after the deluge. About 24,000 of these post-war visitors were natives of Ireland.[4]

The accessible records concern not only Irish-born citizens who had secured American naturalisation, but sometimes members of their families (often American-born). Many applications named accompanying wives or children. In addition, wives, widows, and children born outside the United States could claim passports if a husband or a father was an American citizen, whether by birth or naturalisation. Applicants had to declare their precise place of birth, as well as American address and occupation, previous passport applications and overseas visits, intended destination overseas, and in some cases details of marriage and children. From 1915, applicants had to supply two identical photographs and state their proposed date of travel and purpose in travelling abroad. After the war, naturalised applicants were further instructed to give their father's name, birthplace, and current residence, thus greatly facilitating census searches.[5] By combing the digital index for applicants born in Leitrim, almost five hundred applicants have been identified and matched, in the majority of cases, with Leitrim census returns. The twenty-five natives of Leitrim who applied before passports became commonplace in 1914 have been omitted from the statistical analysis that follows. They tended to be markedly older than later applicants, with only one woman.[6]

The analysis also excludes thirty-one applications made outside the United States, usually by visitors marooned in Ireland who now required a passport to return home. Demand was greatest during the First World War, when a dozen visitors headed for the United States, including four who had been returned to Ireland before the war. The overseas applicants differed somewhat in profile from applicants in America, with a higher median age of 38 and a larger female component (42%). Most applied at the Dublin consulate, but several cases were handled in Belfast and Londonderry. Apart from four Leitrim natives who were heading for destinations in Europe or Asia, all applicants were bound for the United States. The median interval between leaving the United States and seeking to return was 29 months, but eight applicants had been abroad for 5 years or more.[7]

The most lingering 'temporary' resident was Patrick Carroll (formerly a brewery labourer in Lowell, Massachusetts) who resided in Laureen, Gubacreeny, for 13 years from 1906 before applying to return aged 57. Next in line was Charles H. McGourty of Chicago, who spent 12 years 'looking after property' in Leitrim before returning to the United States in 1920 at the age of 70. Perhaps his return was spurred by loneliness: by 1911, he was already widowed and living alone in Drumristin, Drumreilly West. Thomas McGourty, who had left Pennsylvania in 1913 'on a visit to his mother' in Camderry, Cloonclare, returned 7 years later, aged 35, 'to resume my citizenship & to reside there permanently'.

The overseas applicants included three inveterate travellers. Francis Gaynor, whose complex migratory career is unravelled below, made four extended trips home before 1924, when he applied for a passport in the Belfast consulate with the intention of resuming permanent residency. Francis Gordon, who had been living with his children in Leitrim for 6 years before seeking to re-enter the United States in 1920, had already spent 18 months in the county during three previous visits since emigrating to the United States in 1895. James McGourty's multiple passports arose from his work as a wartime motor driver for the Transport Service and the Knights of Columbus (a Catholic fraternity founded in 1882 which organised war relief), and later for the American Graves Registration Service. McGourty was posted to France in 1918, 1919, 1920, 1921, and 1924 along with spells in the United States where two of his passports were procured. Having emigrated in 1886 at the age of 4, he had been naturalised 15 years later in Worcester, Massachusetts.

The migratory consequences of marriage and widowhood are illuminated by several overseas applications from women. Mary Catherine Little was the only Leitrim-born applicant to make her first visit to the United States by dint of her husband's American citizenship. John Little was a Detroit stonemason, naturalised less than a year earlier, who had left Ireland in 1911; she was an actress living in Dublin since 1916.[8] Nellie Seeley sought to return to the United States after 6 years in Drumkeerin, having travelled to Ireland in 1914 on account of her husband's 'business'. In 1907, Mary Ann McKiernan from Leganamer, Garadice, had married a Leitrim-born policeman in Providence, Rhode Island, but returned to her husband's native townland in 1913 because of 'sickness'. John evidently came out to collect her in 1920, as she applied for a passport to the United States in June 1920, 3 months after he had done likewise. Catherine Madden had spent 30 years in Minneapolis and Montana before being widowed in 1916. She spent the next 3 years in Leitrim, Sligo, and Cork, before returning to the United States with her daughter Julia in September 1919. Elizabeth Gilleese Smith, a widowed dressmaker, followed a similar trajectory between Providence and Derreen Lloyd, Gortnagullion, where she resided from July 1914 to June 1919 before returning to the United States.

Many American citizens born in Leitrim initially slipped through the digital net (almost half of all applicants indexed as Irish-born cannot be identified through county searches).[9] This is sometimes attributable to birthplace statements specifying only 'Ireland' or naming a town or parish without specifying the county, but more often to digital mis-transcriptions or original mis-spellings of the word 'Leitrim'. Through dreaming up and checking about 165 variant spellings, it proved possible to augment the initial 'Leitrim' database by almost two-fifths. The most prevalent mis-spellings (with eleven or more hits) were Letrim, Leitrem, Leitrin, Lutrim, Lertrim, and Leitrum; more bizarre renditions included Feitrin, Tetrim, Cohulim, Sedeior, Cooeitrim, Lubrino, and (my favourite) Latrine. A few other missing Leitrim applicants were recovered by searching for dozens of local place names, but other applicants have undoubtedly evaded detection. All told, we may conjecture that up to six hundred Leitrim natives sought passports in the United States between 1914 and 1925, equivalent to about 1% of the county's residual population. Despite its limitations, the American passport dossier is the most extensive and representative source for any historical study of Irish return migration.

II   Profile

The predominance of post-war applications is confirmed in Table 8.1, which shows that less than one-twelfth of all applications by natives of Leitrim between 1914 and 1925 were issued during the 5 years of war in Europe. Only 25 applicants from Leitrim have been identified for the preceding 120 years, during most of which few passports were issued and no statement of precise birthplace was required. A similar pattern applied to Irish applicants in general, with about 85 indexed applications per annum between 1861 and 1913, peaking at 148 in 1889.[10] Though gradually increasing over time, pre-war applications never approached the level recorded in Table 8.1, which rose to 6,345 in 1920. For Leitrim, as for Ireland, the peak year for applications was 1920, when passenger shipping resumed full operation. A second peak occurred in 1922, coinciding with partition and the creation of the twenty-six-county Irish Free State, visitors not being deterred by civil war and unrest in both jurisdictions.

Three-quarters of travellers applied during the traditional migration season from March to August, typically indicating their intention to embark within a week or so of securing a passport or by the first available ship. Applications peaked in April, which accounted for 15% of all applications, remaining at a similar level until July. The least favoured months were December and January.[11] This monthly calendar under-mines the otherwise alluring thesis that reverse movement was increas-ingly concentrated in the winter months when urban unemployment was most severe. It is worth noting that the seasonal concentration of reverse movement from the United States to the British Isles in 1913 was markedly *less* intense than that indicated by Leitrim passport applications.[12]

As Table 8.2 indicates, half of all applicants were resident in New York, with significant outflows (in descending order) from Massachu-setts, Connecticut, Illinois, New Jersey, Rhode Island, Pennsylvania, California, and Ohio. The north-eastern concentration reflected strik-ingly invariant Irish settlement patterns dating back to the Great Famine. Only about 19 of the New Yorkers lived outside the city, most being residents of Manhattan with substantial representation in Brooklyn (39) and the Bronx (11).[13] Virtually all applicants were living in cities or towns, as one would predict from the fabled preference of rural Irish emigrants for settlement in urban America. Outside New York City (with 216 resident applicants), the most prominent cities of residence were New Haven, Connecticut (24), Worcester (23) and Boston (22) in Massachusetts, Providence, Rhode Island (22), Chicago, Illinois (21), Philadelphia, Pennsylvania (11), Jersey City, New Jersey (6), and San Francisco, California (5).

Applicants spanned the full range of occupational categories with the exception of farming, which accounted for only six returners (see Table 8.3). About one-fifth of male applicants were unskilled labourers or servants, only slightly exceeding the numbers in transport, skilled work, or the retail and wholesale trade. Almost one-tenth were public servants, with smaller but notable contingents of clerical and professional personnel. Within these broad categories, there were marked concen-trations of machinists (25), building tradesmen (15), chauffeurs (14), waiters (13), salesmen and buyers (13), Catholic clergy (12), engineers (11), firemen (12), dealers in food and drink (11), and 9 foremen as well as 45 labourers. In addition to the 66 applicants identified as transport workers, some of the engineers and firemen may have worked on the railroad. Among the few gainfully occupied women (57), half were unskilled workers and servants. The most notable sub-categories were nurses (12), maids and domestics (9), housekeepers (7), and wait-resses (4). The broad occupational span of these Leitrim emigrants confirms how far Irish America had progressed from the impoverished and unskilled settlers or transients of the mid-nineteenth century.

Since applicants supplied dates of birth, emigration, and naturalisa-tion, one may reconstruct the major phases of migration for those who eventually made return visits. Table 8.4 reveals that the median age on arrival in the United States was 20 for men and 18 for women, reflecting the celebrated youthfulness of the post-Famine Irish 'exodus'. The inter-quartile range was only 5 years, signifying (for example) that half of all female applicants had emigrated between the ages of 15 and 20.[14] For those who had secured American citizenship, the median interval between reaching the United States and undergoing naturalisation was 7 years. Though the typical interval between naturalisation and application was 4 years, this period varied widely with an inter-quartile range of 16 years.[15] Female applicants tended to be slightly younger, the median age for women being 35 compared with 37 for men. In short, those proposing to return across the Atlantic were mostly mature and well-established citizens, who had seldom sought naturalisation simply to prepare for a home visit.

Passport applications offer tantalising glimpses into family circumstances, through information about the birthplaces of accompanying wives and children, and in many cases of husbands or fathers (see Table 8.5). All but 6 of the 46 accompanying wives were Irish-born, including 9 from Leitrim and 10 from other specified counties (Belfast, Clare, Galway, Kerry, Longford, Mayo, Sligo, Westmeath, and Roscommon *bis*). The 'exogenous' wives were two Scots, a German, and three natives of the United States. Apart from one Leitrimonian, all accompanying children with specified birthplace were American-born. One hundred and forty children were named on applications, with as many as six travelling together, though most applicants proposed bringing only one child.[16] Husbands were specified only by women seeking passports on the basis of marriage to an American citizen. Two-fifths were Irish-born, including 5 husbands explicitly from Leitrim and 9 from other counties (Fermanagh, Kilkenny, Limerick, Londonderry, Longford, Mayo, Roscommon, Tipperary, and Tyrone). In addition to 28 American-born husbands, women from Leitrim had married 5 Englishmen, a Scot, a Dane, a Swede, a German, and an Italian. The most predictable findings relate to fathers, whose birthplace was routinely recorded from 1921. Apart from an Englishman and an American, all fathers were natives of Ireland, Leitrim being the only county specifically named apart from a single scion of Fermanagh.[17]

Applicants were required to provide details of their intended 'country' of destination (such as Ireland, Britain, or the 'British Isles'). As Table 8.6 shows, the vast majority of Leitrimonians were bound for Ireland, sometimes in combination with Britain or Europe. Ireland was given as a destination in 88% of all applications, and may also have been visited by those who merely specified the British Isles or Britain.

One-tenth of voyagers were bound for more exotic parts, mainly in Europe and usually in combination with Ireland. Many of the 43 European travellers intended to visit several countries, including France (42), Italy (11), Belgium (7), Switzerland (7), Germany (6), Denmark, Holland, and Sweden (3 each), and Norway (2). Other applicants proposed a 'Pleasure trip' to Argentina, Chile, and Brazil; two journeys to Cuba; a trip to Ireland via Canada and England; visits to a sister in Australia and a brother in New Zealand; and travel for an engineering project in China via Japan and Hong Kong. Just 12 applications omitted all reference to visiting either Ireland or Britain. While only a few exceeded official requirements by specifying any county destination, we may infer that almost all Leitrim applicants were homeward bound.[18]

By the early twentieth century, it was becoming quite common for emigrants from Ireland and Europe not merely to revisit their homelands but to make repeated return trips across the Atlantic. At least 24 post-1914 applicants went on to apply for another passport before 1925, but many others had previous experience of 'circular' migration. Since applicants were required to declare any previous passports and to specify any overseas visits since naturalisation, we can test the novelty of return visits for those who had emigrated from Leitrim.[19] Previous overseas visits were mentioned by 80 applicants, 35 of whom had previously travelled overseas (mainly to wartime France) as soldiers or sailors not subject to civilian passport protocols. Of the remainder, 34 had headed for Ireland and 6 for the 'British Isles' or Britain.[20] Many others would have made earlier unlisted visits, during the period between emigration and naturalisation (typically about 7 years) when they remained British subjects and 'aliens' in the United States.

The full complexity of migration can be revealed only through reconstruction of individual trajectories. An intricate example is discussed in Dunnigan's study of return migration to Connaught. Patrick McEnroy of Kilroosk and his wife Alice Gilligan of Rossinver reportedly made 'a total of ten trips': sometimes together, sometimes individually, and sometimes with children (one born in Leitrim and another in New York).[21] Of these trips, three are documented in their separate passport applications. According to his 12-month passport application in 1920, McEnroy's object was 'To visit my wife and children who are ill at present and to join wife and family' (Patrick McEnroy, restaurant waiter, born 1873, emigrated 1897). He had never previously applied for a passport, but stated that he had visited Ireland between June 1913 and April 1914. His wife Alice, accompanied by a son born in Leitrim in 1912, had applied in 1916 to visit Ireland and Britain for 6 months, 'for my minor son who is on visit there with my mother' (Alice McEnroy, born 1886, emigrated

1908). Patrick McEnroy and Alice's brother Michael gave the same address in New York and planned to travel together on the *Celtic* in 1920 (Michael Gilligan, oiler and ex-serviceman, born 1894, emigrated 1913, 12-month passport issued 1920).

All told, fourteen passport applicants had made at least two previous overseas trips. Before setting out to visit a brother and 'dispose of property' in 1921, Patrick Carroll (labourer) had spent 3 months in Ireland in 1895 and lived there for 13 years before returning to the United States in October 1919. Patrick Rinn (innkeeper) visited Ireland in 1904 and 1906, returning in 1923 for family and business reasons. Francis Gaynor (iron worker) visited Ireland in 1901–3 and 1910–11, and was enumerated on his father's farm in both 1901 and 1911. Listed in the Irish census as an 'iron moulder' in 1901, he had reverted by 1911 to the lowly status of a 43-year-old 'farmer's son'. He returned to Leitrim in 1919 to arrange 'sale of Real Estate belonging to me'. He again sought a passport in 1921, proposing to 'resume residence indefinitely, to care for my aged father 86 and to look after' property for his mother. Presumably after his father's death, he applied for a passport in Belfast, in order 'to take up permanent residence' in the United States.

Thomas Beirne (stationary engineer) made for Leitrim in 1909, 1914, and 1919. Michael Joseph O'Connor, whose unique declaration of a political motive is discussed in the next chapter, had twice visited Ireland in 1914 and 1915 before his trip to Ireland and France in 1921–2. Michael McMorrow (labourer) sailed for the British Isles in 1911 and Italy in 1916–17, before visiting a sick brother in Ireland in 1921. John Thomas Coulter (shipping clerk) travelled to Fermanagh (1912–17) and Belfast (later in 1917), returning in 1919 to 'leave my wife in Ireland as she is seriously ill'. Thomas Kelly (waiter) visited Ireland in 1903, 1921–3, and again later in 1923 'to settle estate'.

Several inveterate travellers owed their knowledge of the world to service in the forces, usually but not always during the First World War. Edward Donnelly (soldier) had served in Cuba (1898–1902) and the Philippines (1903–8) before visiting his mother in 1922. James McGuire (railway guard and evidently ex-soldier), who returned home in 1921 for the same reason, had spent 18 months in Cuba in 1902–3 and 6 years in the Panama Canal Zone between 1914 and 1920. Peter McPartland was unoccupied when he returned to Ireland in 1920 to visit a sister and enjoy a 'change of climate', having previously spent 6 months back in Ireland between March and October 1914 before serving with the American Expeditionary Force in France. James Carrigan cited 'health' and 'relatives' when applying for a passport in 1920; he had made four trips to France with the naval service between May

1918 and August 1919. Joseph O'Hanlon (machinist), who had travelled with the coastwise sea service following wartime military service, also set out in 1920 to visit his parents in Ireland.

Taking subsequent applications into account, the list of serial returners is completed by Winifred Schumacher (*née* Maguin, wife of a decorator), who visited England and France in 1911, the British Isles and France in 1920 ('to visit relatives'), Ireland and Switzerland in 1921, and France, England, Ireland, Italy, Belgium, and Germany in 1922 (for 'Travel & Study'). Of all Leitrim applicants, Mrs Schumacher (born in 1885) most closely resembled the modern globe-trotter.[22]

III   Physical Characteristics

By 1914, as an essential proof of identity, passports had to carry enough descriptive and visual information to allow the bearer to be matched against the document. Applicants were therefore required to state their stature and provide pithy descriptions of their forehead, eyes, nose, mouth, chin, hair, complexion, face, and 'distinguishing marks' such as scars. Winifred Schumacher, for example, was 5 ft. 5 in. tall, with grey eyes, brown hair, fair complexion, a 'retroussé' nose, and a tattoo spelling out 'Irlandise'. Such self-descriptions were admittedly subjective and might be unduly flattering to the applicant, a flaw that also applies to most modern census and survey data without invalidating self-descriptions as a factual source. Some fancied their noses to be 'Roman', 'aquiline', or 'retroussé'; yet others admitted to noses that were 'short and thick' or 'small and puggy', and even to a chin that was 'round-double'. Unlike the particulars of birth or naturalisation, these descriptions were not made under oath; but they were subject to verification and amendment before submission, encouraged by comparing the applicant sitting in the office with the accompanying photograph.

Table 8.7 helps us to visualise these Americanised home-comers, offering hints about the physical impact of Americanisation and inviting certain comparisons with the home stock. The majority of applicants, particularly men, believed that their eyes were blue or bluish, the residue being evenly divided between grey and various shades of brown. The predominance of blue eyes in twentieth-century Leitrim (and Ireland) was documented in the mid-1930s by the celebrated Harvard survey of Irish physical anthropology, which entailed elaborate examination and measurement of almost 9,000 men and 1,900 women.[23] Having initially excluded the latter, the survey was belatedly extended to provide a role for the fiancée of the main male field worker (C. Wesley Dupertuis), but Helen Dawson's uncompleted survey adopted different procedures, often more rigorous, and was abandoned when funds ran out. The Harvard study indicated that 54% of sampled Leitrim women had blue, grey-blue, or blue-brown eyes, the same proportion as for home-comers.[24] A much higher bluish proportion was recorded for males, reflecting a different system for classifying male eye colour (blue-brown was identified as the dominant Irish hue).[25]

The male investigators were sorely disappointed to find 'very few brown eyes' in Leitrim, where 'special efforts were made to visit the more inaccessible localities in the hope of finding at least a few of these brown-eyed people', since, 'according to legend, Leitrim is the original home and the present resting place of the descendants of the Firbolgs. These people are described as being swarthy-skinned and dark eyed, entirely different from other Irishmen.'[26] Dupertuis would have been delighted to know that thirty-four Leitrim passport applicants combined brown eyes with dark or ruddy complexions, though their Firbolg pedigree remains conjectural.[27]

Hair colour is obviously more correctable than that of eyes, though the day had yet to come when the women of Ireland would mysteriously become blonde while male offspring of the same gene-pool remained dark. Table 8.7 shows that two-thirds of applicants of each sex had brown or dark hair, but women were slightly more likely to display light hair with not a single recorded red-head. These calculations exclude a substantial minority of applicants, mainly male, who were bald, grey, or white. The predominant dark-haired category embraces a rich variety of descriptions such as auburn, bronze, brunette, and chestnut which reveal more about self-perception than about pigment. Once again, the home-comers resembled the home stock in the 1930s, of which about three-quarters had brown or dark brown hair.[28]

Complexion is an attribute highly sensitive to environmental influences, ranging from sunburn to alcohol. Table 8.7 shows a notable contrast between women (overwhelmingly 'fair' or 'clear') and men (of whom over one-third reported dark complexions using epithets such as 'red', 'ruddy', and 'florid').[29] Particularly for women, the prevalence of swarthiness increased with age, mainly at the expense of 'fair' complexions. A case on the cusp was Hannah Tallent, a 58-year-old widow from Glenfarne via Manhattan, embarking on a 'pleasure' trip to Ireland, Italy, and Switzerland, who described her complexion as 'fair & fresh pink'. The trend for male applicants was less clear, with peak incidence of darker complexions among those in their late thirties as well as early fifties. One can only speculate on the relative importance of outdoor exposure and alcohol in promoting swarthiness among older men: sunburn may have been predominant for those in mid-career, drink for men in their fifties as they confronted retirement.

High colour was an issue of great interest to the Harvard investigators, who noted that 'pronounced vascularity' in women diminished sharply with age, whereas in men it tended to increase.[30] The anomalous age trend for women was perhaps attributable to diminishing exposure to wind and even sun in rural Ireland, as women grew older and withdrew from outdoor work. Table 8.8 depicts the relationship between age and vascularity as revealed in passport applications and as reported by the Harvard investigators. Male applicants were three times as likely as women to display ruddiness or other varieties of swarthiness, just as Irishmen in the 1930s were more likely to be vascular than women of the same age group (with the exception of those aged 15–19, unrepresented among passport applicants). Differences between the American and Irish environments may account in part for the incongruity between the distributions of vascularity by age, as documented for applicants and for the Irish at home.

One of the most familiar tools of 'cliometrics' is the measurement of human height, conventionally but sometimes inconsistently adopted as a proxy for levels of income, nutrition, healthiness, and even well-being. Various 'auxanological' studies of nineteenth-century Irish samples of groups such as prisoners and soldiers have indicated that the Irish, despite relatively low earnings and high incidence of poverty, tended to be taller than their English contemporaries, suggesting that the nutritional advantages of potatoes and buttermilk outweighed deficiencies of income or housing.[31] On the other hand, long-run comparisons of disparate data suggest that in Ireland, as in many European countries, mean height has fairly steadily increased since the nineteenth century in response to increasing income and improved living conditions.[32] The returns of height by passport applicants add significantly to the available record, even without extending this study to a comparison between different immigrant ethnicities in the United States. Along with the Harvard dossier, they also enable us to compare the heights of (returning) emigrants and the home population in order to test the hypothesis that emigrants were a superior sub-set of the home stock.

The median height of male applicants was just over 68 in. (5 ft. 8 in.), with only half of the group standing outside the range from 67 in. to 70 in. The full range was 59 in. to 75 in., with twenty-five self-declared 6-footers. For women, the median height was 65 in., half of the group standing between 64 in. and 66 in. Apart from one tiny applicant (50 in.), the shortest woman was 60 in. and the tallest 71 in. These figures do not suggest a population radically different in stature from that of today, or at least of yesterday. Table 8.9 indicates that home-comers of all age groups and both sexes were actually taller than their Irish home counterparts in the 1930s. Only about 1 in. in the case of men, the advantage for female applicants was about 2.5 in., a startling disparity.[33] These differences cannot be attributed to the existence of an unusually tall stock in the Leitrim region (the men were slightly below the mean Irish height in the 1930s, and women were less than an inch taller on average than all 'West Coast' females).[34]

It is conceivable that the relative tallness of the home-comers was in part a product of imagination, due to inflated claims or beliefs about their stature by some applicants. But the anomaly may also reflect selective migration, whereby fitter or stronger people were more likely to venture forth. It must be admitted, however, that no convincing case for selective migration from post-Famine Ireland has yet been presented on the basis of socio-economic evidence, despite persistent assertions that the poorest people from the poorest regions were disinclined to emigrate. As shown below, Leitrim's home-comers were strikingly representative, in their local origins, occupational background, and housing, of the population of origin. This suggests not merely that emigrants were a cross-section of Leitrim society, but also that those who had the means and desire to revisit Ireland were a cross-section of the emigrants. This inference does not, of course, preclude the possibility that, within families, those selected for emigration were the 'fittest' and most robust physical specimens.

The most telling implication of these returns of stature is that height was strikingly invariant when cross-tabulated with other characteristics of applicants. Single women from Leitrim were marginally above average height, refuting the idle speculation that height was an asset in securing a husband in the United States.[35] Further analysis is possible for nearly 300 applicants whose precise place of origin can be established from census matches.[36] The height of applicants from 'congested' electoral divisions, signifying rural poverty, was if anything greater than that recorded for less impoverished districts.[37] Nor was there any height advantage for those coming from South Leitrim, which by several indicators was rather less 'backward' than the rest of the county.[38] Whatever factors tended to stunt or elongate returning emigrants, they seem to have been impervious to regional and socio-economic distinctions within Leitrim.

The mean height of passport applicants may also be compared with later surveys, to test the claim that male height in Ireland has advanced steadily and without interruption over the last century or so.[39] The Harvard comparison challenges this Whiggishly jaunty hypothesis, since the applicants, though taller, were typically born two decades earlier than those examined in 1934–6.[40] Nor is there any firm evidence *within* the two groups that older cohorts tended to be shorter. The age breakdown in Table 8.9 shows that applicants of both sexes who were less than 35 had no height advantage over those in middle age, though the small minorities of applicants over 55 were a trifle shorter. The same pattern applies to those examined in Ireland in 1934–6. As Hooton and Dupertuis observed, 'Probably the stature decline is not too great to be attributed to old age shrinkage and bent posture.'[41]

In the absence of modern data based on direct measurement of Irish heights, auxanologists have relied on the results of a survey questionnaire conducted in 1994–2001 and yielding comparable information for ten European countries. This indicated a mean self-reported height for Irishmen of just over 69 in., about 0.5 in. taller than that of passport applicants (68.6 in.). Though the survey suggested that older respondents were slightly shorter, this may once again have been the effect of shrinkage associated with age rather than progressive heightening of the stock.[42] In the case of women, the mean height of those surveyed (unadjusted for self-inflation) was about 64.5 in., marginally *less* than that of Leitrim passport applicants three-quarters of a century earlier (64.8 in.).[43] It is salutary to compare these findings with a recent survey involving actual measurement of large samples of 'non-Hispanic white' men and women in the United States.[44] This survey yielded median heights of 69.6 in. for men and 64.1 in. for women, very close to the self-reported figures for modern Ireland.[45] Once again, the Leitrim women who applied for American passports were on average slightly taller than American women today. The explanation remains elusive, unless it was the case that Americanised Irish ladies visualised and measured themselves complete with heels.

The fact that every applicant after 1914 had to supply two identical photographs enables us to explore other aspects of the applicants' appearance and demeanour. Analysis is severely restricted by the often poor quality of the available microfilmed images, and the absence of complementary shots in profile to match the superb Leitrim portraits assembled by the Harvard ethnographers. It would be foolhardy on the basis of these photographs to calculate the applicants' cephalic index or 'morphological type' (the euphemism chosen by Hooton and Dupertuis to objectify their failed attempt to establish the enduring prevalence of the 'Keltic' race in the Irish population).[46]

However, as shown in Table 8.7, the photographs convey some significant cultural markers. No less than 96% of male applicants, many of them labourers or porters, presented themselves before the camera in collar and tie. Most appear to have chosen plain dark ties, but the dossier includes at least thirty-one lighter versions, along with fifteen patterned ties and ten with perceptible stripes. Bow ties and stiff collars were worn by eleven applicants apiece, not to mention ten clerical collars. Almost one-sixth of women had hats, seldom donned by men apart from the odd bowler or boater, and women were more likely to wear spectacles. Female hats, occasionally over the top with broad brims or floral decorations, peaked in popularity in 1921 (31%), having been virtually absent in the years of austerity before 1920. Hat-wearing declined steadily and sharply thereafter, characterising only one-tenth of applicants by 1924. The main female accoutrements were necklaces and pendants, visible in over one-quarter of female photographs. Like hats, necklaces were seldom worn during or just after the war, adorning only about one-quarter of female applicants in 1920–2. Unlike hats, the popularity of necklaces rose sharply in 1923–4, being sported by about two-fifths of Leitrim home-comers. These fluctuations, perhaps reflecting broader changes in female fashion, are summarised in Table 8.10.

The only common facial embellishment was a moustache, displayed by over one-fifth of male applicants, with only a handful of beards or whiskers.[47] Apart from the occasional Walrus moustache, most moustaches were discreet and neatly trimmed. Some examples of various styles are depicted in Chapter 10 (Figure 9). Moustaches were most common during the war (44%), and least popular in its immediate aftermath in 1919–20 (15%). The wearing of moustaches recovered thereafter, exceeding one-quarter in 1921 and 1924.

To what extent did such fluctuations reflect broader fashions and cultural practices? The moustache, with its connotations of virility and ferocity, had long been mandatory for British army officers, despite growing concern about hygiene and embarrassment for those with recalcitrant follicles on the upper lip. In March 1916, the *New York Herald*'s special correspondent in France and Flanders noted that 'giddy "Charlie Chaplins"' were in fashion among 'lion-hearted' young officers recently plucked from office jobs: 'I used to laugh at the Charlie Chaplin moustache. I now look upon it as the red, brown, black, or blonde badge of courage.'[48] King George V had a particular aversion to the popular Chaplin style, which was expressly forbidden in October 1916 even when the Army Council ruled that all ranks should be free 'to grow or not to grow, moustaches according to their fancy'.[49]

The results of 'the new moustache order' were keenly awaited in Ireland, leading the drama critic and columnist J. H. Cox to ruminate on the pre-war anti-moustache movement and consequent 'epidemic of shaving'. Cox maintained 'that women did not become assertive till men became clean-shaven. The moustache and the eyebrows are the great belligerent adornments that Nature has given to man. He has foolishly thrown one of them away.'[50] In future columns, Cox confirmed the revulsion against moustaches after the Armistice. In May 1919, he pronounced that 'the rationed war-time moustache is disappearing. Demobilised officers are whipping it and the khaki off together. The American warriors never accepted it. And their decision rules.' Three years later, shortly before the outbreak of civil war, he lamented that 'Irish Army officers apparently have self-determination as regards the moustache', a decision that would 'make it hard to make anything of him – on the stage'. Dublin's office workers were also affected: 'Last evening it was asserted that the City never had fewer men with moustaches. The hairless lip, whose reign seemed threatened five years ago, has more than recovered its sway.'[51]

Yet the positive military connotations of the moustache remained strong, as indicated by an advertisement in the *Irish Times* in early 1924: 'WANTED, as Servant to gentleman, resident Continent, single Man, aged 40 to 50, strong, of military appearance, moustache; send photo; return guaranteed.'[52] It is also noteworthy that leading revolutionaries such as Michael Collins and Ernest Blythe experimented with moustaches, and that over one-quarter of members of the first Dáil Éireann captured in group photographs had moustaches or beards.[53] Shaving remained sporadic in rural Ireland a decade later, as reflected in the photographic dossier compiled by the Harvard ethnographers. Among eight Leitrim specimens of various morphological types, three had moustaches and one had a scruffy full beard (see Chapter 10, Figures 14–16).

In this fairly hirsute environment, the appearance in Leitrim of seventy-three moustached visitors from America would not have seemed abnormal or exotic, despite the reported trend towards shaving in post-war Ireland as well as Britain. Rather than representing the latest in American fashion, the popularity of moustaches among passport applicants may suggest that Irish Americans were resistant to contemporary practice in their adopted country. It has been claimed that the pre-war 'trend toward shaving indicated a decided shift in European and American manliness towards sociability' and 'idealization of youthful energy', as a modern alternative to belligerence. In the United States, this shift was facilitated by the absence of any recent military tradition equating the moustache with virility.[54] Most of the American servicemen who swarmed over Europe and Ireland in 1917–18 were clean-shaven, making them seem doubly exotic. By not conforming to the predominant type of clean-cut and clean-shaven American masculinity, those who visited their homeland with moustaches involuntarily conveyed that they were not yet fully Americanised. This applies most strongly to wartime passport applicants, of whom two-fifths had grown moustaches in defiance of contemporary American military practice.

Nuances of sartorial style and facial expression are best grasped by perusing the photographic montage in Chapter 10. In general, this evokes a solemn procession of respectable citizens in their Sunday best, set apart from their work attire and often rough way of life in both countries. The arrangement and demeanour of family groups is particularly eloquent, especially when restive children or uneasy couples threatened to fracture the impression of contented domesticity that every photographer strove to capture.

IV   Origins

The information recorded by applicants is in itself too restricted to generate a full profile of Leitrimonians who returned home after emigrating to the United States. However, it has been possible to link many applicants with census returns for 1901 (and 1911) in order to document their domestic origins in Leitrim. All but two applicants were born before 1901, and almost two-thirds emigrated after that year. All told, it has been possible to match 214 visitors (45% of all applicants) with census returns (mainly for 1901), and to identify a further 64 census schedules for families from which the applicant was absent.[55] The profile of matched applicants is summarised in Table 8.11. Of those at home on census night, virtually all were Catholics, 92% were literate, only one could speak Irish, four-fifths were occupied (if at all) in farming, and the median age was 12 years. The profile of their parents, including cases where the applicant had already left home, is even more revealing. About one-sixth of both fathers and mothers were unable to read and write, and about one-tenth could speak Irish (fathers more often than mothers). Almost nine-tenths of occupied parents were in farming, with very few labourers or servants. The median age of fathers in 1901 was 51, that of mothers being 45.

These findings invite comparison with our profiles of Leitrim Americans in 1901 and 1911 (see Table 8.12). This indicates that Leitrim-born applicants were rather more likely than American-born residents to be Catholics and literate, and much more likely to be occupied in farming (the median age for all three groups was 10–12 years). The fathers and mothers of applicants also differed little from those of the American-born, apart from higher proportions born in Leitrim and employed in farming rather than farm service. Table 8.13 indicates that the families in which passport applicants had been reared were more likely than American-born residents to live in 'standard dwellings'; were less often found in 1st-class accommodation; and still more likely to have been brought up under thatch, and sometimes even within mud walls. In all three groups, just under half were in 'congested' electoral divisions, but applicants were slightly more likely than American-born residents to come from South Leitrim.

The northern region, which accounted for 40% of Leitrim's population, produced only 35% of passport applicants. This relative concentration of applicants in the south may reflect a gradual northward shift in the regional origins of emigrants, as applicants had typically emigrated a decade or so earlier than the parents of Leitrim's American-born residents recorded in the pre-war census.[56] The applicants were fairly evenly distributed across the five rural districts, whereas the American-born in 1901 were heavily over-represented in the district of Carrick-on-Shannon.[57] The contrasting distributions of the American-born and the former homes of passport applicants are minutely depicted in Maps 6.3 and 6.5, indicating the number recorded in each of Leitrim's seventy-eight electoral divisions.

Apart from these subtle differences in profile, it is clear that the mature emigrants who visited home after the First World War came from the same stock as the American-born children anatomised in the preceding chapter. The visitors were broadly representative of what used to be termed the 'peasantry', with no clear evidence that they tended to come from backgrounds that were either unusually poor or unusually rich. Like emigration itself, its reverse ripples touched all social strata in rural Ireland. Some of the homes in which visitors were reared would have been extended or modernised over the two decades since 1901, but few improvements were recorded in the returns for 1911. The great majority of visitors' family homes had the same number of windows and rooms in both years, and changes in house class and building materials were rare. Allowing for cases where housing reportedly deteriorated over the intercensal decade, only about one-tenth of the housing stock displayed net improvement as indicated by the number of windows and rooms, or by house 'class'. Improvement in the quality of walls or roofs was even less common.[58] The urbanised clerks and engineers and priests and nurses who visited Ireland after the First World War would for the most part have stayed in the unpretentious, austerely furnished dwellings of their parents or siblings, still mainly thatched with three rooms to accommodate the median family of six resident members.[59] Such was the dimly lit theatre in which the dialogue between visitors and 'the old folk' was played out.

V   Typicality

How typical of Irish-born passport applicants were those who had originated in Leitrim? The digital index of applications provides a rough but
ready measure of the county origins of Irish passport applicants
(1914–25), indicating a pronounced excess of visitors born in western
counties, when compared with the population in 1911.[60] Ulster (1.6 per
thousand) and Leinster (3.1) provided very few visitors by comparison
with Munster (6.4) and Connaught (7.9). Leitrim (6.7) ranked eighth
among the thirty-two counties of Ireland, falling somewhat short of the
rest of Connaught as well as Cavan, Longford, and Kerry.[61] Even more
conspicuous as a supplier of emigrants after the 1870s and as a place of
residence for the American-born by 1911, Leitrim had clearly also
become a powerful magnet for American visitors.

   Though not fully compatible with my database, and restricted to the
period up to 1920, Dunnigan's pioneering study of Connaught broadly
accords with many of the findings presented in this chapter. Of just over
100 Leitrim-born applicants identified by Dunnigan, 28% were women
(as in my own database), compared with 30% for Connaught. Dunnigan
likewise reports the predominance of New York as the state of residence,
accounting for 38% of Connaught applicants (as against 49% in my
study). Her histograms imply that the median age of 1,215 Connaught
applicants was 35, while the median interval between emigration and first
passport application was 13 years (compared with 36 and 15 years,
respectively, for my Leitrim).[62] In both studies, the median duration of
passports was 6 months.[63] We may infer that applicants from
Leitrim were broadly representative of the surrounding province and,
by extension, of 'backward' rural Ireland in general.

Table 8.1 *Number of US passport applications by birthplace, 1914–25*

Source	Leitrim (Database)	Leitrim (Index)	All Counties (Index)	Ireland (Index)
Year of Issue				
1914	4	4	147	287
1915	10	10	396	724
1916	15	21	659	1,112
1917	5	7	312	494
1918	3	4	327	577
1919	63	58	2,016	3,685
1920	110	100	3,464	6,345
1921	58	51	1,780	3,351
1922	83	59	3,356	5,671
1923	57	47	2,000	3,923
1924	63	57	2,688	5,295
1925	6	5	342	705
Total	*477*	*423*	*17,487*	*32,169*
% 1914–18	7.8	10.9	10.5	9.9

Note: A digital index covering almost all US passport applications and associated documents (1795–1925) was used to generate initial estimates of the number of applicants whose birthplace was coded as 'Leitrim' or 'Ireland', classified by year of issue. After examination of the application forms for all those ascribed to Leitrim, a reduced database was compiled excluding pre-1914 US applicants (25); applications lodged outside the USA (32); cases in which matching Irish census returns indicate that the applicant was not in fact born in Leitrim (8); applicants in all categories who had previously been issued with a passport (28); and various duplicated, mis-dated, or mis-located entries. Many Leitrim-born applicants were initially missed because of coding errors in assigning place names to counties; but over 150 additional applications were identified by searching for hundreds of aberrant spellings, and for prominent local place names indexed only under 'Ireland'. The database includes naturalised American citizens, and Leitrim-born wives, widows, or children who sought passports on the basis of the American citizenship (whether held through birth or naturalisation) of a husband or father. Ten Leitrim-born accompanying wives and children are not separately enumerated. The columns show the numbers for Leitrim in the database and as indexed, followed by the sum of the numbers assigned in the index to each Irish county and to 'Ireland' (including numerous applications not assigned to individual counties). The index figures are those last updated in February 2017, inflated by categories excluded from my analysis. The index and application forms are accessible at ancestry.co.uk.

Table 8.2 *State of residence of Leitrim passport applicants, 1914–25*

Residence	Number	%
State		
New York	235	49.3
Massachusetts	80	16.8
Connecticut	30	6.3
Illinois	25	5.2
New Jersey	19	4.0
Rhode Island	23	4.8
Pennsylvania	17	3.6
California	9	1.9
Ohio	8	1.7
Missouri	6	1.3
Oregon	4	0.8
Minnesota	3	0.6
Montana	2	0.4
Colorado	2	0.4
Michigan	2	0.4
Texas	2	0.4
Other	10	2.1
Total USA	*477*	*100*

Note: Alaska, Arizona, District of Columbia, Iowa, Maine, Maryland, Nevada, New Hampshire, South Dakota, and Tennessee each supplied one applicant.

Table 8.3 *Occupations of Leitrim passport applicants by sex, 1914–25*

Sex	Male	%	Female	%
Category				
Professional	26	7.8		
Public Service	30	9.0		
Clerical	21	6.3	2	3.5
Trading, Shop-keeping	57	17.1	4	7.0
Transport	66	19.8		
Skilled	56	16.8	23	40.4
Unskilled Labour, Service	71	21.3	28	49.1
Farming	6	1.8		
Total Gainfully Occupied	*333*	*100*	*57*	*100*
Home Duties			70	
None, Unknown	11		6	
Total Applicants	*344*		*133*	

Note: Occupational categories are imprecise because of ambiguous self-descriptions (thus 'firemen' are classified under public service and 'engineers (stationery [*sic*])' as professional, though some in both groups may have been transport workers.

Table 8.4 *Career chronology of Leitrim passport applicants, 1914–25*

From	To	Lowest	Quartile	Median	Quartile	Highest	n
Interval (Full Years)							
Emigration	Naturalisation	2	5	7	11	39	381
Naturalisation	Passport Issue	0	1	4	17	50	382
Emigration	Passport Issue	3	10	15	26	58	458
Birth	Passport Issue	14	31	36	47	76	477
Male		*14*	*32*	*37*	*49*	*76*	*344*
Female		*23*	*29*	*35*	*43*	*70*	*133*
Birth	Emigration	5	18	20	23	44	458
Male		*5*	*18*	*20*	*23*	*40*	*342*
Female		*9*	*15*	*18*	*20*	*44*	*116*
Year of Birth		1844	1874	1884	1890	1902	477
Year of Emigration		1864	1895	1906	1911	1920	459

Note: This table collates the stated dates of birth, emigration to the USA, naturalisation as an American citizen, and issue of passport, analysing the intervals between these events in full years. Except for emigration (normally given only by year), all dates are precise. The distributions of stated years of birth and emigration are also given. For each distribution, the table shows the median interval, lower and upper quartile values, and lowest and highest values.

Table 8.5 *Birthplaces of relatives of Leitrim passport applicants, 1914–25*

Spouse	Wife	%	Husband	%	Child	%	Father	%
Birthplace								
Leitrim	9	19.6	5	5.7	1	0.9	54	21.3
Other Irish County	8	17.4	9	10.3			1	0.4
Ireland Unspecified	23	50.0	35	40.2			196	77.5
Britain	2	4.3	6	6.9			1	0.4
Europe	1	2.2	4	4.6				
USA	3	6.5	28	32.2	107	99.1	1	0.4
Total Specified	*46*	*100*	*87*	*100*	*108*	*100*	*253*	*100*
Unspecified	12		6		32		4	

Note: Statistics refer to birthplaces of 46 wives accompanying male applicants; 87 husbands of women seeking passports on the basis of husband's citizenship; 108 children accompanying applicants; and 253 fathers of applicants in all categories.

Table 8.6 *Destination of proposed trips by Leitrim passport applicants, 1914–25*

Region	Number	% Category	% Total	Notes
1. Ireland	*414*	*100*	*87.5*	
Ireland Only	353	85.3	74.6	
Ireland (Great) Britain	21	5.1	4.4	
Ireland, England, Scotland	5	1.2	1.1	
Ireland, England	32	7.7	6.8	
Ireland, Scotland	3	0.7	0.6	
2. Britain	*47*	*100*	*9.9*	*Ireland not specified*
British Isles	28	59.6	5.9	
Britain	11	23.4	2.3	
England	4	8.5	0.8	
Scotland	2	4.3	0.4	
England, Scotland	2	4.3	0.4	
3. Other	*50*	*100*	*10.6*	*12 cases only 'other'*
Europe	43	86.0	9.1	
Americas	4	8.0	0.8	
Australasia	2	4.0	0.4	
Asia	1	2.0	0.2	
Total Specified	*473*		*100*	*4 cases unspecified*

Note: Stated destinations are assigned to overlapping categories, so that the sum of percentage figures may exceed 100. The first and second categories are mutually exclusive, but only 12 of the 50 applications in the third category specified 'other' destinations exclusively. Within each category, percentages in the second column refer to proportions of the category total. The third column refers to proportions of the grand total. The analysis incorporates some destinations that were crossed out because applicants provided more detail than that officially required.

Table 8.7 *Physical characteristics of passport applicants, 1914–25*

%	Male	%	Female	%	Notes
Eye Colour Specified	341		131		
Blue		60.4		54.2	*incl. blue-grey, etc.*
Brown		20.2		23.7	*incl. brown-grey, etc.*
Grey		19.4		22.1	
Hair Colour Specified	255		119		*exc. white, grey, bald*
Black		17.6		14.3	
Dark		66.7		69.7	
Light		12.9		16.0	
Red		2.7		0	
Complexion Specified	339		131		
Fair		57.2		77.1	
Medium		8.3		11.5	
Dark		34.5		11.5	
Height (inches)	340		131		
Shortest	59		50		
Lower Quartile	67		64		
Median	68.2		65		
Upper Quartile	70		66		
Tallest		75		71	
Accessories	339		131		*from photographs*
Collar, Tie	95.9		0		*incl. 10 clerical collars*
Moustache	21.5		0		
Hat, Cap	1.8		16.0		
Spectacles	8.3		12.2		
Necklace	0		28.2		

Note: Characteristics, including height, were self-declared but often amended by officials. Many digital images of photographs are obscure, so that the proportions of applicants displaying the designated accessories may be under-stated.

Table 8.8 *Vascularity of passport applicants, 1914–25, and Irish population, 1934–6, by age*

Age Group	Applicants			Ireland, 1934–6		
	Vascular	Total	%	Vascular	Total	%
Male						
Under 35	41	133	30.8	1,040	5,586	18.6
35–44	37	95	38.9	507	1,774	28.6
45–54	21	64	32.8	372	1,119	33.2
55+	19	48	39.6	523	1,473	35.5
Total	*118*	*340*	*34.7*	*2,442*	*9,952*	*24.5*
Female						
Under 35	5	65	7.7	268	1,201	22.3
35–54	8	56	14.3	43	392	11.0
55+	2	10	20.0	18	207	8.7
Total	*15*	*131*	*11.5*	*329*	*1,800*	*18.3*

Note: Applicants classified as having 'dark' complexions (including epithets such as ruddy, florid, red, brunette, and sallow) are compared with Irish Roman Catholic males from thirty-two counties and 'West Coast' females of all religious groups displaying 'pronounced vascularity' when examined by the Harvard investigators in 1934–6. No breakdown for West Coast females was published within the age group 35–54. *Sources*: see text.

Table 8.9 *Height of passport applicants, 1914–25, and Irish population, 1934–6, by age*

Age Group	Applicants			Ireland, 1934–6	
	Number	Median	Mean	Number	Mean
Male					
Under 35	133	69	68.7	5,585	67.9
35–44	96	68	68.6	1,775	68.0
45–54	63	68.3	68.7	1,118	67.6
55+	48	68	68.3	1,017	66.5
Total	*340*	*68*	*68.6*	*8,902*	*67.7*
Female					
Under 35	65	65	64.8	1,201	62.6
35–54	56	65	64.9	392	62.4
55+	10	64.5	64.5	207	61.6
Total	*131*	*65*	*64.8*	*1,801*	*62.4*

Note: The self-reported height in inches of applicants in each age group is compared with measurements (converted from centimetres) by the Harvard investigators of Irish Roman Catholic males from thirty-two counties and 'West Coast' females of all religious groups. No breakdown for West Coast females was published within the age group 35–54. No median figures were published for the Harvard survey, but means differed little from medians since the distribution of heights is invariably close to 'normal'. *Sources*: see text.

Table 8.10 *Reflections of fashion in passport photographs, 1914–25*

Accessory	Moustaches			Hats			Necklaces		
Year of Passport	No.	Total	%	No.	Total	%	No.	Total	%
1914–18	11	25	44.0		7	0	1	7	14.3
1919	7	46	15.2	1	16	6.3	3	16	18.7
1920	13	88	14.8	5	22	22.7	6	22	27.3
1921	11	42	26.2	5	16	31.3	4	16	25.0
1922	10	55	18.2	5	28	17.9	6	28	21.4
1923	8	36	22.2	3	21	14.3	8	21	38.1
1924	13	44	29.5	2	19	10.5	8	19	42.1
Total	*73*	*339*	*21.2*	*21*	*131*	*16.0*	*37*	*131*	*28.2*

Note: The number and proportion of male photographs showing moustaches is followed by that of female photographs showing hats and necklaces. Three male and 2 female photographs lodged in 1925 are included in the grand totals.

Table 8.11 *Characteristics of passport applicants and their parents in Leitrim, 1901*

%	Future Applicants	Fathers	Mothers
Characteristic			
Female	15.0	0	100
Born Leitrim	99.5	95.5	89.8
Catholic	97.2	96.7	96.7
Literate	92.1	84.3	83.7
Irish Speech	0.5	12.4	8.1
Widowed	0	5.4	7.7
Occupation			
Farming	80.0	88.8	87.9
Labour, Service	15.4	3.7	3.0
Other	4.6	7.4	9.1
Age in Years			
Lower Quartile	9	45	40
Median	12	51	45
Upper Quartile	16	60	50
Number	*213*	*242*	*246*

Note: Proportions relate to future applicants for American passports and their parents who were resident in Leitrim in 1901, having been confidently matched with family census returns (including two who were resident outside Leitrim). Proportions by occupation exclude unspecified cases. 'Farming' includes those returned as 'farmer's son' etc.; 'Labour, Service' includes farm servants, labourers, and domestics including housekeepers (other than wives). The database includes one applicant resident in Leitrim in 1901, but returned by his employer as a native of Roscommon. The excess of parents over applicants is attributable to the fact that applicants were absent from 64 of the 278 matched households. *Source*: Census of Ireland (1901), family schedules.

Table 8.12 *Comparison between Leitrim Americans and passport applicants,*
1901–11

%	Americans 1901	Americans 1911	Applicants 1901
Migrants			
Female	46.4	46.3	15.0
Born Leitrim	0	0	99.5
Catholic	96.1	96.6	97.2
Literate	76.5	89.2	92.1
Irish Speech	3.9	8.2	0.5
Farming	50.0	55.1	80.0
Labour, Service	13.9	17.9	15.4
Median Age	10	12	12
Number	*153*	*294*	*213*
Fathers of Migrants			
Born Leitrim	83.9	90.2	95.5
Catholic	96.8	100	96.7
Literate	83.9	96.1	84.3
Irish Speech	6.5	7.8	12.4
Farming	71.0	88.2	88.8
Labour, Service	12.9	7.8	3.7
Median Age (Census)	42	45	51
Number	*31*	*51*	*242*
Mothers of Migrants			
Born Leitrim	80.5	72.9	89.8
Catholic	97.6	100	96.7
Literate	95.1	95.7	83.7
Irish Speech	7.3	4.3	8.1
Farming	29.4	70.6	87.9
Labour, Service	5.9	0	3.0
Median Age (Census)	37	40	45
Number	*41*	*70*	*246*

Note: This summary table compares characteristics of American-born residents of Leitrim
(1901, 1911) and of future applicants for American passports whose families were resident
in 1901 (or 1911). In each case, the same characteristics are tabulated for fathers and
mothers of these migrants listed in family census returns. See Tables 6.1, 6.2, 6.3.

Table 8.13 *Housing of Leitrim Americans and passport applicants, 1901–11*

Characteristic %	Americans 1901	Americans 1911	Applicants 1901	Population 1901
Class 1	7.8	3.7	2.2	3.4
2	60.8	73.8	72.7	n.a.
3	30.7	21.8	24.7	n.a.
4	0.7	0.7	0.4	1.2
Thatched Roof	78.4	76.5	91.3	n.a.
Mud Walls	8.5	6.5	11.6	n.a.
Rooms 1–2	22.9	15.3	16.3	27.3
3	50.3	56.5	67.0	53.9
4+	26.9	28.3	16.7	18.7
Standard Dwelling	37.3	41.2	52.4	n.a.
In Congested EDs	49.7	46.3	48.2	48.4
North Leitrim	36.6	38.1	35.1	39.7
South Leitrim	63.4	61.9	64.9	60.3
Number of Households	*153*	*294*	*275*	*14,519*

Note: Proportions relate to the housing of American-born residents of Leitrim (1901, 1911) and of future applicants for American passports whose families were resident in 1901. The housing of each migrant is separately enumerated, even if several migrants belonged to the same household. In certain respects, comparison is possible with the profile of all 14,519 households ('families') in the county. The accompanying house and building return for each townland records the 'class' of dwelling, and enumerates 'perishable' roofs (usually thatched) and walls (usually mud). Houses with three front windows, three rooms, imperishable walls, and perishable roof (Class 2) are here designated as 'standard dwellings'. Electoral divisions (EDs) were designated as 'congested' if their net annual valuation per capita fell short of £1 5s. 'North Leitrim' is equated with the rural districts of Kinlough (part of Ballyshannon union) and Manorhamilton, leaving Carrick-on-Shannon No. 1, Ballinamore, and Mohill to 'South Leitrim'. *Sources*: Census of Ireland (1901), family schedules; townland house and building returns; published report for Co. Leitrim; Royal Commission on Congestion in Ireland, *Second Appendix to Seventh Report*, 25–37, in HCP 1908 (Cd 3786), xl, 431.

9   Visitors from America: Motives

I   'Object of Visit'

The homeward orientation of visitors from America permeates most statements of motive for travel ('object of visit'), often recording superfluous but fascinating details crossed out but not fully erased by Department of State officials. Some applicants responded with exaggerated gravitas to the bureaucratic challenge, as in the case of a waiter reared in a remote townland with 135 houses:[1]

To visit my parents residing in the town of Dargoon County of Leitrim Ireland; to visit my mother which has been in ill health for some time past. (Thomas Stephen Kearney, hotel waiter, 1893, 1915, 1919)

Each applicant whose motives are quoted in this chapter is identified, as in Kearney's case, by the dates of birth, emigration, and application.[2] Those pictured in Chapter 10 are indicated by the figure in which their image appears. Many passport-seekers, as demonstrated below, listed several objects. But 371 applicants (78%) intended to visit relatives, predominantly parents or siblings, along with spouses and children, in-laws, and a nephew (Table 9.1). Only a handful looked forward to visiting 'friends' rather than relatives. This broadly accords with Dunnigan's richly illustrated analysis of motives for applicants born in Connaught, which indicates that two-thirds (66%) of applicants up to 1920 intended to visit relatives. This proportion is deceptively low because of Dunnigan's decision to assign each applicant's often complex motives to only one category.[3]

Parents were specified in nearly half of all applications (47%), with mothers far outnumbering fathers when only one parent was mentioned (reflecting the great excess of widows over widowers). In the majority of cases, however, both parents were still living, though often said to be sick, aged, or infirm. The median age of these filial visitors was 33, with an inter-quartile range of 10 years.[4] Using census returns, it is possible to reconstruct the age profile of many of the parents who were to be reunited with their Americanised children during or after the First World War. Fathers ranged in age from 51 to 87 at the date when passports were issued, while mothers ranged from 45 to 93. The median age of fathers and mothers was 69 and 63, respectively, with an inter-quartile range of 13 years for fathers but only 9 years for mothers.[5] Most fathers were therefore approaching or beyond the normal age of retirement from active farming, whereas most mothers could expect not only to live for a few more years but also to be potential successors to farm occupancy.

This was indeed the phase of the domestic cycle in which issues of inheritance and succession came to a head. Though sometimes still provoking rivalry and resentment between siblings, the impending death or retirement of a farmer increasingly threatened the very survival of the household. By the early twentieth century, many ageing farmers or their widows had no children left at home to squabble over succession. In such cases, the pressure for an emigrant son to take over a property and maintain the lineage was at least as likely to come from a parent, or from other dispersed siblings, as from the emigrant himself. We cannot tell how many applicants were drawn home by the hope of material gain, how many by a latent sense of filial duty inflamed, on occasion, by emotional blackmail. In either case, many visitors must have embarked for post-war Ireland with trepidation as well as nostalgia.

Economic objects were mentioned by about one-sixth of applicants (82). These mostly related to 'business', 'property', or an 'estate', specifying 'personal' and 'family' affairs in roughly equal numbers. It may be assumed that most economic visitors were returning to claim an inheritance, assert an entitlement to property, or perform financial responsibilities as executors or next-of-kin. Only occasionally did applicants explain the precise nature of their business:

I have a farm which I must look after. It is not being managed properly and I intends to sell it or place it in proper hands. (Thomas O'Rourke, stationary engineer, 1872, 1893, 1916)

The more discursive entries illuminate the complexity of the family obligations that pulled emigrants homewards. There was no firm boundary between familial and financial motives, as the following examples indicate.

To be with my parents, also to live on a farm I own there. (Thomas Beirne, stationary engineer, 1880, 1903, 1919: Figure 12)

My parents wants to see me and the[y] are getting old and the[y] have some business to settle. (John Joseph O'Reilly, street cleaning, 1879, 1905, 1920)

Visit my aged father and help him dispose of his real estate. (Marie Finan, housewife, 1875, 1890, 1919)

To see my father who is seriously ill and to sign estate papers which requires the personal presence of myself and wife for signature. (James Boles, grain handler, 1882, 1904, 1919: Figure 3 shows his family)

To see father and look after property. (James Reynolds, waiter, 1885, 1903, 1919)

Sick mother & settle mony that i got. (John Horan, foreman, 1869, 1891, 1919)

To see my mother and settle some property. (Thomas McLaughlin, motorman, 1884, 1910, 1919)

Illness of mother & settle estate. (Thomas Clyne, waiter, 1883, 1905, 1919)

Settle an estate & visit mother. (Terence Ward, machine operator, 1892, 1913, 1920)

To see brothers & sister & get money coming to me. (Michael Moran, steam-fitter, 1881, 1906, 1919)

Parental sickness or infirmity was not simply a source of sadness and regret, but also a stimulus to become involved in the disposal of property and the vexed issue of succession. Taken together, almost nine-tenths of applicants cited either family or property or both when declaring the objects of their visits.[6]

Seventeen applicants were travelling in the course of their employment or for commercial reasons, including a nurse, a maid required for the Grand Tour, a government official, a real estate broker, a textile buyer, a priest, and an actor:

Travel with patient [to Norway, Denmark, and Sweden], accompanying an insane alien to her respective homes. (Hannah McGoldrick, nurse, 1890, 1907, 1921)

Employment [in British Isles, France, and Italy]. (Mary Wrynn, lady's maid, 1892, 1909, 1923)

Official business (immigration service). (John Crown, clerk, US Government, 1870, 1895, 1915)

To inspect the housing conditions abroad on behalf of the Cin[cinna]ti Real Estate Board. (Edward M. Costello, real estate broker, 1855, 1871, 1919)

To buy silk & woolen dress goods. (Robert M. Woodward, buyer, 1864, 1888, 1922)

Visit mother (Ireland); en route (France); business for church (Italy). (Patrick Joseph Smyth, priest, 1878, 1905, 1920: Figure 13)

The actor, to be registered as 'Patrick Connolly known as Frank Shannon', 'the name by which he is known on the stage', offered a breathless explanation for his proposed trip to Britain and presumably Ireland. Having first declared his desire 'to visit my wifes parents' in England, he added a contradictory gloss on the headed paper of the Hotel Jefferson in St Louis, Minnesota:

In making application for a passport, my reasons are: First to see my son, also to see my father & mother. Second, I am engaged to stage 'The Idle Woman' play for Madame [name lost]. (Patrick Connolly, actor, 1874, 1891, 1920)

Several in this category of applicants were involved in relief schemes arising from the war, especially the Knights of Columbus, a prominent Catholic fraternity:

Knights of Columbus war relief work. (James McGourty, motor driver, 1881, 1887, 1919)

Knights of Columbus. (Andrew Gallagher, attorney, 1869, 1888, 1918: Figure 8)

Field Secretary, Knights of Columbus. (John Hackett, ship building, 1864, 1887, 1919)

Red Cross ambulance driver. (Mark Elias Schomberg Kerr, oil-pumper, 1883, 1907, 1917: Figure 7)

Less than one-eighth (56) were conventional tourists, specifying their object as 'travel', 'pleasure', 'vacation', or simply a 'visit' in descending order of frequency. Most of these declared no other motive. A fairly recent arrival living in New Haven, Connecticut, wished to visit Ireland, Britain, and France purely for 'travel and pleasure' (Michael E. Kilcrin, 'restaurant', 1884, 1915, 1923). A prim clerk deleted the unbureaucratic phrase 'and pleasure'. Yet 8 of the 29 tourists hoped to combine amusement with business or family duty, as in the case of a visitor heading for France as well as the British Isles:

To see my parents (Ireland); sight-seeing (England and France). (Matthew Harvey, grocery clerk, 1890, 1911, 1922)

Business and pleasure were more exotically blended in the case of a preacher who proposed to cast the marvellous light upon England, Scotland, Norway, Sweden, Denmark, Holland, Belgium, Switzerland, and Germany, all in the course of 3 months:

Travel & preachin[g]. (David George Downey, Methodist preacher, 1858, 1866, 1921)

The other major motive for return was pursuit of health, mentioned by 31 applicants. This category excludes 49 applications in which the sickness of parents or relatives at home explicitly contributed to the decision to return home. The justified belief that rural Ireland was a healthier environment than urban America was likewise a recurrent theme of emigrant correspondence. Though usually relating to the applicant's own health or sickness, applications occasionally cited the sickness of an accompanying wife, child, or sister as the object of therapeutic travel. Once again, sentiment and self-interest were entangled together:

To benefit my health, see my aged parents. (John O'Beirne, clerk, 1876, 1898, 1922)

My health and poor condition and to visit my mother. (Mary Louise Locke, housekeeper, 1882, 1898, 1920)

Health & see brothers. (John F. McHugh, stock man, 1879, 1908, 1920)

Change of climate & visit sister. (Peter McPartland, unoccupied, 1887, 1904, 1920)

To visit my sister & on acct of my health. (Thomas McKeon, meat business, 1859, 1880, 1920)

Visiting relations and my own health. (Katie Ducker, housewife, 1865, 1884, 1920)

Health(?) and visit my relations at Co. Leitrim father brother sister. (James McManus, engineer, 1872, 1893, 1920)

Benefit of health, rest, & visit relatives. (Mary J. Hyndman, nurse, 1853, 1886, 1916)

Sickness & visit parents. (John McNiffe, guard on railroad, 1884, 1911, 1920: Figure 10)

The sheer diversity and complexity of the motives impelling former emigrants to leave the United States is illustrated by a final selection of declared 'objects':

Visit my aged father 81 years & in ill health & object in wife's visit is to take sick child … and to see aged father who is ill, before he dies. (Frank P. Early, rail operator, 1878, 1898, 1919)

To visit mother & take home my wife. (John Murray, foreman packer, 1877, 1907, 1923)

To settle about a farm of land left to me by the will of my late father and my wife wants to go see her mother. (Dominick Hart, still man (oil refining), 1883, 1902, 1920)

To visit my mother (Ireland); to visit my brothers grave (France). (Hugh Gillen, grocer, 1889, 1908, 1924)

Visiting brother, who is temporarily visiting in Ireland from Australia. (Ellie Masterson, clerk in tea store, 1879, 1899, 1916)

See nephew ordained, see aged and sick bros & sisters. (Thomas M. Tubman, Catholic priest, 1861, 1884, 1920: Figure 13)

Perhaps the most searing statement of motive came from a gardener with three young children born in Fairhaven, New Jersey, as he prepared to return to Ahanlish in December 1915:

To take my motherless children to my mother. (Lawrence Rooney, gardener, 1881, 1900, 1915)

II   Making the Case for a Passport

During the First World War and its immediate aftermath, while passenger shipping was severely curtailed and hazardous, the Department of State refused to issue passports for travel deemed to be inessential. A married housekeeper in New Haven, Connecticut, was refused permission in September 1918 'to see my sick mother':

In view of present conditions, the Department has found it necessary to restrict the issuance of passports to cases of persons who are obliged to go abroad because of some imperative exigency. (Mary Nesbit, housekeeper, 1878, 1888, 1920)

Her fee of $1 was returned, and she was not allowed a passport until March 1920, when the 'exigency' of her mother's illness may have passed. Female applicants were scrutinised with particular scepticism in 1919, when the Department anticipated a flood of women conspiring to consecrate peace with their menfolk in Europe. Most women in the United States would probably have failed the test imposed on Mary Reilly, a widowed housekeeper proposing 'to visit aged parents, brothers and sisters' in August 1919:

I do solemnly swear that I have neither husband, father, nor son who is now an officer or enlisted man with the United States military forces either at home or abroad. I do further swear that I have neither husband, father, nor son who is now employed in Europe in a civilian capacity with the Red Cross, the Young Mens Christian Association, or any other organization of a similar nature; neither have I such a male relative who is now employed in, or attached to, the American Expeditionary Forces in Europe in a civilian capacity. (Mary Reilly, housekeeper, 1881, —, 1919)

Many applicants had to make a strong case, often *ad misericordiam*, to overcome regulatory impediments. This might entail the submission of documents such as family correspondence, medical certificates, and supporting letters, as well as personal statements or affidavits offering detailed justification for the proposed trip. These additional testaments offer sharper insight into the often complex motivation of those impelled to return home in an epoch of crisis and danger.

Some applications appealed to the humanity of officials by portraying the powerful emotional bonds between emigrants and their families at home:

That my said parents are old and infirm, and it is my wish, and the wish of my said parents that I visit them before their death; that my father is 80 years of age past, and my mother is 72 years of age past; that I desire to have my wife and five minor children accompany me on said trip to Ireland to visit with my said parents. (James Gilleece, clerk, 1879, 1907, 1919)

Despite its officious style, this affidavit evoked shared yearning for a final family reunion, the effect being heightened by gross overstatement of the age of Gilleece's parents (67 and 60, respectively, if the census returns for 1901 were accurate).

Two ex-soldiers expressed their family loyalties more simply:

I have recently been discharged from Co. D. 308th Infantry. While in France in answer to several letters from my mother I tried to obtain a furlough to visit her. She was and is very ill. The letters she wrote were lost. I now desire to visit her in her house Mohill, Co. Leitrim, Ireland. (Michael Woods, ship builder, 1893, 1911, 1919)

I desire to visit my brother John Connolly who is in very poor health & who Resides at Glenaniff Co Leitrim Ireland. He often expressed a hope of seeing me & I am very anxious to see him. Recently I was discharged from they U. S. A [rmy] after having served eleven years in this country and abroad. (Thomas Connolly, guard on railroad, 1873, 1901, 1919)

Another applicant made almost flippant reference to his mother's blindness when explaining the need 'to visit sick mother & settle father's affairs (now deceased)':

My mother being in a serious state of health in the County of Leitrim Ireland and expecting death soon as I am informed, desired to see or rather meet me her sight having failed her recently. I am therefore anxious to go and visit her. (William J. Flynn, motorman, 1881, 1904, 1917)

Some applicants asked friends or colleagues to confirm the legitimacy of their applications, including two professional nurses who wished to look after relatives:

I To accompany her sister who already has a Britrish passport and is in poor health and unable to travel alone. II To nurse back to normal health a brother and two sisters who are seriously ill in Ireland. (Margaret Connolly, nurse, 1870, 1888, 1919: Figure 5)

(1) Her aged mother is seriously ill and has sent for her, a competent nurse, to temporarily return to Ireland, and take care of her. (2) To acquire her share in an estate left by her deceased father. (Margaret O'Neill, nurse, 1872, 1891, 1919)

The need for supportive statements from associates in the United States sometimes resulted from the failure to preserve letters from home, which were routinely burned or destroyed by emigrants unmoved by the romantic inclination to pore nostalgically over old correspondence:

That i Thomas McDermott had received many letters from my father in Ireland pleading me to come home as he is living all alone *theire*. i never kept any of the letters never expecting that i would have to produce them before i could get a pass port to Ireland which will be a loss to father and my self if i cannot obtain a pass port. (Thomas McDermott, motorman, New York Railroad Company, 1873, 1907, 1919)

Other friends testified to having read or heard about such family appeals before their destruction. Whole families connived to erase the written record, causing serious bureaucratic problems by eliminating old passports as well as correspondence:

The children found the drawer in my desk open and tore up all the papers they found there and my wife saw that it was no use to keep the passport as it was never used by me, and thought it was no good put it in the stove and burned it. (Patrick McQueeney, chauffeur, 1894, 1914, 1923)

The most poignant cases were made by relatives in Ireland, sometimes naive, often artful. The most succinct of these was a cable from Kate McGuinness to one of two unmarried sisters in New York, each of whom had quite recently visited their parents in Cloonfinan, Drumdoo:

Mother very sick let somebody come Kate. (Bee McGuinness, dressmaker, 1891, 1901, 1923)

A married woman from Rossfriar, Kinlough, hoping 'to see my mother who is aged and ill; and to transact business on property matter', supplied a fragmentary maternal appeal:

I am in the poorest of health. I have tried all the doctors and cures I could, and still I am sinking fast. So I am longing to see you and Ellen home before I die. My poor boy ... (Bridget Quinn, housewife, 1888, 1907, 1919)

Thomas McGuire from Clooncliva, Dromod, was less coherent but equally adept at tugging heart-strings in support of his son's application 'to visit father who is ill, and to settle estate':

My Dear Patk., Come come if you wish to see me. Mary is dead and Joe is lonesome from not without means enough. Say to sisters if you like, you could write. By By ...

Within 8 months, Patrick McGuire again sought a passport 'to visit a sick brother who is an orphan', this time bringing his wife Sabina on the voyage. A United States marshal, referring to his previous visit, testified that:

He has since returned and has just received a letter, notifying him of the death of his father, which necessitates his returning to Ireland. (Patrick McGuire, labourer, 1878, 1900, 1919)

The most elaborate parental appeal was composed by Mary McNiffe of Lisfuiltaghan, Arigna:

We received your most welcome letter this morning and was very glad to hear from you, and to hear that you are very well. I am sorry to have to tell you that I am keeping very ill. I did not like to tell you while you were in the Navy, that I was so bad. You need not tell Hugh, or Tom, that I am keeping so weak, it would make them worry *to* much, about me. I am still under doctors care for this last 12 months and I am keeping very weak all the time, the doctor told me I worried to[o] much about ye, when you were in the Army there, but I could not help *worring* when the three of ye were in joined. So I am sure, dear Patrick if you would get to come home it would do me a lot of good to see you. The doctor told me that to see one of ye home here it would cheer me up and that it would improve my health a lot. I hear that it is pretty hard to get away but I am sure, if you tell the Authorities there that it is to go to see your sick mother that they will be kind enough to let you come especially if you tell them that I had three sons in the U. S. Army. Hoping now to see you soon with best wishes From Your Loving Mother. PS. any time you will say to go back I will not ask to keep you so God bless you and come to see Poor MOTHER. (Patrick James McNiff, waiter, 1894, 1913, 1919)

With its formulaic introduction, emotive exhortation, elaborate petition, and relegation of the key promise to a cramped postscript, this letter conformed to long-established protocols of migratory correspondence which I have analysed elsewhere.[7] Particularly impressive was Mrs McNiffe's advice to win over officials by mentioning the American war service of her three sons, just in case they were not 'kind enough' to respond to the simple impulse 'to see your sick mother'.

Though most family correspondence enclosed with passport applications concentrated on grave problems such as death, illness, isolation, and succession to property, a letter from Arigna to a married sister in Forest Hills, Massachusetts, suggested the prospect of a more relaxed reunion. By May 1920, restrictions on foreign travel had been relaxed and it was no longer necessary to cite dire emergency in order to secure a passport. Indeed, this letter was not an appeal from Leitrim but a response to news that the emigrant was unexpectedly returning 'to see father brother & sister':

Just a few lines to let you know I received your surprise letter yesterday. My father and I are so delighted to hear you are coming home. I hope God sends you safe ... There are so many changes now. We will have a great time with all the young Macks. Jack has got three boys too. I am sure Tom will feel delighted to see Maggie. Kate & Frank took a great notion of marriage – never dreamt Frank would marry so soon. You need not worry about travelling in Ireland at present. You are as safe as in the country *your* in I think ... I'm sure Mollie will get lonely to see you come. I always thought Mollie would take the first trip. Nellie will get a great surprise when she hears you are coming. I hope you get this note before you start your letter has been a long time coming ... In case Jemmie knows you are coming he may make up his mind to be with you he promised to take a trip this summer. Well Maggie everything around will seem strange to you in particulars. My father would have written but I think he never cared for the task of writing. He seems delighted you to come, every day will seem to him like a week. I will now finish trusting in God you get a safe voyage & pleasant weather to return to the old Sod. (Mrs Margaret McManus, 'unemployed', 1886, 1907, 1920)

Despite brother Michael's genial tone, the letter followed convention by incorporating veiled references to Maggie McManus's long silence, and her sister Mollie's stronger bond with 'the old Sod'. What exchange between siblings has ever been utterly untouched by barbs?

Anxiety over property was a major preoccupation for applicants, often entangled with more personal concerns. A New York bartender supported one application in 1919 from a labourer whom he had known for eight years:

He wishes to return to Ireland on account of the old age of his parents, which is about 75 or 80 years old. I have seen several letters from his father, asking him to come home one of which is attached to his application [not found]. As his father is not able to work he wishes his son to return home to look after some property. (Michael Keegan, labourer, 1891, 1911, 1919)

As so often, the antiquity of Michael's parents was greatly exaggerated (in 1901, Thomas and Bridget Keegan were reportedly aged 48 and 46).

The risk of disputes over succession gave a peculiar intensity to Patrick Mulhern's appeal to his brother to return forthwith to Carrick-on-Shannon 'so that the property can be *stratened* out between us':

I know it will cause you a lot of trouble and loss of time coming over here but you see John it is so important that you must be here before anything can be done with the property. (John Mulhern, dock builder, 1879, 1895, 1917)

Property disputes, like illness and infirmity, could drag on for many years, as Thomas Kelly discovered. Having spent nearly 2 years in Cullagh between October 1921 and July 1923 trying to assert his claim, Thomas Kelly was again homeward bound in October 1923, obliging him to complete an affidavit to explain his protracted absence from the United States:

I was interested in a farm of land a dispute arose and had to be settled in court and I had to remain to attend to my personal interest in this estate which is not settled yet. (Thomas Kelly, waiter, 1883, 1906, 1923)

Especially during and just after the war, applicants offering health as a motive routinely supplied medical certificates, revealing not only particular afflictions but also medical assumptions about the benefits of an Irish environment and a sea voyage:

He is suffering with a rather uncommon condition, spleno-ungelogenous leukemia, and I have advised him to return to Ireland. (James McHugh, watchman, 1879, 1907, 1915: Figure 8)

Mr John McNiff 34 yrs is under my care suffering from anaemia which has resisted ordinary treatment I advise him to take a vacation and a sea trip if possible to restore his health. (John McNiffe, guard on railroad, 1884, 1911, 1920: Figure 10)

I hereby certify that Patrick McLoughlin 33 Trumbull St Worcester Mass is afflicted with sciatica, that I have attended him professionally and have advised him to go to Ireland as I think a change would be beneficial for him. (Patrick McLoughlin, labourer, 1875, 1907, 1919)

My reasons for wanting to go are, the failing health of an aged mother, whom I have not seen for seven years, also my own ill health. My doctor has advised an ocean voyage for this. (Mrs Mary Murphy, 1896, 1913, 1920)

A shipping clerk and his 'desperately sick' wife ('such worthy people', as the pastor of Brooklyn's Methodist Episcopal Church remarked) also headed for a healthier home:

She is suffering from a chronic gastritis with probably gastric ulcer … She is desirous of returning to Ireland and owing to her condition will be unable to travel alone. (John Thomas Coulter, shipping clerk, 1876, 1898, 1919: Figure 4)

Perhaps the most revealing explanation for taking an Irish cure was supplied by a machinist worn down by the war but alert to the benefits of free hospitality. With support from a doctor who deemed her 'nervously tired', she set out her reasons for return:

To regain my health and to see my aged mother during the War I worked In the International Motor Co. Plainfield and from continuous work my health broke down. My reason for going home is I have not funds enough to *thake* a trip for my health over here and if I get home it will cost me nothing for board. It would also help me a lot to see my mother whome I have not seen in 9 years and I would like to see her before she dies. My husband Edmund B. Coghlan of Supply Co. 113th n. s. Inf. been [being] 11 months in France and at the same time working 10 hours each day in a war plant shop has me a complete nervous wreck. (Mary Foley Coghlan, machinist, 1896, 1908, 1919)

III   Marooned in Ireland

Many visitors from America who had arrived in Ireland (or Europe) before the outbreak of war or shortly afterwards found themselves marooned, their return impeded by the curtailment and increasing danger of passenger shipping across the Atlantic. Those who nevertheless decided to risk the journey, usually after the Armistice as that risk diminished, were obliged to apply for a 'departmental' passport through an American consul or vice-consul (or, in urgent cases, an 'emergency' passport). Many applicants were required to submit an 'affidavit to explain protracted foreign residence and to overcome presumption of expatriation', offering a synopsis of their reasons for travelling overseas and for failing to return earlier. These retrospective accounts of visits to Ireland are of considerable value to the historian of migration.

Several overseas applicants who had returned to Ireland to visit parents remained there for the entire span of the war. This was typically explained either by the need to look after Irish relatives for a protracted period, or by the impracticability of returning earlier. Since the aim of applicants was to demonstrate their intention to return permanently to the United States, they were unlikely to declare other factors that might have kept them in Ireland, such as profiting from the wartime boom in agriculture. Several affidavits referred to the recent resolution of long-term family commitments. Thomas McGourty had arrived at Camderry 'on a visit to my mother' in June 1913, and stayed there for eight years:

I returned to Ireland on a visit to my aged parents, and a brother of mine who had been looking after them left home, thus compelling me to look after my parents. My father has since died and my mother is going to make her home with a sister, and I now desire a passport to enable me to return to the United States to reside there permanently. (Thomas McGourty, 1885, 1904, Belfast 1921)

Thomas Keegan of New Haven, Connecticut, spent more than a decade in Corgallion, Mohill, before applying in October 1919 to travel back to the United States:

I came to this country to visit my aged parents, both of whom were invalids, and on the death of my father seven years ago I remained on to care for my mother who died in March last. Having now no ties in this country I am desirous of returning to my home in the United States. (Thomas J. Keegan, labourer, 1881, 1899, Dublin 1919)

Keegan, resplendent in bow tie when photographed in front of his wife, who was sporting a severe bun, and theatrically attired step-daughter, omitted the most salient context for his departure from Leitrim. Only seven weeks earlier he had married a widow back from Scotland, and was ready to bear off his bride (and her daughter) to the New World he had left behind in February 1909.[8]

Marriage in Ireland to an American citizen could secure a fast track across the Atlantic, as Mary Mulreeney found when she married Patrick

Clancy, a naturalised American, in St Mary's Church, Killanummery, on 14 August 1916. Having accompanied 'his sick brother' back to Ireland in May 1916, Clancy wrongly believed that his new bride could be added to his passport for the return journey. Mary, who had also been in Drumahaire since May 1916, seven years after emigrating to the United States, was given an emergency passport so that she could follow her husband, who had arranged to sail a few days earlier.

Two other overseas applicants explained in detail how complex property transactions had long impeded their return to the United States. Charles McGourty had spent twelve years 'looking after his property' in Drumristin, Drumreilly West, before seeking to return to the United States in May 1920:

To rescue the property rented by my brother who died intestate; after which it took me two years to acquire title to the property from the Land Commission; I then put the property up for sale but could get no bids and I could not sell the property until March 9th, 1920. (Charles H. McGourty, 1850, 1872, Dublin 1920)

Francis Gaynor from Curraghnabonia, Oughteragh, had made several trips to Ireland since emigrating in 1885, being at home in both 1901 and 1911. He made a further visit in 1922 but overstayed the term of his passport, necessitating a visit to the Belfast consulate:

I came over to Ireland in 1922 for the purpose of disposing of my father's property as he was too old (89 years) to manage it himself. Since I came to Ireland I have done my best to sell this farm but up to the present I have not done so. It is my intention whether this property is sold or not to return to Providence, R. I. accompanied by my wife at an early date, leaving the farm in capable hands to be auctioned. (Francis Gaynor, moulder, 1867, 1885, Belfast 1924: Figure 4)

Several applicants drawn back by family pressures attributed their prolonged presence in Leitrim to war conditions. Francis Gordon, who had spent three spells in the Barr of Farrow, Glenboy, between 1885 and 1914, had returned there in April 1914 and stayed for 6 years, working as a salesman:

I came to Ireland to get my children but on account of the war I felt unable to do so. I remained in Ireland on account of their education which has been completed and they are now at work in Ireland. I intend to remain in the United States at least six years and probably the rest of my life. (Francis Gordon, 1869, 1895, Dublin 1920).

The American consul in Dublin approved Gordon's application, though 'somewhat doubtful' that he would return permanently, having no property in the United States and having left his children in Ireland.

More straightforward were two cases of visitors who had returned to Leitrim just before the outbreak of war and who returned shortly after the 'cessation of hostilities'. Michael Gill, formerly a fireman in Boston who had evidently also worked in New York, secured testimony from a namesake (perhaps sister):

I have on several occasions heard Michael Gill – 302 West 30th St express his intentions of his contemplated trip to Ireland for the purpose of visiting his parents. Especially since the death of his mother which occurred in 1917, owing to war conditions he has been unable to obtain passport until now. Very *Respect* Mary Gill. (Michael J. Gill, fireman (stationary), 1887, 1906, Dublin 1919)

A widowed dressmaker who had returned to Derrien (Lloyd), Gortna-gullion, less than a fortnight before the outbreak of war, explained her 5-year stay succinctly:

(1) To visit sick brother and other relatives. (2) Difficulties and risk of travel during submarine menace. – I would have returned to America long since but for the difficulties in procuring a steamship ticket, owing to lack of accommodation on shipboard. (Elizabeth L. Gilleese Smith, housekeeper and dressmaker, 1882, —, Dublin 1919)

Three applicants who had been drawn back to Ireland by health problems expressed frustration that the war had held back their return. Nellie Seeley and two children were separated from her husband for 6 years:

I came to Ireland on the Doctor's advice, owing to the illness of two of my children and when here and the children had recuperated sufficiently I could not get back then owing to the activity of enemy submarines. All my children have been born in the United States and my husband is a native born American citizen and myself and children are going back to rejoin my husband. (Mrs Nellie D. Seeley, housekeeper, 1893, 1907, 1920)

Patrick Carroll's recuperation in Boyannagh, Gubacreeny, occupied 13 years, though at least he had his wife's company:

I underwent a surgical operation at St. John's Hospital Lowell Mass. in March 1906 My Doctor (Dr. Irish) ordered me to Ireland my country of origin to recuperate I came to Ireland in June of that year accompanied by my wife and was never sufficiently strong to enable me to undertake the return journey to the United States until the war broke out and since then it was impossible for me to get back. (Patrick Carroll, brewery labourer, 1862, 1888, Londonderry 1919)

Two and a half years later, Carroll was off again 'to dispose of property and visit brother', confirming the complex entanglements which made it impossible for many emigrants to permanently sever the home connection.

Ireland's fabled salubriousness had brought Bernard Shanley back to Leitrim in June 1914, but unlike more fearful visitors he decided to return to the United States in August 1916 despite the persistent threat of submarine attacks:

I was advised by my physician in New York City that my son, Thomas Shanley, who was then suffering from chronic eczema, must have a change, and I came to Ireland on his account and also because of my wife whose health was also bad in New York ... The reason I have not returned to the United States is that conditions of travel have been so dangerous that I have feared to return earlier. (Bernard Shanley, clerk, 1876, 1897, Dublin 1916)

Shanley planned to return first 'and to have my wife and child follow as soon as their state of health and conditions warrant'. A year and a half had passed since his son had been 'discharged cured' from the Children's Hospital in Temple Street, Dublin.

The pathetic case of Sarah Gregory of Brooklyn (Figure 3), first brought to light in Dunnigan's pioneering thesis, gives rare insight into the impact of domestic turmoil on international migration.[9] Sarah McGloin was reared in Drummons, Aghanlish, where the otherwise standard farmhouse with three rooms and three front windows was notable for its imperishable roof. In August 1916, she sought a passport to 'visit mother' in Ireland, accompanied by her two daughters aged 4 and 2. Sarah was 27 years old, 5 ft. 7½ in. tall, with high forehead, grey eyes, straight nose, brown hair, and fair complexion. Her photograph depicts a gaunt woman with two glum children, both neatly attired with white bows in their hair. An official remarked that 'this woman's face still bears the result of a beating her husband gave her the other day, for which he got ten days. While he is in jail, her friends want to send her back to her mother in Ireland, and I am in favour of issuing a passport under the circumstances.'

Three years later, in August 1919, she applied in Dublin for a passport to return to the United States. In explaining her 'protracted foreign residence', she declared that she had been 'visiting relatives' and cited 'the great risks attendant upon ocean travel during submarine menace, especially with young children. I now wish to return to reside with my husband in the United States.' Sarah produced her husband's baptismal entry, and a certificate of their marriage in 1909 in the Catholic Church of the Transfiguration, Brooklyn. Her daughters, who had sprouted impressively since 1916, still wore white bows in their hair, and Sarah was as gaunt as ever. Sarah was in no hurry to depart, finally travelling with her daughters on the SS *Columbia* from Londonderry to New York in July 1920. Their 'home' was given as 78, South 9th Street, the

Brooklyn address where James Gregory, a chauffeur, was 'rooming' when the federal census was conducted a few months earlier. Earlier census returns for 1910 and 1915 locate the Gregorys at other Brooklyn addresses, James having first been a 'hostler' or stableman and then a teamster.[10]

No further trace has been found of either James or Sarah Gregory, but their daughters Margaret and Mary both eventually married, claimed social security benefits, and lived on until the 1990s. In 1930, both were living in Brooklyn. Margaret, returned as 21 but who was in fact 18, was one of several resident teachers in a 'practical school' in North 5th Street. It was Mary whose situation reflected the disorientation and troubles of her early years: she was listed as a 'prisoner', performing laundry work at the House of the Good Shepherd in Hopkinson Avenue.[11] The Gregorys' return to Brooklyn had not been an unqualified success.

IV   Two Activists

The motives of two visitors merit exceptionally close attention because of their significant involvement in Irish politics, though only one application gave any hint of this:

Settle estate, private business, attend world wide Irish conference. (Michael Joseph O'Connor, trucking and commercial(?), 1872, 1893, 1921)

M. J. O'Connor was a well-established New York businessman with an address on 5th Avenue. He became an American citizen in 1902, 9 years after emigrating from Moville, Co. Donegal. His father had been a publican in the small town of Leitrim, midway between Carrick-on-Shannon and Drumshanbo, presiding over nine rooms and a servant girl in 1901. Having made two short visits to Ireland in 1914 and 1915, O'Connor applied for a 3-month passport just before Christmas 1921, with the intention of embarking on the SS *Potomac* on New Year's Eve.

O'Connor was the only Leitrim applicant to indicate a political motive in an era of turmoil and revolution involving many returned Americans. The Irish Race Congress, held in Paris in late January 1922, was an extravaganza intended, when convened on Dáil Éireann's third birthday, to impress the world with Ireland's unflagging unity in the pursuit of self-determination. Instead, riven by the 'split' occasioned by the Anglo-Irish Treaty, it became a forum for faction-fighting and sniping, despite strenuous attempts to present a common front.[12] News of de Valera's resignation as president and divisions within the Dáil and its ministry had precipitated the abrupt withdrawal of fifty-five delegates of the American Association for the Recognition of the Irish Republic.[13] O'Connor and

half a dozen others were left to represent the wealthiest and most influential element of the 'Irish race'. The organising secretary, Katherine
Hughes, informed delegates that 'previous to this decision five delegates
had set out some weeks in advance for personal reasons, and these men
were now in attendance at the Congress'.[14] Regrettably for the evening
cultural programme, this impromptu American delegation did not
include the tenor John McCormack, who telegraphed his 'infinite regrets
cannot get to Paris for Irish Race Congress. Dates have been booked for
over six months. Impossible to change.'[15]

O'Connor joined scores of others purporting to 'represent' Ireland,
Scotland, England, Newfoundland, Australia, New Zealand, Argentina,
South Africa, Brazil, France, and Italy. The North Americans were
actually outnumbered by both Argentinians and Australians, who
mustered seven delegates apiece.[16] In the absence of more prominent
figures at the preliminary Saturday session, O'Connor was elected to a
vital committee controlling 'general procedure and agenda'. Initially
unobtrusive, he offered some interesting 'suggestions for Irish trade with
America' on the Thursday, stating that he had been instructed to
approach Irish textile houses with a view to forming links with a group
of New York businessmen. With a nod and a wink towards Harry Boland
and the secret society men, O'Connor declared that the New York group
was 'in the hands of men who are true and reliable in every way. When
I say in every way, there are men in this hall who will understand what
I mean.' Though the Republic's consul in New York (Joseph Connolly)
had given him no letters of introduction to northern firms, in view of the
current sectarian unrest, O'Connor was 'very confident that I will be
permitted to go to some of these houses because I had my early training
in Belfast'. As he warmed up, nostalgia for Arigna began to cloud his
judgement as he contemplated the future of Irish mining: 'Right where
I was born in the West of Ireland, we have the greatest coal mines in the
world, and in one district there are twenty-nine tin mines lying
undeveloped.'[17]

On the previous day, O'Connor had proposed the formation of a new
body 'for the purpose of federating Irish organisations and respectively
co-ordinating and developing their efforts', embracing 'political, cultural, economic, and athletic organisations'. This provoked an ill-
tempered and meandering debate on membership criteria, the role of
foreign bodies in controlling its activities, and the future of militant
republicanism. After much manoeuvring, O'Connor was nominated to
its central committee, despite an apparent agreement to limit membership to those living within a day's travel of Dublin. Speaking 'for an
organisation in my own state of a quarter of a million', he promptly

nominated de Valera as president of the new 'world organisation' (Fine Ghaedheal, or Family of the Gael). He lavished praise on 'the last man to surrender' in Easter Week, implausibly claiming that while in America de Valera had 'made more friends than any man I ever knew who came from a foreign country, owing to his unselfishness, dignity, and the clear, orderly way in which he conducted his campaign'.

O'Connor went on to promise that the committee 'can look at least to the United States for twenty thousand or thirty thousand dollars to start with'. Yet he emphasised that overseas funding would depend on inclusiveness: 'I think we cannot draw the line at all in making this an Organisation of Irish men and Irish women or of Irish birth.'[18] He may have been thinking of his close associate in Paris, Joseph John Castellini of Cincinnati (who disingenuously presented himself as 'simply a poor, plain business man, never was in politics').[19] In any case, Michael Joseph O'Connor had made a powerful impression in Paris, even if Fine Ghaedheal never managed to fulfil its grandiose promise by securing adequate funds, let alone organising and directing the Irish race worldwide. The organisation's legacy was its name, which in simplified form (as Fine Gael, oddly rendered into English as United Ireland) was resurrected by the Treatyists in 1933.

If O'Connor, like Fine Ghaedheal, has been generally forgotten, another Leitrim visitor from New York was to attain lasting celebrity. James Gralton gave no hint of any political motive when he applied for a 6-month passport to visit Ireland (altered by a clerk to 'British Isles') in May 1921. This was his first such application and his only overseas trip since becoming an American citizen in 1915:

Visit mother & health. (James Gralton, chauffeur, 1886, 1907, 1921)

His description and photograph depict a rather dour figure, who might have passed for 65 rather than 35: shortish yet stooped, of dark complexion and bald, with an oblong face, grey eyes, pointed chin, straight nose, and no distinguishing marks.[20] James Gralton (1886–1945) was a farmer's son from Effrinagh in Drumsna electoral division, to the east of Carrick-on-Shannon. In 1901, he was living with his parents and five siblings in a 'standard dwelling' (thatched with three rooms and three front windows), where they remained in 1911 after his departure from Queenstown in 1907. Though his parents had no Irish, a younger sister could speak the language by 1911.

The Graltons are reputed to have been 'Fenians' (though in rural Leitrim this may merely have signified involvement in agrarian agitation). James Gralton had a varied early career, working as a grocery boy in Carrick, a bartender in Dublin, a soldier in the Royal Irish Regiment before deserting to avoid service in India, a docker in Liverpool, and a miner in Wales. Once in the United States, he served in the navy and worked as a barman and taxi-driver.[21] Exploration of genealogical sources reveals further complications. On arrival from Queenstown in April 1907 to join a sister in Brooklyn, he had brown hair, blue eyes, a fair complexion, and an extra inch and a half by comparison with 1921. Occupied as a fireman, he had already spent 2 years in Texas. Three years later, he appeared in the census as an unemployed driver of ice-waggons, boarding with a laundress. In 1925, he was again a boarder and a mere 'laborer'; by 1930, he had reverted to chauffeur, this time working for a wholesale bakery. When registering for the draft in 1942, he had regained an inch and some hair (now 'gray'), developed a ruddy complexion, and acquired tattoos on both arms. These records illustrate the vagaries of so many migratory careers, and the anomalies and contradictions to be found in so many official documents.[22]

Gralton became a radical Irish republican in the United States, joining the Communist Party and forming a James Connolly club. He is reported to have raised money for the IRA before returning in June 1921 to Leitrim, where he trained local Volunteers. As the SS *Cedric* was not due to leave New York until 11 June, he experienced at most three weeks of the 'War of Independence', suggesting that his initial military contribution was to train uniformed 'Truciliers' in the open, without fear of arrest or violence, in preparation for ceremonial inspections by senior officers.[23] He also erected the 'Pearse–Connolly Memorial Hall' on the family farm in Effrinagh, using voluntary labour. The hall was run by an amalgam of republicans, farmers, and trades unionists, and was used for republican courts and settlement of land disputes. Gralton was imprisoned by the National Army for forcible dispossession, and he returned to the United States just before the eruption of civil war.[24] He remained active in Irish affairs, joining New York's Leitrim republican club in 1927, and returned to Ireland in March 1932, 'partly due to the death of his brother Charles, who had run the farm, and the poor health of his parents'. The Irish Free State was in turmoil, de Valera's Fianna Fáil having just formed a minority government despite accusations of complicity with the IRA and communism ('the Red Scare').

During his 18 months back in Ireland, Gralton achieved international celebrity as a victim of church and state. Having joined an IRA group after expulsion from Fianna Fáil, he outraged the clergy and all major political parties by his espousal of social radicalism and alleged promotion of loose morals and prostitution in his hall, which was burned down on Christmas Eve 1932. In March 1933, he was served with a deportation order as an undesirable alien. While he was on the run for the next

5 months, a campaign on his behalf received little support outside his own locality, being disavowed by the IRA's army council and a local Fianna Fáil deputy as well as the clergy. Back in America after his eventual arrest and deportation, Gralton failed to secure election as a Communist in Manhattan, and sealed his connection with Leitrim by marrying a Drumsna woman shortly before his death. His reputation as a dissident radical hero, who defied clericalism, conservatism, and intolerance in the Irish Free State, has been fostered by several books and memoirs, Donal O'Kelly's 'folk-play' *Jimmy Gralton's Dancehall* (2010), and Ken Loach's rollicking good yarn, the film *Jimmy's Hall* (2013). If Gralton was an agent of 'Americanisation', the radical version of Americanism that he embodied was as much at odds with the prevailing outlook in the United States as in Ireland.

Politically far apart, Gralton and O'Connor both displayed the hybrid characteristics of many politically active Irishmen whose adult life was spent mainly in America. O'Connor, through his dream of a world organisation for the Irish race, sought to associate those born in Ireland, like himself, with a much broader and loosely defined penumbra of people of Irish descent or simply with Irish sympathies, mirroring the intrinsic dualities of all successful 'Irish' bodies in the United States. Gralton, like so many Irish socialists with direct experience of American syndicalism or socialism, struggled to graft his American-fostered radicalism on to his ingrained Irish nationalism. The ultimate failure of both enterprises reflected the social and cultural gulf between rural Ireland and urban America, and the practical obstacles facing any returned American with strongly developed 'hyphenated' values. Though international migration created and sustained powerful 'transnational' networks, these often found themselves at odds with prevailing opinion in both Ireland and the countries of Irish settlement.

Table 9.1 *Object of proposed trips by Leitrim passport applicants, 1914–25*

Category	Number	%	Notes
1. Visit Relatives	*371*	*78.4*	
Parents	222	*81.6	*Father 33, mother 88, both 101*
Siblings	49	*18.0	*Brother 20, sister 13, both 16*
Other Specified Relatives	18	*6.6	*Spouse/child 11, in-law 6, nephew 1*
Total Specified	*272*	*73.3*	
Unspecified Relatives	99	26.7	
2. Visit Friends	*9*	*1.9*	
3. Business	*82*	*17.3*	
Business, Estate, Property	20	24.4	*BEP*
Family BEP	16	19.5	
Personal EP	12	14.6	
Personal Business	8	9.8	
Look after EP	6	7.3	
Employment	13	15.9	
Commercial	3	3.7	
Church	1	1.2	
Unspecified Business	3	3.7	
4. Tourism	*56*	*11.8*	
Travel	31	55.4	
Pleasure	16	28.6	
Vacation	4	7.1	
Visit	5	8.9	
5. Health of Visitors	*31*	*6.6*	
6. Accompany Another Person	*9*	*1.9*	
7. Other	*6*	*1.3*	
Total with Specified Object	*473*	*100*	*Unspecified in 4 cases*

Note: Stated objects are assigned to seven overlapping categories, so that the sum of percentage figures exceeds 100. Percentages in italics refer to the proportion of all 473 applications in which an object was specified. Within each category, percentages refer to proportions of the category total. This also applies to the overlapping sub-categories of specified relatives (asterisked).

10   Visitors from America: Faces

This chapter restores faces to seventy-eight Leitrim American visitors, parading a wide range of moods, styles, and physical attributes. The passport images are arranged thematically, and basic information such as occupation is supplied for each subject. Family groups and married couples are followed by women (stylish and otherwise) and several male categories (particular attention being given to ties and moustaches). Many of those chosen have been introduced in preceding chapters. Hundreds of interesting photographs could not be used because of the poor quality of accessible images, though a few grainy or fuzzy faces were too distinctive to be omitted.

The passport montage is followed by photographs of nine men of Leitrim taken by Harvard ethnographers in the mid-1930s, representing morphological types. Some of these types have rough matches among the passport images. The bearded Francis McGovern and Patrick Milton (Figure 10) resemble the aged 'Nordic Alpine' (Figure 14). James McHugh (Figure 8), Michael McMorrow (Figure 9), and even James Henigan (Figure 12) call to mind the 'Dinaric' representative (Figure 15). John Short (Figure 10) has some facial affinity with the 'Nordic Mediterranean' (Figure 16). Yet it is not practicable to firmly assign passport applicants to Harvard types, as one could only surmise the 'cephalic index' of long-headedness from their photographs and facial descriptions. Subjects are named in the order of appearance on each page.

Description of figures

Figure 1 Family groups, often unintentionally, convey a good deal about human relationships as well as pictorial conventions. Peter McGloin (labourer), Michael McMorrow (marine engineer), Peter Gilbane (carpenter), Patrick Stratton (storekeeper), Peter Flynn ('special officer'), and Patrick Byrne (retired police sergeant) all intended to travel with their wives and children. These families with both parents present seemed composed before the camera, though Gilbane had to restrain a squirming son. All wished to visit Irish relatives except McMorrow, who was prompted by 'sickness and travel', and Sergeant Byrne, who was travelling for 'pleasure'. Byrne had married a Bostonian; the other wives whose birthplace was recorded were both Irish.

Figure 2 Many mothers applied to travel with children, while their husbands either stayed at home or travelled on separate passports. Among the happier mothers were Alice McEnroy, Ellen Gilogly, Teresa Devlin, Annie Walker, pert Mary Kate Smyth, and Mary O'Hara. Devlin, the only widow in this group, was the first to emigrate (in 1897). All proposed to visit Irish relatives, but McEnroy was also looking forward to collecting a son from Ireland. All had married Irish men except Walker (an American) and O'Hara (an Englishman, despite his surname).

Figure 3 To a jaundiced modern eye, there are hints of disappointment and stress in the faces of Katherine Brennan, Catherine Madden, Margaret Boles, Rose Clancy Flynn (with solemn son in sailor suit), and the unfortunate Sarah Gregory (see above, page 199). All except Madden (the elegant widow, who was already in Ireland) intended to visit Irish parents. Gregory and her daughters are depicted before leaving for Ireland in 1916 and again 3 years later, when they proposed to return to Brooklyn. Only Brennan and Flynn had Irish husbands, Gregory having married an American. Margaret Boles from Edinburgh and her children are pictured without her husband, a grain handler from Leitrim who travelled on a separate passport.

Figure 4 The body language of the six chosen couples conveys remoteness more often than intimacy. The husbands were John James O'Brien (electrician), John Sweeney (truckman), Hugh O'Rourke (foreman), Henry Burns (coachman), John Thomas Coulter (shipping clerk), and Francis Gaynor (a former iron worker who had emigrated in 1885). The Coulters were distinctly the frostiest couple, whereas the grave Gaynors were intimate enough to touch elbows on a garden bench. Most were visiting Irish relatives, but Sweeney was also intent on 'personal business and pleasure'. All the wives were Irish except the butch Burns, whose birthplace was not recorded.

Figure 5 These six women of assorted 'types' were granity Bridget Walsh (nurse), kindly Harriet Daly, Mary O'Leary the Irish colleen, Margaret Connolly (another nurse, erect and masterful), defiant Catherine McHugh (chocolate-dipper), and wistful Mary McGowan (waitress).

The first three had married Irishmen, Walsh having been widowed for 18 years; the rest remained single. All were visiting relatives, though Nurse Connolly was also accompanying a sick sister to Ireland. Daly was bound for Australia to visit a sister, a reminder of the convolutions of international migration.

Figure 6 Six more or less stylish women have been selected here: Rose Anne McGovern (nurse), Bessie Vizion (wife of an American), Elizabeth O'Brien (wife of Irishman), Katherine McLaughlin (wife of Irishman), Mary Grimes (waitress), and Margaret McNiff (houseworker). All proposed to visit Irish relatives. Hats, not then forbidden in passport photographs, were unmistakable declarations of style: Vivion's floral chimney-pot and O'Brien's feathered traffic-cone were particularly over the top, while McLaughlin's portrait appears to be a hazy study in fur.

Figure 7 Would-be stylish men were more restrained, discreetly sporting a white kerchief (James McHugh, salesman), neat coiffure (debonair Mark Elias Schomberg Kerr, oil-pumper), demure waistcoat (John Flynn, steam-fitter), folded arms and sleek hair (Patrick J. Muldoon, cooper), and bow tie (James Earely, retired city fireman). Kerr was bound for France as a Red Cross ambulance driver; McHugh's object of travel was the purchase of merchandise in the British Isles and France; and Flynn was engaged in engineering work in the Far East. The remainder hoped to visit Irish relatives or property (Earely also hoped to benefit his health).

Figure 8 Almost all male applicants wore ties, only occasionally patterned or light coloured. The chosen extroverts were John James Kelly (electrical worker), John J. McLaughlin (conductor), James McHugh (watchman), James McCue (floor-man), Edward White (retired, with bow tie), and Andrew Gallagher (attorney). Kelly's spotted tie offset the gloomy effect of his moon glasses, while McHugh's elaborate patterns contrasted nicely with his bushy moustache. McHugh, who was suffering from leukaemia, hoped the trip would improve his health. All except Gallagher, off to France for the Knights of Columbus, were bound for Ireland, but only Kelly and McCue proposed to visit relatives. McLaughlin was looking forward to a 'pleasure trip' to his home country and White to 'travel' throughout the British Isles.

Figure 9 Few fashion statements are more nuanced than one's choice of moustache. Those selected are a 'lampshade' moustache (Michael Bohen, chauffeur), two 'walruses' (Michael McMorrow, labourer, and Thomas James Murphy, seaman), and three 'chevrons' (Michael Cullen, foreman, John Molloy, steel-worker, and Patrick J. O'Connor,

Peter McGloin (labourer)

Michael McMorrow (marine engineer)

Figure 1 *Family groups*

Peter Gilbane (carpenter)

Patrick Stratton (storekeeper)

Figure 1 (*cont.*)

Peter Flynn ('special officer')

Patrick Byrne (retired police sergeant)

Figure 1 (*cont.*)

Alice McEnroy

Ellen Gilogly

Figure 2 *Mothers with children: I*

Teresa Devlin

Annie Walker

Figure 2 (*cont.*)

Teresa Devlin

Mary O'Hara

Figure 2 (*cont.*)

Katherine Brennan

Catherine Madden

Figure 3 *Mothers with children: II*

Margaret Boles

Rose Clancy Flynn

Sarah Gregory (1916)

Sarah Gregory (1919)

Figure 3 *(cont.)*

John James O'Brien (electrician)

John Sweeney (truckman)

Figure 4 *Six rather formal couples*

Hugh O'Rourke (foreman)

Henry Burns (coachman)

John Thomas Coulter (shipping clerk)

Figure 4 *(cont.)*

Francis Gaynor (former iron worker)

Figure 4 (*cont.*)

Bridget Walsh (nurse)

Harriet Daly

Figure 5 *Assorted women travellers*

Mary O'Leary

Margaret Connolly (nurse)

Catherine McHugh (chocolate-dipper)

Figure 5 *(cont.)*

Mary McGowan (waitress)

Figure 5 (*cont.*)

Rose Anne McGovern (nurse)

Bessie Vizion

Figure 6 *Stylish women*

Elizabeth O'Brien

Katherine McLaughlin

Mary Grimes (waitress)

Figure 6 *(cont.)*

Margaret McNiff (houseworker)

Figure 6 *(cont.)*

James McHugh (salesman)

Figure 7 *Would-be stylish men*

Mark Elias Schomberg Kerr (oil-pumper)

John Flynn (steam-fitter)

Patrick J. Muldoon (cooper)

Figure 7 *(cont.)*

James Earely (retired city fireman)

Figure 7 *(cont.)*

John James Kelly (electrical worker)

John J. McLaughlin (conductor)

Figure 8 *Extrovert tie-wearers*

James McHugh (watchman)

James McCue (floor-man)

Edward White (retired)

Figure 8 (*cont.*)

Andrew Gallagher (attorney)

Figure 8 (*cont.*)

Michael Bohen (chauffeur)

Michael McMorrow (labourer)

Figure 9 *Styles of moustache*

Thomas James Murphy (seaman)

Michael Cullen (foreman)

John Molloy (steel-worker)

Figure 9 (*cont.*)

Patrick J. O'Connor (government official)

Figure 9 (*cont.*)

Patrick Ginty (police detective)

John Short (labourer)

Figure 10 *Diverse men*

John McNiffe (railroad guard)

John Joseph McGoldrick (salesman)

Francis McGovern (solicitor)

Figure 10 (*cont.*)

Patrick Milton (merchant)

Figure 10 *(cont.)*

John McGovern (barber)

Figure 11 *Assorted male 'types'*

Peter Kenny (hotel footman)

Peter Maguire (driver)

Figure 11 (*cont.*)

John McGovern (barber)

James Callahan (machine-shop worker)

James McGurn (clerk)

Figure 11 *(cont.)*

James Mulvey (blacksmith)

Thomas Henigan (farmer)

Michael McPartlan (longshoreman)

Figure 12 *More male 'types'*

Michael Travers (longshoreman)

Thomas Beirne (stationary engineer)

Michael James O'Rourke (labourer)

Figure 12 *(cont.)*

Father Thomas M. Tubman

Father John Joseph O'Neill

Father Patrick Joseph Smyth

Figure 13 *Roman Catholic priests*

Father James John Farrelly

Father Peter Keany

Father Francis McCaffrey

Figure 13 (*cont.*)

81-year-old 'Nordic Alpine' type

20-year-old 'Predominantly Nordic' type

42-year-old 'Nordic Alpine' type

Figure 14 *Men of Leitrim (Harvard ethnographers' photos)*

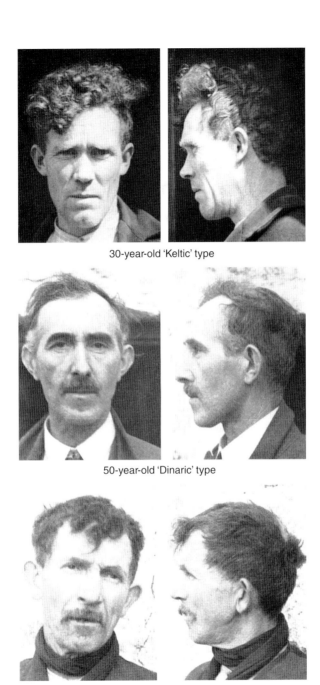

30-year-old 'Keltic' type

50-year-old 'Dinaric' type

64-year-old 'Pure Mediterranean' type

Figure 15 *Harvard ethnographers' 'types': I*

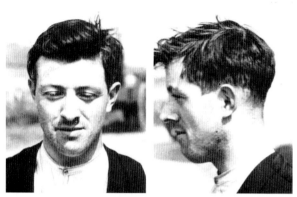

24-year-old 'Nordic Mediterranean' type

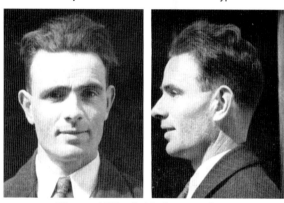

28-year-old 'Nordic Mediterranean' type

29-year-old 'East Baltic' type

Figure 16 *Harvard ethnographers' 'types': II*

government official). Other applicants sported the odd 'painter's brush' or 'toothbrush' (Charlie Chaplin), but 'imperials' were unrepresented. Bohen intended to 'visit friends' in Ireland and Britain, Cullen wished to sell his property in Ireland, Molloy was travelling for 'pleasure', and O'Connor was shepherding a deported alien to Britain; only McMorrow and Murphy were visiting Irish relatives.

Figure 10 Six diversely expressive applicants were the slick Patrick Ginty (police detective), self-conscious John Short (labourer), bold John McNiffe (railroad guard), worldly-wise John Joseph McGoldrick (salesman), bearded Francis McGovern (solicitor), and wildly hirsute Patrick Milton (a merchant from Chattanooga, Tennessee, who had emigrated in 1864). Ginty's shiny suit and ostentatious Panama boater might as fittingly have adorned a crook as a detective. All proposed to visit relatives or conduct family business in Ireland.

Figure 11 Assorted male 'types' are exemplified by the studious John McGovern (barber), smoothly hairless Peter Kenny (hotel footman), neatly scrubbed Peter Maguire (driver), sturdy Daniel McMorrow (fireman), Draculean James Callahan (machine-shop worker), and clubbable James McGurn (clerk). All proposed to visit Ireland, mostly to visit relatives; Callahan was intending to join his daughter there. None had emigrated to the USA before 1888, when McGovern left Ireland for New York.

Figure 12 The rough countryman in city gear is represented by the simian James Mulvey (blacksmith of Anaconda, Montana), belligerent Thomas Henigan (farmer), startled Michael McPartlan (longshoreman), weepy Michael Travers (longshoreman), stolid Thomas Beirne (stationary engineer), and perplexed Michael James O'Rourke (labourer). They were recent arrivals, having emigrated between 1904 and 1915. With the exception of Mulvey, all lived in New York and intended to visit Ireland to see relatives or deal with property. McPartlan, Travers, and O'Rourke also intended to travel to France in 1922, O'Rourke at least having served with the wartime American army.

Figure 13 Applicants in the Roman Catholic priesthood included the genial Thomas M. Tubman, calmly confident John Joseph O'Neill, apprehensive Patrick Joseph Smyth, bleak James John Farrelly, sinister Peter Keany, and prissy Francis McCaffrey. Farrelly is the subject of a case study in Dunnigan's thesis, 'Irish Return Migration'. Apart from Keany, whose objective was to travel to the British Isles and France, all proposed to visit Irish relatives. 'Business for church' also summoned Smyth to Italy and France. Apart from Tubman and Farrelly, who had emigrated in 1884 and 1892, all had entered the USA since 1903.

Figure 14 The photographs taken by Harvard ethnographers provide an arresting record of the appearance and attire of ten men of Leitrim in the mid-1930s. Though less often formally dressed than the passport applicants, five wore ties for the occasion and two had scarves. Two each had beards and moustaches. They were selected to represent the 'morphological' types by which Hooton and Dupertuis chose to classify their subjects. As mentioned in Chapter 8, the ethnographers failed to demonstrate that the Irish were predominantly 'Keltic', and found no significant traces in mountainy Leitrim of the 'Pure Mediterranean' ('Firbolg') physiognomy. These types were defined by combinations of various physical attributes: head shape (long or round), eye colour, and hair colour, with occasional reference to height or the shape of noses. Figure 14 contrasts a well-kempt 'Predominantly Nordic' 20-year-old with two 'Nordic Alpines': a scraggily bearded 'Nordic Alpine' 81-year-old and a scantily moustached 42-year-old. These types accounted, respectively, for 8% and 18% of 734 men surveyed in the Leitrim region. The youth had red hair, green-brown eyes, and a long head; the old man of the mountains had red-brown hair, blue eyes, and a round head; while his fellow Nordic Alpine had brown hair, blue-brown eyes, and a round head.

Figure 15 These images represent three distinct types: 'Keltic', 'Dinaric', and 'Pure Mediterranean'. These types accounted, respectively, for 26%, 16%, and just 1.1% of men measured in the Leitrim region. The curly-haired 'Keltic' 30-year-old had red hair, blue eyes, and a round head. The tall 'Dinaric' 50-year-old with a moustache had dark brown hair, blue-brown eyes, and a long head. The scraggy, stubbly 64-year-old 'Pure Mediterranean' had dark brown hair, darkish brown eyes, and a round head, providing a cherished relic of the fabled 'Firbolg'.

Figure 16 portrays two 'Nordic Mediterraneans' aged 24 and 28, and an 'East Baltic', types found among 29% and 1.2% of men measured in the Leitrim region. Both 'Nordic Mediterraneans' had dark brown hair, blue-brown eyes, and very round heads. The 'East Baltic' 29-year-old had red hair, blue-brown eyes, and a round head. Like the younger 'Nordic Mediterranean', he dressed informally and plastered his roughly cut hair with plenty of Brylcreem, a product unavailable to passport applicants having been launched in 1928.

Epilogue: Questions Unanswered

This book has portrayed an American expatriate population very different from the cultural emissaries of American values to be found in nineteenth-century Britain or Europe. Only a small, if fascinating, minority belonged to the mainly urban elite that dominated American settlement elsewhere. Ireland was surely the only European country whose American-born population was overwhelmingly shaped by previous emigration. As revealed by passport applications, this also applied to American citizens of rural Irish birth who visited Ireland in the aftermath of the First World War. Both groups were strikingly representative of the rural poor from which they had sprung, and among whom they lived when 'at home' in Ireland. At least in the case of the thousands of American-born children and sometimes their parents who sheltered with Irish kinsfolk in the early twentieth century, Ireland's 'Americans' were more likely to be regarded with pity than with envy, being apparently 'losers' in the game of international migration. This fundamental contrast to the prevailing stereotype of American wealth and success meant that 'Americanisation' was a far darker experience in Ireland than in Britain. Yet it was also more solidly grounded in personal interaction and direct observation, because the American human presence was proportionately far greater and more diffused in Ireland.

In its inception, this demographic study was not intended to stand alone. I had aimed to cover a broader canvas. I had long since remarked that those at home reacted to American and exotic influences in different ways: by aping 'foreign' fashions and life-skills; by doggedly reviving 'archaic' practices (potato-eating, the match, Irish-speaking); or by combining both traditional and modern world-views through the exercise of imagination (reverse 'hyphenation'). A second instalment would have depicted the broader transnational experience of Ireland's forgotten Americanisation, examining the balance of trade in each flow, whether of money or skills or sentiment.

As a contribution to the history of Ireland and Irish people, this might have led to a fundamental reinterpretation of many key processes associated with post-Famine 'modernisation'. Past historians have used the elusive concept of 'Anglicisation' to explain the decline of the Irish language, the spread of literacy in English, the diffusion of 'bourgeois values', the patterns of Irish economic growth and reorganisation, the focus of Irish politics on the question of 'nationality', and widespread adherence to a parliamentary model of democracy. It may be found that, in each of these fields, Americanisation exercised a comparable influence. The 'English' language and literature that suffused Ireland were increasingly tinged by American influences; the thirst for English literacy and the concomitant decline of Irish were dictated by the skills required for successful emigration; Irish aspirations for upward social and occupational mobility were American-inflected; American models of marketing and trading reshaped Irish business practice; and all Irish political factions (nationalist and unionist, violent and 'constitutional', conservative and radical) were deeply influenced by American political models and the quest for American funding. This strongly suggests that the course of modern Irish history is inexplicable without confronting Americanisation. Likewise, the reverse impact of transatlantic migration on Europe cannot be fully understood without systematic study of Ireland, the most transnational yet still the most elusive of all nineteenth-century homelands.

A critical issue for any such study is the degree to which Ireland's Americanisation process was exceptional in the British and European context. It is obvious that American cultural products (such as books, journals, music hall acts, and cinema) were often brought to Ireland by British-based publishers or impresarios, and that Ireland shared in the growing European identification of American culture with modernity. Yet this process of increasingly global cultural diffusion must be set against the impact of personal contact and exchange between Irish residents and their American friends or relatives. Because no other country had comparably intense migration to America, no other country was so deeply and densely exposed to these personal American influences. Personal exposure American influences tended to challenge or undermine the mainly positive stereotypes generated by mass marketing of 'American' cultural products – not least because so many emigrants returned home, or fostered their children with Irish relatives, because of insufficient income or living space in American cities. The 'New World' in which Irish emigrants had invested so much faith and hope, if not always charity, had failed to sustain many of the immigrant poor. Direct human contact, though only one of many channels for Americanisation, was crucial in setting Ireland apart from its neighbours in the ways that it responded to this profound cultural challenge.

Unfortunately, illness has made it impracticable for me to pursue these themes. I hope that other scholars will recognise the potential of 'Americanisation' to underpin a major recasting of post-Famine Irish history, and to challenge some deeply entrenched assumptions about the character and timing of Ireland's 'modernisation' and 'globalisation'.[1] Meanwhile, I wish to pay tribute to the growing array of historians of the Irish who have done so much to liberate their subject from the self-imposed restrictions by which it was, until recently, confined and distorted. It has been my honour and pleasure to play some part in that exhilarating enterprise.

David Fitzpatrick
September 2018

Notes

1 The US Passport Collection Database, 1795–1925, is available online at: www.ancestry.co.uk/search/categories/img_bordercross.

I. BEYOND EMIGRATION

1 For development of these points, see my articles cited in the next footnote.
2 Much of this chapter presents, in much revised form, arguments and evidence set out in sections of my four contributions to *A New History of Ireland*, W. E. Vaughan (ed.), vols 5 and 6: 'Emigration, 1801–70' and 'The Irish in Britain, 1801–70', in vol. 5 (Oxford University Press, 1989), 567–622, 623–60; 'Emigration, 1871–1921' and 'The Irish in Britain, 1871–1921', in vol. 6 (Oxford University Press, 1996), 606–52, 653–702. I am grateful to Robert Faber (formerly of Oxford University Press) for permission to incorporate this material, to which I have added a more extensive and detailed statistical analysis of migration flows.
3 *Fourth Report of the Select Committee of the House of Lords appointed to inquire into the Operation of the Irish Poor Law*, 819–21, in House of Commons Papers (HCP) 1849 (365), xvi (evidence of Thomas Larcom). Paupers were charged to the union at large unless resident in a particular District Electoral Division (DED) for the period stated.
4 Published census returns by birthplace for thirty-one counties (Antrim, Down, and Belfast being combined because of anomalous enumeration) were used to compute (a) natives of a county resident elsewhere in Ireland, and (b) persons from elsewhere in Ireland resident in a county, as a proportion of that county's population at each census between 1841 and 1911. To avoid distortion because of anomalous figures for Dublin and the Belfast district, the correlations between county distributions are limited to the other twenty-nine counties. For outward displacement (a) in 1841 and 1871, we obtain $r = +.96$. For inward displacement (b), $r = +.88$. The correlation between the distributions for outward and inward displacement was $r = +.73$ (1841), $r = +.69$ (1851), and $r = +.78$ (1871).

5 After 1861, no census tabulation of migrant occupations was provided. As in all subsequent references to 'over-representation' etc. of an occupation (or other category) within a certain group, our index gives the ratio of (a) to (b), where (a) is the proportion of occupied members of that group following the stated occupation, whereas (b) is the proportion of persons occupied in Ireland following the same occupation.

6 For outward displacement (a) in 1871 and 1911, we obtain $r = +.93$. For inward displacement (b), $r = +.92$. The correlation between the distributions for outward and inward displacement was $r = +.78$ (1871) and $r = +.81$ (1911).

7 Census of Ireland (1841), 450–1, in HCP 1843 (504), xxiv.

8 Cormac ÓGráda, 'Seasonal Migration and Post-Famine Adjustment in the West of Ireland', *Studia Hibernica*, 13 (1973): 48–76. See also Ruth-Ann Mellish Harris, *The Nearest Place that Wasn't Ireland: Early Nineteenth-Century Irish Labor Migration*, PhD thesis, Tufts, 1980; published under the same title by Iowa State University Press, 1994).

9 For passengers to Britain (1841) expressed as a proportion of each county's population, the coefficient of variation (CV) = .98 (thirty-two counties). The corresponding figure for all 'permanent' emigrants leaving Irish ports between May 1851 and December 1860 is CV = .28.

10 *Report and Tables relating to Irish Migratory Agricultural and Other Labourers* (annual, 1880–1915, under variant titles), in HCP.

11 *Report from the Select Committee on Tenure and Improvement of Land (Ireland) Act*, 194, in HCP 1865 (402), xi (evidence of William Keane, bishop of Cloyne (1857–74).

12 Arnold Schrier, *Ireland and the American Emigration, 1850–1900* (Minneapolis: University of Minnesota Press, 1958), 129–43; Marjolein 't Hart, 'Irish Return Migration in the Nineteenth Century', *Tijdschrift voor Economische en Sociale Geografie*, 76(3) (1985): 223–31; 't Hart, 'Heading for Paddy's Green Shamrock Shore: The Returned Emigrants in Nineteenth-Century Ireland', MA thesis, University of Groningen, 1981; Poor Inquiry (Ireland), *Appendix G: Baronial Examinations*, 134, in HCP 1836 (39), xxxiv, 1.

13 't Hart, 'Irish Return Migration'.

14 G. R. C. Keep, 'Some Irish Opinion on Population and Emigration, 1851–1901', *Irish Ecclesiastical Record*, 5th ser., 84 (1955): 384 (citing *Belfast News-Letter*, 13 July 1874).

15 *Copy of Statistical Tables relating to Emigration and Immigration … in the Year 1876*, 12–16, in HCP 1877 (5), lxxxv, 632–6. This unique return gives immigration from each country by *port*, enabling us to estimate the number of Irish immigrants for comparison with that of emigrants (assuming that all passengers at Irish ports and one-tenth of those at Liverpool were Irish). These estimates indicate that net outward movement of steerage passengers during 1876 was only 838 to the US, 122 to British North America, 686 to Australia, and 192 elsewhere. New outward movement of cabin passengers to the last three destinations was 10, 59, and 106 in turn; while net interchange of cabin passengers with the US was inward, amounting to 915 passengers.

16 For each of the eight quinquennia between 1876 and 1880 and 1911 and 1915, the repatriant ratios for the US were 56, 27, 37, 52, 59, 52, 47, and 73. The corresponding ratios for British North America were 40, 23, 29, 47, 58, 28, 29, and 37. The ratios for Australasia diverged somewhat, being 14, 17, 32, 72, 67, 62, 37, and 27.

17 Drew Keeling, *The Business of Transatlantic Migration between Europe and the United States, 1900–1914* (Zurich: Chronos Verlag, 2012).

18 The only detailed annual returns for British subjects (including Irish nationals) travelling between ports in the UK and the US relate to 1913: *Copy of Tables relating to Emigration and Immigration from and into the UK in the Year 1913*, in HCP 1914 (295), lxix, 941. The proportions leaving or reaching the UK in the first and final quarters, respectively, were 28.7% and 12.5% (immigrants to UK from US), 18.1% and 15.3% (emigrants from UK to US), 29.7% and 13.1% (temporary visitors from US to UK), and 14.4% and 29.9% (temporary visitors from UK to US).

19 For convenience in this section, the terms 'America' and 'American' denote only the USA. Canada (otherwise British North America) is separately tabulated among 'other countries'.

20 The repatriant ratios for British subjects with colonial and foreign residence were 162 and 378, respectively.

21 This calculation incorporates passengers of British colonial birth, separately enumerated from 1908 but excluded from the returns by nationality used for Tables 1.1 and 1.2. The repatriant ratio for colonials alone (1908–11) was 204, while the ratio for those of British or Irish nationality alone (1903–11) was 44%. We may conclude that the effect of excluding colonials from these computations is trivial.

22 The fact that not all British subjects entering or leaving Irish ports were Irish residents, while not all Irish residents entered or left Irish ports, precludes an exact comparison between Irish and British incidence of 'permanent' as against temporary migration.

23 Permanent migration of aliens with British residence was much greater (8,807 inwards and 18,080 outwards), as was temporary migration of aliens with British residence (1,720 inwards and 937 outwards). In the British case, it is likely that many of these migrants were of European origin rather than Britons who had taken up citizenship elsewhere.

24 This strand is subsumed within the huge mass of alien passengers without UK residence, including 180,171 inward passengers from the USA with foreign residence and 296,565 outward passengers to the USA (mostly Europeans in transit via UK ports). There was virtually no temporary migration of aliens with Irish residence (18 inwards and 4 outwards).

25 J. D. Gould, 'European Inter-Continental Emigration, the Road Home: Return Migration from the USA', *Journal of European Economic History*, 9(1) (1980): 55–60. Similar calculations by 'race or people' rather than birthplace produce an Irish repatriant ratio of 1 to 6, also the lowest of Gould's series.

26 Michael MacGowan, *The Hard Road to Klondyke* (London: Routledge, 1962), 139.

27 MacGowan, *Hard Road*, 145; P. D. Murphy, 'Village Characters, II: The Returned Emigrant', *Ireland's Own*, 29 (30 May 1917), 364.

28 John Millington Synge, *The Aran Islands, in Collected Works*, 4 vols (Oxford University Press, 1962–8), vol. 2, *Prose*, ed. Alan Price (1966), 96.

29 *Minutes of Evidence taken before Her Majesty's Commissioners on Agriculture* [Richmond Commission], 1013, in HCP 1881 (C 2778–I), xv (evidence of Charles Hare Hemphill, concerning Kerry); Devonshire Commission, *Reports by Fox*, 57.

30 George A. Birmingham (Revd. J. O. Hannay), *The Lighter Side of Irish Life* (Edinburgh: T. N. Foulis, new edn, 1924), 213–14.

31 *Report of the Royal Commission on the Land Law (Ireland) Act, 1881*, 42, in HCP 1887 (C 4969), xxvi, 74 (evidence of A. Newtown Brady, Connemara).

32 Birmingham, *Lighter Side*, 211.

33 't Hart, 'Irish Return Migration', 225.

34 Royal Commission of Congestion in Ireland [Dudley Commission], *Appendix to Ninth Report*, 133, in HCP 1908 (Cd 3845), xli; *Appendix to Tenth Report*, 50, in HCP 1908 (Cd 4007), xlii; *Appendix to Fifth Report*, 167, in HCP 1907 (Cd 3630), xxxvi (evidence of Revd. John Fallon, Revd. Michael McHugh, and John Fitzgibbon, respectively). See also Schrier, *Ireland and the American Emigration*, 130–1.

35 *Emigration! Where Shall I Go? By an Australian Colonist* (London: W. Tweedie, 1869), 13.

36 *Report of Her Majesty's Commissioners of Inquiry into the Working of the Landlord and Tenant (Ireland) Act, 1870, and the Acts amending the Same* (Bessborough Commission), *Appendix D*, q. 1546, in HCP 1881 (C. 2779–III), xix (evidence of Daniel O'Donnell).

37 *Royal Commission of Inquiry into the Procedure and Practice and the Methods of Valuation … Minutes of Evidence*, 889, in HCP 1898 (C 8859), xxxv (evidence of James Berry).

38 Ibid., 660 (evidence of Thomas Barry).

39 Dudley Commission, *Appendix to Ninth Report*, 221, in HCP 1908 (Cd 3748), xxxix, 1001 (evidence of Farrell Reynolds).

40 *Report from the Select Committee on Law of Rating (Ireland) … Minutes of Evidence*, 328, in HCP 1871 (423), x (evidence of Michael FitzHenry Sweetman).

41 Robert Lynd, *Home Life in Ireland* (London: Mills & Boon, 1909), 121.

42 J. H. Tuke, 'With the Emigrants', *Nineteenth Century*, 12 (July 1882), 152.

43 Michael O'Riordan, *Catholicity and Progress in Ireland* (London: Kegan Paul, 1906), 292.

2. COSMOPOLITAN IRELAND, 1841–1911

1 Cormac Ó Gráda, *Jewish Ireland in the Age of Joyce: A Socioeconomic History* (Princeton University Press, 2006); Brian Reynolds, *Casalattico and the Italian Community in Ireland* (Dublin: UCD Foundation for Italian Studies, 1993), to which Jane Leonard kindly drew my attention; Kyle Hughes, *The Scots in*

Victorian and Edwardian Belfast: A Study in Élite Migration (Edinburgh University Press, 2013).

2 An earlier version of this chapter under the same title was presented to a conference held in Adelaide in 2015 in honour of my late beloved friend Eric Richards. It appeared in *Emigrants and Historians: Essays in Honour of Eric Richards*, ed. Philip Payton (Adelaide: Wakefield Press, 2017), 14–38.

3 For a pioneering introductory survey, see Irial Glynn, 'Returnees, Forgotten Foreigners and New Immigrants: Tracing Migratory Movement into Ireland since the late Nineteenth Century', in *Transnational Perspectives in Modern Irish History: Beyond the Island* (London: Routledge, 2014), 224–50.

4 Though the tool for searching the family returns by the names of thirty-two counties and thirty-one countries is potentially valuable, many foreigners are hidden within the 'other' category – currently comprising 260,982 persons in 1901 and 266,329 in 1911 – which it is not yet possible to sort by place name. The category includes many entries specifying cities (notably Belfast) or states rather than counties or countries, others with unrecognised prefixes such as 'Co.' or 'in', and numerous mis-transcriptions.

5 'Outsiders' and 'incomers', 'overseas-born', 'colonials', and 'foreigners' refer, respectively, to those born outside Ireland, outside the UK, in British possessions or India, and outside the empire.

6 If the overseas-born proportion of the population in 1861 ($n = 32$) is correlated with those for 1841, 1851, 1871, and 1911, the corresponding correlation coefficients (r) are +.88, +.87, +.83, and +.80. The strength of covariance is measured by r-squared (.77, .76, .69, and .64). For 1841 and 1911, the coefficient is +.70 (r-squared = .48).

7 Census returns for 1911 recorded 375,325 Irish in England and Wales and 174,715 in Scotland, compared with 90,237 English and Welsh and 38,486 Scots in Ireland. In proportion to the host population in 1911, however, Britons comprised 2.9% of the Irish population, whereas the Irish-born proportion of the British population was only 1.3%.

8 Unfortunately, it is not possible to extract British-born military (or naval) personnel through digital searching of the census for 1901 and 1911, because the column indicating military service in barracks returns was not indexed under occupation.

9 As already mentioned, the birthplace of most natives of the USA was given as 'America', a category also including unknown numbers from other countries. I have followed the example of many published census tabulations by aggregating figures for the entire region. The regional category of natives of America in 1911 (12,763) incorporated the following descriptions: 'America' unqualified (7,371), USA (5,049), South America (268), Argentina (31), North America (18), Mexico (11), Chile (5), Peru (3), Uruguay (2), and Costa Rica, Greenland, Guatemala, Haiti, and Santa Cruz (1 each).

10 The number of colonial sailors was negligible (2, 25, and 18 in the three census years), but a post-Famine explosion was evident in the presence of British sailors in 1851 (343, 4,920, and 4,563, respectively).

11 In 1871, the emigrant population peaked at 1,856,000 in the USA and 223,000 in Canada, falling by 1911 to 1,352,000 in the USA and 93,000 in Canada.

12 The increase of 355 in the Italian population (1861–71) was due almost entirely to the presence of 290 additional Italian seamen in 1871.

13 Of 128 identified natives of China, 62 were Episcopalians, 35 Roman Catholics, 22 Presbyterians, and 9 Christians of other denominations.

14 The ratio of Indians in Ireland (3,681) to Irish in India (12,244) was 30.1%, though the disparity for females was far smaller (1,983 to 2,291, a ratio of 86.6%). For an abstract of recorded birthplaces based on census reports for each British possession, see 'Tables relating to the British Empire', table 2.7, in Census of England and Wales (1911), *General Report*, appendix D, 352–61.

15 The search by birthplace yields 817 Canadians and 1,003 Australians (though the aggregate of county figures for the Australian-born is 1,034). Of the Australians, 219 were in Dublin, 199 in Antrim and Down, and 79 in Cork. These figures exclude many Canadians and Australians whose birthplace was returned by state, province, or city.

16 According to the 'Tables relating to the British Empire' in 1911, 139,434 natives of Ireland were enumerated in the Commonwealth of Australia, 92,874 in the Dominion of Canada, and 330 in Newfoundland (still a separate colony).

17 If the 1911 county distribution of colonials ($n = 32$) is correlated with those for Britishers and non-American foreigners, the respective coefficients of correlation are +.76 (r-squared = .58) and +.80 (.65). For Britishers and non-American foreigners, the association (+.53) is much weaker as a result of the anomalous distribution of British army barracks (r-squared = .28). In each case, the number of incomers is expressed as a proportion of the county population in 1911.

18 If the 1911 county distribution of Americans ($n = 32$) is correlated with those for colonials, Britishers, and non-American foreigners, the respective coefficients of correlation are −.03 (r-squared = .00), −.34 (.12), and −.40 (.16).

19 If the 1911 distribution of female proportions (Table 2.7, $n = 17$) is correlated with those for 1871, 1881, 1891, and 1901, the respective coefficients of correlation are +.69 (r-squared = .47), +.71 (.51), +.84 (.71), and .79 (.63).

20 The link between an even sex-balance and family migration did not, however, apply to Irish emigration, which was remarkable both for its even sex-balance and the predominance of individual migration.

21 If the 1911 distribution of proportions aged under 20 (Table 2.7, $n = 17$) is correlated with those for 1871, 1881, 1891, and 1901, the respective coefficients of correlation are +.73 (r-squared = .53), +.34 (.12), +.85 (.73), and .94 (.88). The wobble in 1881 is attributable to aberrant figures for some very small nationalities.

22 If the 1911 distribution of Dublin proportions (Table 2.7, $n = 17$) is correlated with those for 1871, 1881, 1891, and 1901, the respective coefficients of correlation are −.04 (r-squared = .00), +.55 (.31), +.57 (.32), and +.63 (.40).

23 If the 1911 distribution of Irish proportions for each nationality (Table 2.4, $n = 16$) is correlated with those for 1871, 1881, 1891, and 1901, the

respective coefficients of correlation are +.69 (*r*-squared = .47), +.71 (.51), +.84 (.71), and .79 (.63).

24 It should be noted, however, that the British exclusion of British subjects led to understatement of the true number of American and other specific nationalities by between one-quarter and one-third. For the entire foreign-born population of Britain, the proportion identified as British subjects was 19% (1851), 20% (1861), 29% (1871), 34% (1881), 17% (1891), 27% (1901), and 24% (1911); the number of foreign-born British subjects was not enumerated in 1841. The only published breakdown by specific nationalities refers to London in 1851, when the proportion of British subjects was 22% for Americans and 12% for other foreign-born. The fact that birthplace was commonly returned simply as 'America' precludes precise comparisons for the USA alone (if all those returned in the Irish census as natives of the USA or simply 'America' are assigned to the USA, the Irish component rises to 45.6%).

25 The proportions that follow are based on the number of each nationality following occupations with 40 or more foreigners, the total occupied population not being sub-divided by nationality. For the entire foreign population, the proportion of all occupied persons in these selected categories (excluding 'scholars' and 'students') was 75.2% (1871), 69.9% (1881), 73.0% (1891), 80.1% (1901), and 77.2% (1911).

26 Seamen fell short of a majority of Greeks and Spaniards in 1881, but again formed the majority of occupied Greeks in 1891 and 1911 and of Spaniards in 1901.

27 Census of Ireland, *General Report*, p. 100.

28 Census of Scotland (1911), vol. III, *Report*, xiv.

29 Census of Scotland (1861), *Report*, lx.

30 Census of England and Wales (1861), *General Report*, 39.

31 In 1871, there were insufficient foreign musicians to qualify for inclusion of this category.

32 A decade earlier, 27 of the 32 ice-cream vendors were born in Italy, according to a digital search of the returns for 1901. For a statistical analysis of the occupations of Italians in Ireland (1851–1911), including discussion of ice-cream vendors, see Reynolds, *Casalattico*, 46–54.

33 The leading surnames of Ireland's Italian immigrants in 1911 (incorporating variant spellings) were Forte (19), Fusco (11), Magliocco (8), Morelli (7), and Matassa (7). Entries in the telephone directories for the Republic of Ireland (2009) and Northern Ireland (2000) included Forte (20), Fusco (25), Magliocco (3), Morelli (12), and Matassa (9). The widespread abandonment of 'land-lines' has reduced the value of this source for more recent years. For the astonishingly concentrated and persistent regional origins and occupations of the Italians in Ireland, and for references to Forte, Fusco, and Matassa as local personal and place names, see Reynolds, *Casalattico*, esp. 56, 84, 153.

34 For a multi-faceted analysis of Jewish (and Russian) occupations and social mobility, see Ó Gráda, *Jewish Ireland*, 45–93 (chs 3, 4).

35 The number of each nationality returned through a digital search invariably falls short of that given in the published census, the percentage ratio of the

two numbers for each birthplace being Britain (86.7%), India (98.0%), 'America' and USA (77.9%), Russia (99.6%), France (85.1%), Germany (88.0%), and Italy (89.7%).

36 The only serious anomaly is for the French, of whom 41% were female according to the published census report compared with 47% through a digital search. Note that 15% of the French were missed through digital searching, the highest proportion of misses for any nationality apart from Americans (22%).

37 1,901 of 1,977 Russians (96%) were digitally categorised as 'Jewish' (including 55 with variant descriptions ascertainable from inspection of those of 'other' religions). The Russian-born Jewish group accounted for 38% of the 4,945 Jews revealed through a search by religion and birthplace. The published reports give slightly higher totals (1,985 Russians and 5,148 Jews or Hebrews).

38 Census returns of religion by birthplace were occasionally compiled in Australia and Canada, but never in Britain or the USA. See Donald Harman Akenson, *Being Had: Historians, Evidence, and the Irish in North America* (Port Credit, Ontario: P. D. Meany, 1985), for trenchant discussion of the failure of historians of Irish emigration to the USA to learn from the far superior Canadian census statistics.

39 Figures relating to Episcopalians include those classified in the digital index as Church of Ireland and Church of England; Presbyterians include adherents of the Church of Scotland.

40 Presbyterians (20% of Canadians in Ireland), however, were over-represented by comparison with Episcopalians (42%). In Ontario (1931), those of 'Irish race' included Anglicans (20%), Presbyterians (13%), United Church (33%), and Catholics (27%): Census of Canada (1931), *Reports*, vol. IV, tables 45, 49. The United Church, combining Presbyterians and Methodists, was formed in 1925. The Catholic component for the entire dominion was somewhat higher (32%).

41 Of 3,572 digitally identified natives of India in 1911, 47.6% were Episcopalians, 43.7% Roman Catholics, 5.0% Presbyterians, and 2.2% Methodists (there were 3 Hindus, 2 Buddhists, 1 Zoroastrian, but no Muslims).

42 See David Fitzpatrick, 'Ireland, 1801–1914', in Andrew Porter (ed.), *Oxford History of the British Empire* (Oxford University Press, 1999), vol. III, 494–521.

43 I am grateful to Jane Leonard for information on Crosslé, who served with the Royal Australian Medical Corps in the First World War, and Mecredy, his schoolfellow at Portora Royal School in Enniskillen, who emigrated to New Zealand before settling in Sussex.

44 John Cousins, gateman at Musgrave's iron foundry (48), his wife Evelina Henrietta (34), eldest daughter Agnes Angelina (13), and 3 younger children, were resident at Cluan Place (Albertbridge) in 1901, and at Madrid Street a decade later. His Methodist younger brother (James's father) was another James, a seaman (58), living nearby on the Ravenhill Road in 1901. The Orange and Indian backgrounds of J. H. Cousins are not mentioned in Francis Clarke's entry in the *Dictionary of Irish Biography*, ed. James McGuire

and James Quinn (Cambridge: University Press, 2009), vol. II, 919–20, or in James H. and Margaret E. Cousins, *We Two Together* (Madras, 1950), esp. 1–22.

45 In addition to inmates listed as lodgers, boarders, or visitors (enumerated in Table 2.8), many foreigners unrelated to the family or institutional 'head' (especially French and Germans) were irregularly returned as 'crew', 'religious', 'governess', 'assistant', etc.

46 The exceptions to this trend of intercensal increase in the number of Americans per 10,000 were Connaught (1861–71) and Leinster (1881–91).

47 The only exception was Leinster (46% were aged under 20 in 1911).

48 If the 1911 distribution of the American proportion in each county (n = 32) is correlated with those for 1841, 1861, and 1871, the respective coefficients of correlation are –.08 (r-squared = .01), +.21 (.04), and +.22 (.05). When the distribution for 1841 is correlated with those for 1861 and 1871, the coefficients are +.58 (r-squared = .34) and +.41 (.17).

49 If the 1911 distribution of the American proportion in each county's population (n = 32) is correlated with the distribution of recorded emigrants from Irish ports to the USA (1876–1914), expressed as a proportion of the county population in 1891, the coefficient of correlation is +.53 (r-squared = .28).

3. AMERICA ON SHOW, 1901–11: PROFILE

1 For a mainly qualitative analysis of elite Americans in Britain, see Stephen Tuffnell, 'Nationalism, Cosmopolitanism and Empire in Britain's American Expatriate Community, *c.* 1815–1914', DPhil. thesis, University of Oxford, 2013.

2 Though Canadians were not separately tabulated in published census reports, a partial list can be assembled from the digital index (omitting many indexed under 'other birthplaces', which, on individual inspection, were clearly in Canada). For the same reason, many elite Americans have been unavoidably omitted from those identified under particular occupational terms.

3 The database of selected occupational categories includes 530 members of the elite in 1901 and 629 in 1911, 206 of whom were enumerated as such in both censuses. The net number of individuals examined was therefore 953.

4 For males aged 20 or more, the proportion in elite occupations in 1901 was 19.8% (USA) and 59.1% (Canada). The corresponding proportions in 1911 were 15.6% and 51.7%, respectively. Because many Americans and Canadians were missed when assembling the elite database from the digital index to the census, the age data is also drawn from that index rather than from the more reliable and complete published figures for Americans (but not Canadians) aged 20 or more.

5 In 1901, the proportion of 154 co-resident spouses born in each region was as follows: Ulster (24.7%), the rest of Ireland (50.0%), Britain (13.6%), North America (8.4%), and elsewhere (3.2%). The corresponding proportions for 193 co-resident spouses in 1911 were 21.2%, 51.8%, 15.0%, 10.4%, and 1.6%. Wives constituted 87.5% of co-resident spouses in 1901 and 91.7% in 1911.

6 In 1901, the proportion of 105 co-resident mothers born in each region was as follows: Ulster (38.1%), the rest of Ireland (44.8%), Britain (7.6%), North America (6.7%), and elsewhere (2.9%). The corresponding proportions for 145 co-resident mothers in 1911 were 37.2%, 47.6%, 8.3%, 6.9%, and none. In 1901, 2 mothers came from India and 1 from Norway.

7 In 1901, the proportion of 67 co-resident fathers born in each region was as follows: Ulster (44.8%), the rest of Ireland (47.8%), Britain (6.0%), North America (1.5%), and elsewhere (none). The corresponding proportions for 101 co-resident fathers in 1911 were 49.5%, 43.6%, 4.0%, 2.0%, and 1.0%. In 1911, 1 father came from India.

8 In 1901 and 1911, the proportions of American households including a co-resident spouse were 29.1% and 30.7%, respectively. Corresponding proportions for households with mothers were 19.8% and 23.1%, compared with 12.6% and 16.0% for households with co-resident fathers. Note that a substantial minority of 'married' Americans were enumerated without a spouse on census night (29 in 1901 and 34 in 1911).

9 Though strenuous efforts have been made to ensure the accuracy of details given for named individuals, I plead for the indulgence of readers who discover errors when pursuing cases of interest to them.

4. AMERICA ON SHOW: PEOPLE

1 While avoiding a mechanical recitation of often complex place names, I aim to provide enough information to allow informed readers to locate each individual. For rural addresses, this may include both townland and electoral division (the basis of census enumeration), or the name of a country seat (often irregularly spelt). Counties surrounding cities such as Dublin are referred to as Co. Dublin etc. As birthplaces were usually returned only by county, the prefix 'Co.' is omitted. When more particular details of birthplace appear (such as 'Merrion' or 'New York'), they have been reproduced.

2 To ensure consistency in defining the 'peculiarities' of each sector, the values of selected variables have been ranked in descending order for fourteen occupational sectors (excluding law, engineering, and manufacturing, which all fell short of 20 members in both 1901 and 1911). The top three scores are deemed extremely high, the bottom three extremely low. For sectors achieving an extreme score in *both* 1901 and 1911, the fact is noted in the introduction to the relevant section (to avoid wearisome repetition, the term 'extremely' is alternated with various synonyms). The nine selected variables are: (1) median age in years, (2) the proportion of elite members who were matched in the other census, (3) head of household, (4) Roman Catholic, (5) female, (6) unmarried, (7) Canadian-born, and (8) in households containing kin and (9) fellow-Americans.

3 The number of rooms was returned as 7 in 1901 and 10 in 1911.

4 Lawrence W. McBride, *The Greening of Dublin Castle: The Transformation of Bureaucratic and Judicial Personnel in Ireland, 1892–1922* (Washington, DC: Catholic University of America Press, 1991). This model is challenged by Fergus Campbell in *The Irish Establishment, 1879–1914* (Oxford University Press, 2009).

5 No additional consular agents born outside the USA have been identified for 1911.

6 Between 1901 and 1911, Usborne moved from a house with fifteen rooms and twenty windows to another address in Queenstown with only ten rooms and seven windows. Usborne was returned as an adherent of the Canadian Apostolic Church in 1901, but the Church of Ireland in 1911.

7 In 1876, William Charles Hume of Polworth owned 1,048 acres in Wicklow valued at only £171: *Return of Owners*, 100; see also *Walford's County Families* (1889 edn), 547. For fuller citations and discussion of such sources, see notes to following chapter.

8 McArdle served as an officer from 1881 to 1900 and died in 1912; Hume served from 1859 to 1898 and died in 1919: Jim Herlihy, *The Royal Irish Constabulary: a complete alphabetical list of officers and men, 1816–1922* (Dublin: Four Courts, 1999).

9 A statute of 1858 created the General Council of Medical Education and Registration of the United Kingdom, elected by practitioners.

10 On 19 January 1910, Benjamin St George Lefroy (1865–1946) married Kathleen Grace, younger daughter of Lt.-Col. Hugh Lefroy of 'Carigglas': *Irish Family Records*, 710.

11 The sector incorporates two miscellaneous professionals (a brewer's analyst and a professional horse trainer).

12 The Catholic proportion ranked second out of the fourteen major sectors in 1901, but fourth in 1911; the female proportion ranked fourth in 1901 and third in 1911.

13 Since religious orders were often unspecified in census returns, many convents have been matched with detailed entries in the annual *Irish Catholic Directory* or *Thom's Official Directory*. Directories have also been consulted to establish, where possible, the names of hotels and bars.

14 In 1876, the Revd. William Sherlock, then canon of Christ Church, Bray, owned 1,201 acres in Kildare valued at £1,397: *Landowners of Ireland*, 411.

15 The musical and evangelical activities of the Sims family are chronicled in the next chapter.

16 In 1888, Benjamin Courtney Hobson, born in Woodstock, Oxford, Ontario, married Caroline Sinton (1860–94) at the Friends' Meeting House in Hillsborough: Harrington family tree, digitally accessible through ancestry.co.uk.

17 Thomas Henry (1844–1908), Frederick Charles (1851–1928), and Edward Benjamin Cleeve (1849–1925), born in Shipton, Sherbrooke Co., Quebec, were sons of Edward Elms Cleeve (1814–85) and Sophia Olivia Journeaux (1822–1904), an Irishwoman of Huguenot extraction who died in Limerick: Cullen (Newpot, Co. Tipperary) family tree, digitally accessible through ancestry.co.uk. Sir Thomas Cleeve was evidently absent from Ireland in 1901.

18 Website of Hazlebrook Confectionery Co.

19 There were 9 North American waiters and bar staff of both sexes in 1901, and 10 in 1911.

20 See Alan F. Parkinson, *Belfast's Unholy War: The Troubles of the 1920s* (Dublin: Four Courts Press, 2004), 229–37.

5. AMERICA ON SHOW: SPECIAL CASES

1 For the formal definition of 'extreme' values applied to each occupational sector throughout this analysis, see Chapter 4, n. 3.

2 Most North American wives of aristocrats and gentry would have been returned without occupation, and therefore missed in the construction of my database. An example, traced incidentally in connection with Mary Early Davison, was the British Columbian wife of Sir Richard Musgrave.

3 In 1876, the Duke of Manchester's Irish estates covered 12,198 acres in Armagh with an annual valuation (roughly equivalent to the rental value of agricultural land) of £17,164: *The Landowners of Ireland: An Alphabetical List of the Owners of Estates of 500 Acres of £500 Valuation and Upwards, in Ireland, with Acreage and Valuation in Each County*, comp. U. H. Hussey de Burgh, Land Agent (Dublin: Hodges, Foster, and Figgis, 1878), 304–5. His English estate of 15,014 acres was valued at £22,518: *The Great Landowners of Great Britain and Ireland: A List of All Owners of Three Thousand Acres and Upwards, worth £3,000 a Year...*, comp. John Bateman, FRGS (London: Harrison, [1876] 1883), 297.

4 On 14 November 1900, William Angus Drogo Montagu, 9th Duke of Manchester (1877–1947), married Helena, daughter of Eugene Zimmerman of Cincinnati.

5 *The Times* (19 September, 29 November 1900; 19 October 1901; 28 February 1902).

6 *The Times* (30 November 1901).

7 *The Times* (12 May, 8, 19 December 1931).

8 The Plunket estate occupied 3,834 acres in Monaghan, Cork and Dublin valued at £3,527: *Landowners of Ireland*, 369.

9 In 1894, William Lee, 5th Baron Plunket (1864–1920), married Lady Victoria Alexandrine Hamilton-Templeton-Blackwood, youngest daughter of Frederick, 1st Marquis of Dufferin (governor-general of Canada, 1872–8): *Burke's Peerage Baronetage and Knightage* (1938 edn), 1977. In 1876, Dufferin (then a mere earl) owned 14,313 acres in Co. Down valued at £16,572 (elsewhere given as 18,238 acres valued at £21,043): *Landowners of Ireland*, 139; Bateman, *Great Landowners*, 141.

10 Plunket's father, 5th Baron Plunket and archbishop of Dublin, had been a senior officer in the Masonic and Orange orders in Ireland, and a powerful supporter of the Irish Church Missions to the Roman Catholics whose proselytism had temporarily transformed the religious demography of Connemara.

11 In 1876, the Avonmore estate covered 3,269 acres in Mayo and Tipperary valued at £1,103; Robert Evans, 'formerly a magistrate' of Gortmerron House, Dungannon and George's father, owned 1,116 acres valued at £956: *Landowners of Ireland*, 14, 150.

12 Algernon William Yelverton, 6th Viscount of Avonmore (1866–1910), had married Mabel Sara Evans (d. 1927) in 1890: *Burke's Peerage* (1938 edn). For her father George Evans (1828–1905) of Gortmerron House, Dungannon, see *Burke's Landed Gentry of Ireland* (1912 edn), 209.

13 In 1876, Richard Grove Annesley owned 1,757 acres in Cork valued at £1,429: *Landowners of Ireland*, 8.

14 In 1907, Richard Arthur Grove Annesley (b. 1870) married his second wife, Hilda Margaret (b. 1868), younger daughter of Sir Francis Edmund Macnaghten, 2nd Baronet Macnaghten of Dundarave, Bushmills, Co. Antrim. Following the death at the Somme of the 6th and 7th baronets, the succession passed to their uncle, Sir Francis Alexander Macnaghten, 8th Baronet (b. 1863), Hilda's first cousin. On 6 July 1905, he had married Beatrice, daughter of the late Sir William Ritchie of the Canadian Supreme Court: *Burke's Peerage* (1938 edn), 129, 647–9. In 1876, the Macnaghten estate covered no less than 8,281 acres in Antrim, Armagh, and Londonderry valued at £8,577: *Landowners of Ireland*, 298.

15 Hundreds of families with Irish seats, who might otherwise have been included in the *Landed Gentry*, appear incidentally in the pedigrees published in *Burke's Peerage*.

16 *Walford's County Families of the United Kingdom*, a useful compendium published annually from the 1860s, gave less information about more families than *Burke's Landed Gentry*.

17 Mervyn Montgomery Archdall (b. 1869) was the fifth son of Hugh Montgomery Archdall of Drumadravy, Co. Fermanagh, a captain in the 52nd Light Infantry; his wife was Ida, daughter of John Gustav Thaung of Bjornamo, Sweden: *Burke's Irish Family Records* (1976), 33–4.

18 Eleven rooms were enumerated in 1911.

19 In 1900, John Thomas Rashleigh Lucas (b. 1863) married Grace Ellen (d. 1950), fourth daughter of Charles Donovan of Ummara House, Timoleague, Co. Cork. Rashleigh was the only son of Jasper Lucas of the Manor House, a major in the 47th regiment who presumably served in Canada. Charles Donovan's membership of the clan O'Donovan is implied by a cross-reference to that family, though I have failed to establish his precise relationship to 'the O'Donovan' of Hollybrook House, Skibbereen: *Burke's Irish Family Records*, 740. The Dunmanway estate does not appear in *Landowners of Ireland*.

20 *Return of Owners of Land of One Acre and Upwards, in … Ireland*, BPP, 1876 (C-1492), 61. This return, derived from the schedules of valuation of tenements (land and buildings) initiated by Sir Arthur Griffith in the 1840s, was the basis for de Burgh's *Landowners of Ireland*. De Burgh solicited useful biographical information from many of those listed, in some cases providing additional details of property held as 'superior landlords' (often the bulk of a 'landed estate') rather than as 'immediate lessors'. In general, however, the returns understate the size and value of estates because of the ubiquity of 'middlemen'. They also ignore the charges (such as 'head rents') imposed even on 'landowners', arising from the fact that ultimate ownership of all property resided in the Crown, which had granted large tracts to institutions such as the established church, only for church lands to be sublet to 'landowners'.

21 Since the land purchase acts excluded demesnes, 'untenanted' lands held under several forms of leasehold, and urban property, the transfer of ownership was incomplete.

22 The occupant in 1901 was Hamilton Joseph Bunbury, an unmarried militia captain from London with four servants. Bunbury (1866–1949) had succeeded to a cousin's Carlow estate in 1886, becoming privy chamberlain to Pope Pius XI in 1923: family history accessible at turtlebunbury.com.

23 All seven servants were Episcopalians. No Willcox is listed in *Landowners of Ireland* or *Burke's Landed Gentry*.

24 The architect of Lisnabrucka House, near Recess, was Laurence Aloysius McDonnell of Dublin: Irish Architectural Archive, *Dictionary of Irish Architects, 1720–1940* (online edn); information accessible on buildingsofireland.ie.

25 In 1876, John T. Devereux of George's St, Wexford owned 397 acres in Wexford valued at £1,235, implying a mainly urban estate: *Return of Owners*, 94.

26 Michael Scanlan, owner of 1,105 acres valued at £721: *Landowners of Ireland*, 406.

27 George Ramsay of Clag[g]an House, Cookstown owned 392 acres in Co. Londonderry valued at £165: *Return of Owners*, 264. Like Kennedy, he did not figure in *Burke's Landed Gentry*.

28 Patrick Kennedy of Tuam owned 57 acres in Co. Galway valued at £47: *Return of Owners*, 296.

29 Richard's eldest son John (1810–82) of Oakley Park and Carrickoreely, Co. Limerick, died unmarried. In 1876, he retained only the Limerick estate (5,011 acres valued at £2,559), though living at Edenmore Raheny, Co. Dublin. Oakley Park passed to George Woods Maunsell (1815–87), a magistrate for Kildare and Dublin city, whose combined estates of 3,438 acres were valued at £2,771, including 702 acres valued at £444 in Kildare: *Landowners of Ireland*, 312.

30 In 1859, Richard Dixie Maunsell (1816–85) of Whitehall, Co. Dublin (and Ailesbury Rd, Dublin, according to the rector of Innistonagh, Co. Tipperary), married Alicia Fanny (d. 1907), daughter of Malcolm Laing of Spanish Town, Jamaica (formerly of Pasdale, Orkney and Taplow, Bucks and nephew of the eponymous historian of Scotland). The rector was the third of six sons (and six daughters) of Richard Maunsell (1785–1866) of Oakl[e]y Park, who had acquired the estate in 1812: *Burke's Irish Family Records*, 809–10; *Burke's Landed Gentry of Ireland* (1912 edn), 469.

31 The only Catholics were an Irish house maid and a French governess; five servants and three visitors were English-born, and a nephew from Edinburgh was also present.

32 In 1891, Sir Richard John Musgrave, 5th Baronet of Tourin (1850–1930) married Jessie Sophia of Rock House, Ardmore, Co. Waterford, daughter of the Hon. R. Dunsmuir of Victoria, British Columbia. This Irish baronetcy became extinct on his death: *Burke's Peerage* (1938 edn), 1822–3. For the 1st baronet's career, see James Kelly, *Sir Richard Musgrave, 1746–1918: Ultra-Protestant* (Dublin: Four Courts Press, 2009).

33 Peter Warburton Jackson, JP, of The Park, Cheltenham and Novarra, Bray, held 20 acres in Co. Wicklow valued at £592; William Henry Jackson, of Mountjoy Square and Killarney House, Bray, held 5 acres in Co. Wicklow

valued at £553 and an acre in Dublin valued at £715: *Landowners of Ireland*, 234.

34 There is no evidence to connect Stella Smith, the 50-year-old spinster staying in Rugby Road in 1901, with the John Smith of Belfast who owned 2,219 acres in Co. Antrim valued at £1,005 in 1876: *Landowners of Ireland*, 416.

35 *Burke's Irish Family Records*, 342. In 1876, Lady de Burgho (*sic*) of Island House, Castleconnell, Co. Limerick, occupied 372 acres in Wexford valued at £208 (and 3,844 acres valued at £2,290 in Limerick): *Landowners of Ireland*, 121. Ballynapierce may have belonged to that estate.

36 Joseph Meadows of Cathis, Co. Wexford, owned 414 acres in the county valued at £391: *Return of Owners*, 94. His townland address in 1901 was Leachestown, Killinick.

37 David Hicks, 'Mountshannon House, Castleconnell', in icksbook.blogspot (2015). In 1876, Lady Louisa Isabella Georgina FitzGibbon of Mountshannon (heir to the 3rd, and last, Earl of Clare) owned 13,494 acres valued at £8,120 (including 10,316 acres valued at £6,694 in Limerick and the remainder in Tipperary): *Landowners of Ireland*, 162.

38 Henry Vincent Jackson of 'Junne', Roscrea owned 2,853 acres valued at £1,665, roughly equally divided between King's County and Co. Tipperary, Inane House being on the county boundary: *Irish Landed Families*, 233.

39 Robert J. Marshall married Marnie C. Nevins in Philadelphia in 1889: Pennsylvania index of marriages digitally accessible via ancestry.co.uk. Robert's father was also Robert; Jackson's wife was Mary Celia in the census return; and her presumed eldest child (Robert, Jr) was 11 in 1901.

40 Binty's father, named as Dr Andrew A. Stoney of Aldershot, owned 210 acres in King's County valued at £231: *Return of Owners*, 50.

41 Tester–Nevin family tree, digitally accessible via ancestry.com.

42 *Burke's Irish Family Records*, 938.

43 Rolf and Magda Loeber, *A Guide to Irish Fiction, 1650–1900* (Dublin: Four Courts Press, 2006), 1032–3.

44 Ellen Clarke and Annie Evans (not yet authors) were both living at the same addresses in 1911 as they were in 1901.

45 The play was performed at the Abbey Theatre: *IT* (20 April 1925).

46 Vint was returned as American in 1901 but Canadian in 1911.

47 The term 'curator', later a senior position requiring expertise, may have signified a caretaker in 1911.

48 *IT* (6 April 1901).

49 *IT* (14, 15 April 1911).

50 *Weekly IT* (11 November 1910).

51 *IT* (28 December 1910).

52 *IT* (20, 26 November 1875); *Western People* (16 February 1901), digitally accessible via Irish Newspapers Archives.

53 See Damian Evans, 'The Creation of Meaning and Identity in the Dublin Jazz Scene, Past and Present', PhD thesis, Dublin Institute of Technology, 2016, 35–6; Douglas C. Riach, 'Blacks and Blackface on the Irish Stage, 1830–60', *Journal of American Studies*, 7(3) (1973): 231–41.

54 Except in 1879, this 'negro troupe' was variously named as Brown's, Burns', and Bram's Blacks: *BNL* (3 March 1879, 30 April 1887, 7 January 1888, 9 September 1889).
55 *BNL* (26 July 1883, 28 September 1885, 7 April 1891, 14 January, 8 May 1893).
56 *Northern Whig* (1 April, 25 March 1901).
57 Eugene Watters, *Infinite Variety: Dan Lowrey's Music Hall, 1879–97* (Dublin: Gill & Macmillan, 1973), 28.
58 Ashcroft's other 'famous' songs were 'The Crockery Ware (The Flitting)', 'A Quarter to Two', 'Norah Kearney', 'Wreck of the Ragamuffin', 'McGinty, the Swell of the Sea', 'Mind You that Now', and 'Swimming Match': *IT* (29 July 1901).
59 Watters, *Infinite Variety*, 19, 123–4.
60 *Weekly IT* (18 May 1901).
61 Watters, *Infinite Variety*, 124.
62 The term 'proselytism' is routinely used in Mormon official documents.
63 Each census report included a detailed tabulation of all denominational self-descriptions with the number of occurrences (also given for each county and city). There were no recorded Mormons etc. in 1861, 43 in 1871, 1 in 1881, 58 in 1891 and 1901, and 97 in 1911. In 1911, 50 Mormons were enumerated in Belfast, 17 in Co. Dublin, and 3 in Dublin city: Census of Ireland (1861–1911).
64 Letters of Davidson, Jones, and Pierson to President Joseph F. Smith (26 December, 23 April, 18 September 1910).
65 Cutting from *The Millennial Star* (7 June 1900); Baker to Committee of the Apostles (27 March 1899); Baker to President Lorenzo Snow (3 April 1899).
66 A useful conspectus of the history of Mormonism in Ireland since 1840 is provided on Wikipedia, an authority that I have never hitherto cited.
67 *IT* (4 October 1877).
68 *BNL* (8 July 1882; 12 February, 9, 14 March 1894; 11 May 1885; 22 September 1894).
69 *IT* (22 April 1911).
70 *Evening Herald* (22, 24 April 1911), reporting remarks by the Protestant archbishop of Dublin, the dean of St Patrick's, and the rector of St Luke's (the leading Orangeman T. C. Hammond).
71 *IT* (28 May 1912).

6. AMERICANS IN LEITRIM, 1901–11: PROFILE

1 The population of designated towns (incorporating townland returns for clusters failing in certain years to meet the criterion of twenty occupied houses) has been abstracted from the detailed county census reports (1841–1911). Figures for 1851–81 are slightly inflated by the unavoidable inclusion of institutions (apart from workhouses). The proportion living in towns was 7.4% (1841), 7.8% (1851), 8.0% (1861, 1871), 8.3% (1881), 8.6% (1891), 9.1% (1901), and 9.4% (1911).

2 The counties with the highest proportions resident on agricultural holdings in 1911 were Leitrim (90.8%), Roscommon (90.3%), Mayo (86.4%), Donegal (86.0%), Cavan (85.8%), and Longford (82.0%), which together formed a bloc of excessive rurality in the north midlands and north-west.

3 The counties with the highest proportions of agricultural residents living on holdings valued at less than £15 were Mayo (91.0%), Leitrim (83.8%), Donegal (81.7% ?), Galway (79.5%), Roscommon (76.9%), and Sligo (75.6%). For statistical analysis of the close correlation between these distributions, along with other variables measuring social unrest, see David Fitzpatrick, 'The Geography of the War of Independence', in John Crowley, Donal Ó Drisceoil, and Mike Murphy (eds), *Atlas of the Irish Revolution* (Cork University Press, 2017), 534–43.

4 Leitrim ranked third to Galway and Kerry in the frequency of reported 'agrarian outrages' relative to population (1879–82), third to Cavan and Monaghan in the proportion of Catholics belonging to the United Irish League (March 1913), and second to Longford in the equivalent proportion for Sinn Féin (January 1919); but only twelfth in the proportion enrolled in the IRA (July 1921) and twentieth in the frequency of fatalities attributable to conflict (January 1917–December 1921). For details and sources, see Fitzpatrick, 'Geography'.

5 Leitrim's net population loss between 1841 and 1851 (27.9%) was exceeded only in Roscommon (31.6%), Mayo (29.4%), Monaghan (29.2%), Sligo (29.0%), Longford (28.7%), and Cavan (28.4%). Leitrim's proportionate loss between 1851 and 1911 (43.2%) ranked eighteenth among Ireland's thirty-two counties. Ireland's total population declined by 19.9% (1841–51) and 33.0% (1851–1911).

6 Ig, an often deployed Princeton proxy for marital fertility setting the number of registered births against the number expected from an American Hutterite population with the same age distribution of married women, amounted to 83% of the Hutterite standard (1871–81), 75% (1881–91), 75% (1891–1901), and 78% (1901–11). Leitrim's marital fertility ranked sixth, seventeenth, sixteenth, and eighth among the thirty-two Irish counties in each successive decade. For a pioneering introduction to the ingredients of Irish demographic change, see Robert E. Kennedy, Jr, *The Irish: Emigration, Marriage, and Fertility* (Berkeley: University of California Press, 1973).

7 These figures embody Hajnal's Singulate Mean at Marriage (SMAM), an index based on the proportions unmarried among equivalent age groups at successive censuses. Leitrim's SMAM for men and women, respectively, was 30.3 and 25.0 years (1821 cohort), 30.1 and 26.3 (1831), 30.8 and 25.7 (1841), 30.9 and 25.7 (1851), and 32.0 and 27.9 (1861). Leitrim's county rankings (in descending order of age) for men were 21, 24, 15, 21, and 16; for women, they were 28, 31, 27, 27, and 12.

8 The unmarried proportion of men aged 45–54 (46–55 for 1841) recorded at each census was 6.7% (1841), 7.4% (1851), 10.4% (1851), 12.9% (1871), 13.2% (1881), 15.2% (1891), 22.2% (1901), and 26.2% (1911). Corresponding percentages for women were 8.7, 8.0, 9.3, 10.5, 9.3, 10.8, 16.0, and 16.3. Leitrim was invariably among the counties least marked by

'celibacy', successive county rankings for men being 28, 29, 27, 26, 26, 28, 24, and 25. Corresponding rankings for female celibacy were 28, 29, 30, 29, 30, 28, 27, and 30.

9 The survivorship ratio for men aged 15–55 was 75.0% (1846 cohort) and 74.4% (1856 cohort); corresponding figures for women were 74.6% and 71.7%. These calculations are based on mortality rates derived from the number of registered deaths in successive age groups and the corresponding censal populations, traced over four successive decades.

10 With the exception of the female cohort of 1856, for which Leitrim ranked fourteenth among the counties, its survivorship ratios were surpassed in only three or four counties, being exceeded in Mayo and Roscommon (in all three cases), along with Cavan (for both male cohorts) and Clare (for 1856 males and 1846 females). In Dublin, only 47.1% of the male cohort for 1846 could expect to survive four decades later.

11 For Leitrim males, the ratio of registered deaths under one year to births was 7.5% (1870s), 6.9% (1880s), 6.4% (1890s), 5.4% (1900s), and 4.8% (1910s). The corresponding ratios for females were predictably lower (6.7%, 6.3%, 5.9%, 5.7%, 5.0%, and 4.6%). The only counties with occa- sionally lower incidences of infant mortality were Fermanagh (boys, 1870s), Sligo (girls, 1870s and 1880s), Cavan (girls, 1880s), and Roscommon (boys, 1910s; girls, 1890s and 1910s).

12 This summary is based on successive censal returns giving the birthplaces of residents of each county, offering snapshots of displacement rather than any index of migratory flows (see Chapter 1 for detailed analysis of inter-county movement).

13 The proportion of Leitrim's population aged 5–24 in 1851 *not* accounted for by its population aged 15–34 in 1861 was 38.9% (fourteenth in county ranking). Corresponding cohort depletion ratios for subsequent decades were 39.6% (1861–71, fourth in county ranking), 35.7% (1871–81), 41.4% (1881–91), 38.2% (1891–1901), and 37.6% (1901–11). Cohort depletion over the Famine decade was 50.5% (1841–51), but a significant minority of that loss is attributable to excess mortality. Depletion over the longer period preceding the first census for the Irish Free State was 42.1% (1911–26).

14 The annual volume of recorded emigration from Leitrim amounted to 2.0% of its entire censal population (May 1851–December 1855), 1.6% (1856–65), 1.4% (1866–75), 2.0% (1876–85), 1.9% (1886–95), and 1.2% (1896–1905 and 1906–14). The corresponding county rankings were twenty-third, tenth, sixteenth, first, fourth, eighth, and second.

15 Between 1876 and 1914, the proportion of Leitrim emigrants from Irish ports making for the United States was 90.0%, distantly followed by Great Britain (4.2%), Canada (3.4%), Australia (2.1%), and New Zealand (0.2%).

16 The reported number of female emigrants for every 100 male emigrants from Leitrim was 97.0 (1851–5), 100.3 (1856–65), 89.1 (1866–75), 104.6 (1876–85), 104.5 (1886–95), 137.3 (1896–1905), and 97.4 (1906–14). The corresponding county rankings were twenty-second, seventh, fourth, eighth, tenth, fourth, and eighth. Since females tended to emigrate at an earlier age

than males, comparison of cohort depletion rates by sex is unreliable (being based on the depletion of a designated age group).

17 Of Leitrim's emigrants from Irish ports, 8.5% were returned as married or widowed (1883–1914), the lowest county proportion. The proportion of emigrants aged less than 15 years declined from 22.2% (1851–5) to 6.7% (1886–95) and only 3.3% (1906–14), Leitrim's county ranking being twenty-ninth (1886–95) and twenty-seventh (1906–14).

18 The annual outflow aged 20–24 amounted to 6.7% of the equivalent censal age group (1851–5), 4.9% (1856–65), 5.8% (1866–75), 7.9% (1876–85), 9.3% (1886–95), 6.2% (1896–1905), and 7.6% (1906–14). The corresponding county rankings were twentieth, tenth, nineteenth, second, fourth, eighth, and second.

19 'North Leitrim' (N) is equated with the 'rural districts' of Kinlough and Manorhamilton, leaving Carrick-on-Shannon No. 1, Ballinamore, and Mohill to 'South Leitrim' (S). Leitrim had no 'urban districts', as constituted after the reorganisation of local government in 1899. Unless otherwise stated, all regional and district statistics are derived from published census returns.

20 Population decline between 1871 and 1911 was 33.8% (N) and 33.3% (S); the proportion living on agricultural holdings in 1901 was 93.6% (N) and 90.7% (S); the proportion of agricultural residents on holdings valued at less than £4 per annum in 1901 was 25.5% (N) and 16.7% (S).

21 The proportion living in households with one or two rooms was 35.3% (N) and 21.9% (S); the proportion in 'congested districts' was 46.0% (N) and 50.0% (S). Electoral divisions were designated as 'congested' if their net annual valuation per capita fell short of £1 5s. For those in Leitrim, see Royal Commission on Congestion in Ireland [Dudley Commission], *Second Appendix to Seventh Report*, 25–37, in HCP 1908 (Cd 3786), xl, 431.

22 For Kinlough, population decline (1871–1911) was 38.0%; the proportion on agricultural holdings was 94.4%; the proportion of that group on holdings valued below £4 was 28.1%; and the proportion in 1 or 2 rooms was 38.0%.

23 The proportion returned as Irish-speakers in 1911 (virtually all bilingual) was 8.4% (N) and 4.7% (S); the proportion of migratory labourers in 1880 was 1.08% (N) and 1.07% (S), Scotland being the destination for 51.7% of northerners and 24.0% of southerners.

24 Cohort depletion was 33.5% (N) and 37.1% (S) in 1871–81; 40.9% (N) and 41.6% (S) in 1881–91; 38.3% (N) and 38.2% (S) in 1891–1901; and 38.0% (N) and 37.4% (S) in 1901–11.

25 Until 1901–11, when its cohort depletion ratio (38.8%) exceeded that for all other districts, Kinlough had invariably ranked last among the five districts. In the three preceding decades, the ratio for Kinlough was 30.8% (1871–81), 37.4% (1881–91), and 32.2% (1891–1901). Note that Kinlough had proportionately *fewer* migratory labourers and Irish-speakers than neighbouring Manorhamilton.

26 The density of British-born residents per 10,000 inhabitants in 1911 was 88.6 (N) and 56.0 (S), the difference being almost entirely attributable to Scottish settlement preferences. The corresponding proportion for foreign-born residents was 48.5 (N) and 48.7 (S). Leitrim's 25 natives of India and the Empire were concentrated in the South (18).

27 The published birthplace tabulations for Leitrim (1911) returned 298 Americans (including one from South America), 232 Scots, 206 English, 16 colonials, 9 Indians, 5 Africans, and 5 Europeans (from France (2), Germany, Russia, and Sweden). The digital index reveals that the colonials included 9 Australians, 4 Canadians, and a New Zealander.

28 Leitrim ranked twenty-third among Ireland's thirty-two counties in the proportion of Americans who were female (47.0%), but fourth in the proportion aged under 20 (77.2%).

29 The database, excluding 4 Canadians in each year and one South American (1911), comprises 153 individuals (1901) and 294 (1911). Of these, the number simply returned as born in 'America' was 117 (1901) and 197 (1911); simply in the 'United States', 12 (1901) and 46 (1911); and in specified locations in the USA, 18 (1901) and 47 (1911). New York (City and State) accounted for 10 of the final group (1901) and 30 (1911). Because Leitrim had rather few inhabitants mis-assigned in the digital index to 'other birthplaces', it has been possible to identify and incorporate all of the Americans in that category. The published American population of Leitrim (including natives specifically of the USA but excluding Canadians and the South American) was 148 (1901) and 297 (1911).

30 Unlike the country-wide analysis presented in Chapter 3, this database excludes those returned as Canadian-born and also those Leitrim residents, ostensibly born in the county, who were matched with Americans returned in the other census. Five natives of Canada were traced, 4 of whom were located in Ireland in both 1901 and 1911. About a dozen persons returned as Americans in each census were matched with persons ostensibly born in Leitrim in the other census: these individuals are incorporated in the analysis of matches, but not in the separate tabulations for 1901 and 1911. The effect of omitting these groups from analysis is negligible in the case of Leitrim.

31 In 1911, 83.3% of occupied heads of households containing an American were farmers or farmers' relatives, whereas only 3.3% were labourers or servants. The corresponding proportions in 1901 were 77.1% and 7.9%.

32 Though Leitrim's 294 Americans resided in only 191 separate households, these figures aggregate the environment of all 294 individual Americans.

33 The proportion of Americans in what may be termed 'standard' second-class dwellings with these attributes was 41.2% in 1911, compared with 37.3% in 1901.

34 The proportion of Americans in North Leitrim was 36.6% (1901) and 37.9% (1911). When compared with the overall distribution of inhabitants in each census year, the Index of Over-Representation (IOR) in 1901 was 92 (N) and 105 (S); in 1911, the IOR for Americans was 96 (N) and 103 (S). This index is the quotient of the proportion of Americans in each region and the proportion of the population in the same region, expressed as a percentage.

35 By comparison with the proportion in congested divisions of all residents of agricultural holdings, the IOR for Americans in 1901 was 109 (N) and 99 (S); in 1911, the IOR for Americans was 94 (N) and 96 (S). Their over-representation in the North (1901) resulted from an unusually high concentration in congested divisions of Kinlough district (IOR=112).

36 By 1911, 5 matched Americans were resident in Dublin, Down, Mayo, and Roscommon (2), Clare being given as the birthplace of the 6 Leitrim residents no longer given as American-born.

37 Of 68 'settlers', 42.6% were female in 1901, 86.8% were unmarried, 48.5% had a parent present, 45.6% were in congested divisions, and 38.3% were relatives (other than children) of the household head. The median age of settlers, as of Leitrim Americans as a group, was 10 years. It has not been practicable for me to comb the civil marriage registers for each individual case, though the register entries are now accessible via IrishGenealogy.ie.

38 Of 71 settlers, 45.1% were female in 1911, 81.7% were unmarried, 45.1% had a parent present, 40.8% were in congested divisions, and 32.4% were relatives (other than children) of the household head. The median age of settlers was 21 years in 1911.

39 No attempt has been made to match the census returns with death registrations, since the registers do not specify birthplace and since many Leitrim Americans had locally common names.

40 Calculations refer to all 82 individuals returned in either census as American-born, for whom an Irish match was identified in the other census.

41 Among matched Americans, 6 aged by less than 9 years, 9 by 9 years, 35 (43%) by 10 years, 15 by 11 years, and 17 by more than 11 years.

42 Thirteen were promoted (4 children, 6 relatives, and 3 non-relatives who became family members) and 14 were demoted (6 children who became relatives in 1911, a head and a wife, and 6 relatives who became non-relatives). Fifty-five settlers (57%) belonged to the same categories in both years.

43 Of 34 settlers with a father, 3 had none in 1901 and 10 had none in 1911; of 43 with a mother, 5 had none in 1901 and 9 had none in 1911.

44 Seventeen of the 82 settlers (21%) moved to a different townland, of whom 2 remained in the same electoral division; 6 settlers moved between Leitrim and another county.

45 All 6 older non-Americans in 1901 were born in Scotland (they belonged to 3 households, but as usual these statistics refer to each individual American rather than each separate household with Americans). Three of the 10 older non-Americans enumerated in 1901 were born in Cavan (1) and Fermanagh (2).

46 As a proportion of all non-American siblings, those born outside Leitrim amounted to 11.5% in 1901 and only 5.8% in 1911.

47 Of 9 spouses in 1901, 4 were natives of Leitrim, 2 of Cavan, and the remainder of Donegal, Westmeath, and Scotland. No American-born co-resident spouse was recorded at either census.

48 In 1911, 7 mothers of Leitrim Americans were returned as married without co-resident husbands, compared with 13 widows. In addition, 2 female Americans were so returned in each census year, along with 1 male without a co-resident wife in 1911.

49 As shown in Tables 6.1 and 6.2, there was little difference between the housing of Americans with and without co-resident parents, as indicated by the relative proportions in houses of the 3rd or 4th classes, with perishable

roofs, and with perishable walls. Those without resident parents tended to be slightly inferior. In both categories, the median number of both rooms and front windows was three.

50 The three remaining cases were marked by the loss of one parent through death after 1901 (a father and a mother), and the remarriage of a widowed father.

51 In those three cases, the American offspring were living in Dublin, Roscommon, and elsewhere in Leitrim in 1911.

52 The five remaining parental combinations in 1901 were 3 couples, 1 widowed father, and 1 father whose wife was absent.

53 For Gralton's migratory career, see above, pages 202–4.

54 Based on a search of the indices of civil marriages (1901–41) and deaths (1901–66), for which the original register entries may be consulted via Irish-Genealogy.ie. This resource is not yet accessible for later periods.

55 Annie, like Lizzie Mahon, has not been traced in the available civil registers of marriages and deaths for Leitrim (see previous note). Being a decade younger, Annie Scanlon might have married or died at a later period for which these records are inaccessible.

1 The exclusion of Canadians from the 'American' database for Leitrim is explained in the preceding chapter.

2 Kate Kelly's birthplace was assigned to America in 1911, and Mary McLoughlin's to Leitrim in 1901.

3 Henry Greenblath (pedlar) lived with his wife and 14-year-old daughter, both born in Russia; three younger children born in Dublin; and two other Russian Jewish boarders (a pedlar and a tailoress) in addition to Fine in Martin Street, Fitzwilliam ward: Census of Ireland (1901), family schedule.

4 Anna Godley became the mistress of Killygar after the death of her parents in 1906 and 1907. Her father, Archibald Godley, DL, JP, was the fifth son of John Robert, whose eldest son John Arthur became Permanent Under-Secretary of State for India and (in 1909) Lord Kilbracken: *Burke's Peerage and Landed Gentry* (1938 edn), 1431–2.

5 Though the definition of a 'multiple' American used for statistical purposes is not restricted to those with American-born siblings, American parents and other American co-residents were far less numerous.

6 The households headed by Shorts in Lissagravan were numbered as 22 (Francis Short), 24 (Pat), 41 (Terence), 43 (Pat), 44 (Cecelia), and 45 (James); Rose Short lived with her widowed daughter Rose McHugh at No. 47. Cecelia's house had imperishable walls, but three other Short houses were mud cabins; all were thatched.

7 Since John McManus had been married for only 40 years in 1911, he may not have been the father of Benson's 42-year-old wife.

8 The term 'disappearance' refers only to entire groups of American siblings within households, without implying that every member of the 1901 household had left by 1911.

9 Winifred McPartlan of Drumdarkan, Riverstown, mother of American-born Michael (11 in 1901), was widowed during the intercensal decade (her husband had been an Irish-speaking agricultural labourer).

8. VISITORS FROM AMERICA, 1914–25: PROFILE

1 This was introduced by a US government order in 1915, followed by an Act of Congress in 1918. Diane Rose Dunnigan, 'Irish Return Migration from America at the Turn of the Nineteenth Century, 1890–1920', PhD thesis, NUI Maynooth, 2011, pp. 22–3.
2 This form of the oath, prescribed under the Naturalization Act, 1906, is no longer applied.
3 This applies to the most substantial study of Irish return movement using passport records, Dunnigan, 'Irish Return Migration', esp. chs 2 and 3. Dunnigan's otherwise painstaking analysis of passports sought by emigrants from Connaught gives no clear indication that the great majority returned in 1919–20 rather than around the 'turn' of the century.
4 According to a digital search of applications made accessible by the National Archives (Washington, DC) through ancestry.co.uk (see Table 8.1), 28,975 passports were issued between 1919 and 1925 to applicants born in Ireland. On the assumption that the true number of individuals involved was five-sixths of the aggregate number of applications (as for Leitrim, analysed below), about 24,000 natives of Ireland applied for passports in the USA during that period.
5 The first applications giving the name, birthplace, and residence of fathers were lodged in 1919, and by 1921 all passport forms for naturalised citizens incorporated these elements.
6 Twelve men and one woman from Leitrim were issued with pre-war passports (for a median duration of 6 months), ranging between 1872 and 1912. Though less informative in earlier years, these applications indicate that pre-war applicants tended to be much older, with a median age of 54. Their median dates of birth and emigration were 1839 and 1863. More came from Massachusetts than New York and two were priests (including Bartholomew McKeany from Bondville, Massachusetts, who secured no less than five passports for short visits between 1898 and 1908). In addition, one pre-war overseas application was lodged (in 1906).
7 Eighteen men and thirteen women born in Leitrim applied for passports overseas between 1914 and 1925 (seventeen in Dublin, five in Belfast, three in Londonderry, and the remainder in Queenstown, Lausanne, London, Paris, and Shanghai). Their median dates of birth and emigration were 1881 and 1899. Thirteen applicants had previously been resident in New York. Statistics for the interval between departure from the USA and return exclude four applicants heading elsewhere and one (a wife resident in Dublin) who had never lived in the USA.
8 Another applicant who had never lived in the United States was Violet Post from Manorhamilton, who twice applied for passports in 1918 in order to settle her affairs and visit her husband (a banker from Rhode Island) in

France and Switzerland. Though declaring an intention to take up permanent residence in the United States, she did not intend to do so imminently.

9 According to the digital index, as last updated in February 2017, the number of applicants (1914–25) born in Ireland was 32,169, whereas the sum of the number of applicants born in each of the thirty-two counties was 17,487 (54%).

10 The mean annual number of applicants indexed as born in 'Ireland' was 59.4 (1861–70), 78.3 (1871–80), 87.3 (1881–90), 92.6 (1891–1900), 98.7 (1901–10), and 117.0 (1911–14), with fairly regular oscillation over a cycle of 5–6 years between peak values.

11 The percentage of Leitrim applications issued in each month (1914–25) was 2.7 (January), 4.4 (February), 8.6 (March), 15.3 (April), 15.1 (May), 13.4 (June), 13.2 (July), 8.0 (August), 6.7 (September), 5.5 (October), 3.8 (November), and 3.4 (December).

12 The only detailed annual returns for British subjects (including Irish nationals) travelling between ports in the UK and the USA relate to 1913 (see Chapter 1). The proportions leaving or reaching the UK between March and August were 55.9% (immigrants to UK from USA), 61.0% (emigrants from UK to USA), 55.8% (temporary visitors from USA to UK), and 62.1% (temporary visitors from UK to USA). The comparable proportion for Leitrim passport applications was 74.3%.

13 Many other addresses in boroughs such as Brooklyn and the Bronx districts were presumably subsumed under New York City following its administrative absorption of surrounding cities and towns in 1898.

14 The 'inter-quartile range' is the difference between the values recorded for applicants placed at the lower and upper quartile, when all applicants are arranged in ascending order of age. Among 101 applicants so arranged, the lower quartile, median, and upper quartile values would be those recorded for the applicants ranked 26, 51, and 76, respectively.

15 The median interval between arrival and application was 15 years, not 11 years or so, as might be expected from the sum of the intervals between arrival and naturalisation (7 years) and naturalisation and application (4 years). This anomaly is attributable to the inclusion of applicants (mainly women relying on male citizenship) who had not themselves been naturalised.

16 Thirty-seven out of 76 applicant parents named a single child, 22 named 2, 13 named 3, with 4 larger groups.

17 Returns of *current residence* for 109 fathers (omitting 143 who were dead and 5 of unknown status) located 76 in Leitrim, 3 in other Irish counties, 24 in 'Ireland', and 6 in the USA.

18 Only 10 applications specified a county of destination, almost always Leitrim (Donegal and Longford each attracted 1 applicant, while another was bound for both Queen's and Leitrim).

19 In some cases, earlier applications were not indexed under Leitrim and are therefore absent from my database of first applications (1914–25), accounting for most of the 24 cases in which reference was made to issue of a previous passport.

20 Other civilian applicants had visited France (as a diplomat) and Alaska; 3 visitors to Britain or the British Isles also went to France or Italy, and

2 visitors to Ireland also went to Britain and England, Italy, and France. Of 35 in the services, 5 served in the navy, 1 was a seaman, and 29 were in the army (including 7 cases in which men with previous overseas experience were naturalised in military camps).

21 It is unclear whether these 'ten trips' were single or return journeys: Dunnigan, 'Irish Return Migration', 110.

22 The dates of birth and emigration for each of these multiple travellers are as follows: Edward Donnelly (1882, 1904); Patrick Rinn (1878, 1895); Francis Gaynor (1867, 1885); Thomas Beirne (1880, 1903); Michael Joseph O'Connor (1872, 1893); Michael McMorrow (1880, 1901); John Thomas Coulter (1876, 1898); Thomas Kelly (1883, 1906); Winifred Schumacher (1885, unknown). In 1922, Schumacher claimed to have been born in 1888, exactly 3 years later than hitherto stated.

23 Earnest A. Hooton and C. Wesley Dupertuis, *The Physical Anthropology of Ireland, with a Section on the West Coast Irish Females by Helen Dawson* (Cambridge, MA: Peabody Museum of Archaeology and Ethnology, Harvard University, *Papers*, xxx, Nos 1–2, 1955).

24 1,856 women were examined in seven counties, including 68 in Leitrim; the blue-eyed component accounted for 56.4% of all women examined and 54.4% in Leitrim: Hooton and Dupertuis, *Physical Anthropology*, table XXVII-10 (unpaginated).

25 8,909 men were examined in thirty-two counties, including 616 in Leitrim; overall, 42.4% had blue eyes with 43.9% blue-brown. In the sub-region dominated by Leitrim, 44.4% of eyes were blue and 45.1% were blue-brown: Hooton and Dupertuis, *Physical Anthropology*, table IV-14.

26 Putative Firbolgs were probably subsumed in the rare 'Pure Mediterranean type' (with only 33 male and 55 female examples throughout Ireland, including 8 men in the Leitrim region and 5 women in the county): Hooton and Dupertuis, *Physical Anthropology*, 7, 143, 280, table XXVIII-1.

27 The sub-group excludes blue-brown eyes but includes all swarthies (17 dark, 14 ruddy, 1 each red, florid, and brunette).

28 The proportion with dark or dark brown (excluding black) hair was 80.0% (Leitrim females), 75.5% (West Coast females), 72.0% (Leitrim district males), and 76.7% (Irish males). As with eye colour, inconsistencies of classification preclude rigorous comparison between men and women or between home-comers and the Harvard sample: Hooton and Dupertuis, *Physical Anthropology*, tables XXVII-10, IV-13.

29 In descending order of usage, the female epithets for complexion were fair (88), medium (14), light (10), dark (5), brunette (3), ruddy (3), white and sallow (2 each), and blonde, normal, olive, and 'fair and fresh pink' (1 each). The male epithets were fair (153), ruddy (68), dark (41), light (33), medium (27), white (4), clear, florid, and red (3 each), sallow (2), and blonde, ordinary, and 'fair, ruddy' (1 each).

30 Hooton and Dupertuis, *Physical Anthropology*, 289, 293, table XXX-2; E. A. Hooton and C. W. Dupertuis, 'Age Changes and Selective Survival in Irish Males' (American Association of Physical Anthropologists and the Wenner-Gren Foundation for Anthropological Research, *Studies in Physical Anthropology*, No. 2, 1951), 44 (table XLI). Statistics cross-tabulating male vascularity and age were not presented for sub-regions such as Leitrim.

31 See Cormac Ó Gráda, *Ireland: A New Economic History* (Oxford: Clarendon Press, 1994), 18–23, 105–10, 243–5.
32 See, for example, Timothy J. Hatton and Bernice E. Bray, 'Long Run Trends in the Heights of European Men, 19th–20th Centuries', *Economics and Human Biology*, 8 (2010): 405–13. This article compares cross-tabulations of height by cohort (using survey data collected between 1994 and 2001 for the European Community Household Panel) with earlier data including, in the Irish case, mean figures derived from the Harvard survey (arbitrarily reduced by 2% to achieve 'cohesion' with other observations). Hatton and Bray draw heavily on an earlier synthesis by Jaume Carcia and Climent Quintana-Domeque, 'The Evolution of Adult Height in Europe: A Brief Note', *Economics and Human Biology*, 5 (2007): 340–9.
33 The Harvard investigators measured men ranging from 57.5 in. to 79.5 in., and women ranging from 51.6 in. to 73.6 in.: Hooton and Dupertuis, *Physical Anthropology*, tables III-2, XXVI-3.
34 Mean height for the entire male and female samples was 67.9 in. and 62.4 in., respectively; the mean height for Leitrim women and men from the district surrounding Leitrim was 67.7 in. and 63.1 in., respectively: Hooton and Dupertuis, *Physical Anthropology*, tables III-2, XXVI-3. Male statistics for mean height by age group appear in Hooton and Dupertuis, 'Age Changes', 10 (table VII).
35 The median height for 90 ever-married female applicants was 65 in., compared with 66 in. for 41 single applicants. The median age of the two sub-groups was almost identical (36 and 37, respectively).
36 For definitions and sources, see note to Table 8.13.
37 The median height for 15 women from congested divisions was 66 in., 2 in. greater than that for 21 women from uncongested divisions. The median height for 119 men from congested divisions and 121 from elsewhere was 69 in. in each case. Once again, there was no noteworthy difference in median age (32 and 31 years for women, 34 and 35 years for men).
38 The median height for 22 women from South Leitrim was 66 in., 1 in. greater than that for 14 women from North Leitrim (a slightly older sub-group). The median height for 134 men from South Leitrim and 105 from North Leitrim was 69 in. in each case. Median age in each category was 29 and 32.5 years for women, 35 and 34 years for men.
39 Despite contrary claims in Hatton and Bray, 'Long Run Trends', 410–11, there is no clear evidence that Irishmen born in the later twentieth century were taller than passport applicants or those measured by the Harvard team.
40 The median date of birth of male applicants was 1883, whereas that of male Harvard subjects was about 1905 (their median age being 30 in 1934–6).
41 Hooton and Dupertuis, 'Age Changes', 10 (note to table VII), discussing the gradual decline in mean height from the peak recorded for men aged 35–39.
42 Hatton and Bray, 'Long Run Trends', 411. Hatton and Bray reduced the raw mean figures by 0.8 cm by way of compensation for self-inflation. The *unadjusted* mean height for those born in each quinquennium from 1950–5 (6 years) to 1976–80 was 68.9 in., 69.4 in., 69.3 in., 69.6 in., 69.7 in., 69.8 in.: Garcia and Quintana-Domeque, 'Evolution', 343 (table 1).
43 The mean height for those born in each quinquennium from 1950–5 (6 years) to 1976–80 was 64.1 in., 64.1 in., 64.3 in., 64.6 in., 64.8 in., and 64.7 in.: Garcia and Quintana-Domeque, 'Evolution', 343 (table 2).

44 Cheryl D. Friar et al., 'Anthropometric Reference Data for Children and Adults: United States, 2011–2014: Data from the National Health and Nutrition Examination Survey' (Hyattsville, Maryland: US Department of Health and Human Services, *Vital and Health Statistics*, series 3, No. 39, 2016).

45 For all non-Hispanic whites aged 20 or more, median recorded height was 69.6 in. for men and 64.1 in. for women (the mean figures were 69.7 in. and 64.1 in., respectively). As in the other distributions discussed above, older subjects tended to be slightly shorter, perhaps because of shrinkage. For men aged 20–39, 40–59, and over 60, median height was 70.2 in., 69.9 in., and 69.0 in.; the corresponding median figures for women were 64.9 in., 64.4 in., and 63.0 in.: Fryar, 'Anthropometric Reference Data', 16 (table 12), 14 (table 10).

46 The term 'racial survey' was used alongside the less tendentious analysis of 'morphological types', also designated as 'sub-races' or 'perhaps only "breeds"': Hooton and Dupertuis, *Physical Anthropology*, 11, 142. In the sub-region dominated by Leitrim, 26.2% of men were categorised as 'Keltic', 29.2% as 'Nordic Mediterranean', 17.8% as 'Nordic Alpine', and 15.7% as 'Dinaric'. 'Keltic' signified 'the dark-haired, blue-eyed, long-headed type' also found 'in Gaelic Scotland, in Wales, in the Isle of Man, and to some extent in England, and in Brittany'; it was interpreted as a bequest of 'the third Keltic or Laginian invasion'. See Hooton and Dupertuis, *Physical Anthropology*, 244 (table XIII–5).

47 Two men had beards and 3 had whiskers, usually in combination with a moustache.

48 *IT* (26 March 1916).

49 Sir Nevil Macready, *Annals of an Active Life*, 2 vols (London: Hutchinson, 1924), vol. 1, 257–9.

50 J. H. Cox, 'Sunday Survey', *Sunday Independent* (22 October 1916).

51 J. H. Cox, 'To-day and Yesterday', *Irish Independent* (19 May 1919, 25 May 1922, 10 January 1923).

52 *IT* (13 February 1924).

53 Based on scrutiny of captioned group photographs of those attending meetings on 21 January and 10 April 1919 (accessible through NLI, digital photograph collection). Of 52 pictured individuals, 3 had beards with moustaches and 12 had moustaches alone.

54 Christopher Oldstone-Moore, 'Mustaches and Masculine Codes in Early Twentieth-Century America', *Journal of Social History*, 45(1) (2011): 47–60, esp. 54.

55 Before 1901, 160 applicants emigrated, 182 between 1901 and 1910, and 117 thereafter (the date of emigration was not recorded in 18 of 477 applications). Of 278 matches with the census for 1901 (including 214 cases where the applicant was present, including 3 only in 1911, and 64 family matches), 164 are firm, 92 are probable, and 22 are the stronger of two credible identifications. Applications have also been matched with 261 family census returns for 1911, of which 87 name the applicant.

56 As shown in Table 8.4, the median year of emigration for passport applicants was 1906, their median year of birth being 1884. By comparison (see Table 6.3), the median year of birth for co-resident mothers of American-born residents in 1901 was 1863, and 1870 for mothers enumerated in 1911

(the median dates for fathers being 1858 and 1865, respectively). These accompanying parents would therefore have tended to leave Ireland a decade or so earlier than the representative passport applicant.

57 The proportion of the census population (1901) resident in each rural district was 7.5% (Ballyshannon), 32.2% (Manorhamilton), 12.8% (Bawnboy), 18.8% (Carrick-on-Shannon), and 28.6% (Mohill). The corresponding percentages for matched households were 5.8, 29.3, 14.5, 19.2, and 31.2. Carrick-on-Shannon's share of the American-born was 20.1% in 1911 and no less than 27.5% in 1901.

58 In 255 out of 276 matched cases (excluding 2 outside the county), information was available for housing in both years (256 cases for rooms). The number of cases showing improvement and decline, respectively, was as follows: walls (16, 5); roof (7, 1); front windows (42, 17); rooms (56, 26); house class (38, 13). The percentage of cases where no change occurred was as follows: walls (91.2%); roof (96.9%); windows (74.9%); rooms (68.0%); class (80.0%). Net improvement (cases of improvement less cases of decline) applied, respectively, to 4.3%, 2.6%, 11.8%, 11.7%, and 9.8% of all matched cases.

59 A majority of applicants were reared in 'standard' dwellings (52%), compared with only about two-fifths of Leitrim Americans enumerated in either census.

60 County rankings may be severely distorted by the spelling of county names, Leitrim being a name easily mis-transliterated from handwriting by optical-recognition software. Counties with distinctive spelling such as Cavan and Galway were probably seldom mis-transliterated, leading to excessively high apparent incidence of indexed applications by comparison with 'Leitrim'.

61 The counties with most visitors per thousand were Cavan (9.8), Galway (8.7), Longford (8.6), Roscommon (8.4), Sligo (8.3), Kerry (7.8), and Mayo (7.3). An apparently comparable tabulation for the period 1890–1920 is seriously flawed and cannot be used as a basis for regional analysis: Dunnigan, 'Irish Return Migration', 84.

62 Dunnigan, 'Irish Return Migration', 87, 90, 100, 92, 108, 110. The absence of detailed statistical tables leaves various anomalies in Dunnigan's analysis unresolved. The number of applicants assigned to Leitrim for the period 1890–1920 (108) falls far short of my own database for the same period (169, including 20 who only applied overseas), though Dunnigan's more eclectic approach unearthed several Leitrim applicants missing from my database.

63 The maximum period of validity was 2 years except between 1915 and 1920, when passports were restricted to 6 months: Robertson, *The Passport in America*, 256–7.

9. VISITORS FROM AMERICA: MOTIVES

1 The townland of Dergvone in Killarga electoral division had 31 houses and 135 inhabitants in 1901: Census of Ireland (1901), county report.

2 Oddities of spelling (italicised) and syntax in the quoted statements have been retained, but capitalisation and punctuation have been regularised. Additional letters required to clarify a mis-spelt word are given in brackets: thus,

'the[y]'. Some extracts incorporate inferred letters or words missing from the available images.

3 Dunnigan, 'Irish Return Migration', 116.

4 The quartile values for 220 visitors intending to visit parents were 29 and 39 (median 33), with ages ranging between 21 and 60. If restricted to 140 cases in which the age of a parent is also known from census schedules, the age distribution is slightly younger (median of 32 with quartile values of 29 and 35).

5 The quartile values for fathers were 62 and 75, and for mothers 59 and 68 (a much more densely clustered distribution). The ages at date of passport issue are based on those returned for 92 fathers and 120 mothers enumerated in 1901 (occasionally supplemented from 1911 census returns), excluding a few cases of parents mentioned in applications who had in fact died by 1911 (perhaps indicating loose use of the plural 'parents'). Preference is given to the 1901 returns because the ages of older people were systematically over-stated in 1911, reflecting the introduction in 1909 of old-age pensions from the age of 70.

6 Only 34 of 301 declarations of motive made no reference to visiting relatives or friends, attending to business, estate, or property, or accompanying family members. This residual group includes those whose objectives were restricted to employment, commerce, tourism, and so forth.

7 David Fitzpatrick, *Oceans of Consolation: Personal Correspondence between Ireland and Colonial Australia* (Cork University Press, 1994).

8 Thomas and Mary Keegan were married in Rowan district on 21 August 1919; Mary's daughter Mary Ellen Shanley was born in Musselburgh on 11 April 1914 (attached summary of 'identifying documents').

9 Dunnigan, 'Irish Return Migration', 131.

10 Passenger lists for vessels arriving at New York, and census enumeration forms for the decennial Federal Census and the New York State Census (1915) are digitally accessible through ancestry.co.uk.

11 Based on Federal Census returns for 1930, and the index to United States Social Security Applications and Claims (1936–2007), digitally accessible through ancestry.co.uk. The index states precise dates of birth and death and names both parents, in Margaret's case supplying her mother's maiden name.

12 David Fitzpatrick, *Harry Boland's Irish Revolution* (Cork: University Press, 2003), 270–3. A passport clerk inaccurately identified the event as 'Irish Race Conference'.

13 This organisation had been instigated by Harry Boland, on behalf of de Valera, to outflank and out-fund the Friends of Irish Freedom (FOIF) and Clan na Gael, controlled by de Valera's rivals John Devoy and Daniel Cohalan. The Canadian Self-Determination for Ireland League also can-celled its delegation.

14 Miss Katherine Hughes had become foundation secretary of the Irish National Bureau of Devoy's FOIF in Washington, DC, in spring 1919, but resigned in June 1920 to 'resume her residence in Canada, where, for many years, she was active in public affairs': FOIF, *Newsletter*, No. 50 (12 June 1920); FOIF, Minutes (8 May 1920), in American Irish Historical Society (New York), FOIF Papers, 4/8, 6/3.

15 *Proceedings of the Irish Race Congress in Paris, January, 1922* (Dublin: Fine Ghaedheal Central Secretariat, 1922), 28, 31.

16 Irish Race Congress, typed minutes, in Mary MacSwiney Papers, UCDA, P48a/354/2.

17 *Proceedings*, 20–2, 155–7.

18 *Proceedings*, 83, 194, 198, 212, 227. See also briefer accounts in *Irish Independent* (26, 28 January 1922) and *Freeman's Journal* (28 January 1922); Diarmuid Hayes, Michael Hayes, Douglas Hyde, and Eoin MacNeill, 'Report on the Irish Race Conference [*sic*], February 1922', in Michael Kennedy et al. (eds), *Documents on Irish Foreign Policy, vol. 1: 1919–22* (Dublin: RIA and Department of Foreign Affairs, 1998), 390–7, at 396.

19 *Proceedings*, 109. Joseph J. Castellini, a prominent anti-Treatyist and associate of Joseph McGarrity, nominated O'Connor to the central committee of the new body.

20 Gralton eluded the digital passport index for Leitrim because his birthplace was mis-transliterated as 'Feitrin'.

21 In most respects, this biographical sketch closely follows Diarmaid Ferriter's pithy entry in *DIB*.

22 This information is derived from records from the National Archives accessible digitally at ancestry.co.uk, including the manifest of alien passengers arriving in New York from Queenstown on the *Oceanic* (19 April 1907); enumeration schedules for the US Federal Census (1910 and 1930) and the New York State Census (1925); Draft Registration Card (27 September 1942). Other accessible documents include the outward passenger list for the *Celtic* from Queenstown to New York (18 June 1922), and the list of American citizens arriving in New York on the *Britannic* from Queenstown on 20 August 1933, noting Gralton's deportation from the Irish Free State.

23 Ferriter (in *DIB*) states that Gralton 'returned to Ireland on 2 June 1921', but in fact this was the date of his passport application.

24 Outward passenger list for the *Celtic* from Queenstown to New York (18 June 1922): accessible through ancestry.co.uk. He sailed midway between the 'Pact' general election and shelling of the Four Courts, not 'shortly after the beginning of the civil war' as stated by Ferriter (in *DIB*).

10. VISITORS FROM AMERICA: FACES

1 Dunnigan, 'Irish Return Migration'.

EPILOGUE

1 A workshop conceived by the author on 'The Americanisation of Ireland, 1841–1925: Culture and Society' was organised by his former graduate students, Dr Fionnuala Walsh and Dr Ciaran Wallace, in Trinity College Dublin in 2019. The speakers expanded upon the additional themes raised here. It is envisaged that the proceedings, together with further unpublished work by David Fitzpatrick on these themes, will be published in due course under the editorship of Dr Walsh.

Index

Tables are indicated by bold type.